SIMPSON

IMPRINT IN HUMANITIES

The humanities endowment
by Sharon Hanley Simpson and
Barclay Simpson honors
MURIEL CARTER HANLEY
whose intellect and sensitivity
have enriched the many lives
that she has touched.

The publisher gratefully acknowledges the generous support of the Simpson Humanities Endowment Fund of the University of California Press Foundation, which was established by a major gift from Barclay and Sharon Simpson.

The Road Out

The Road Out

A Teacher's Odyssey in
Poor America

Deborah Hicks

UNIVERSITY OF CALIFORNIA PRESS

Berkeley   Los Angeles   London

University of California Press, one of the most distinguished university presses in the United States, enriches lives around the world by advancing scholarship in the humanities, social sciences, and natural sciences. Its activities are supported by the UC Press Foundation and by philanthropic contributions from individuals and institutions. For more information, visit www.ucpress.edu.

University of California Press
Berkeley and Los Angeles, California

University of California Press, Ltd.
London, England

Library of Congress Cataloging-in-Publication Data

Hicks, Deborah.
    The road out : a teacher's odyssey in poor America / Deborah Hicks.
        p.   cm.
    Includes bibliographical references and index.
    ISBN 978-0-520-26649-0 (cloth : alk. paper)
    1. Poor [low income?] girls—Education—Ohio—Cincinnati.   2. Poor whites—Education—Ohio—Cincinnati.   3. Poor girls—Books and reading—Ohio—Cincinnati.   4. Poor girls—Ohio—Cincinnati—Anecdotes.   Hicks, Deborah—Anecdotes.   I. Title.
    LC4093.C56H53   2013
    371.822—dc23   2012010483

Manufactured in the United States of America

21 20 19 18 17 16 15 14 13
10   9   8   7   6   5   4   3   2   1

In keeping with a commitment to support environmentally responsible and sustainable printing practices, UC Press has printed this book on Natures Book, a fiber that contains 30% postconsumer waste and meets the minimum requirements of ANSI/NISO Z39.48–1992 (R 1997) *(Permanence of Paper).*

I want to be lifted up
By some great white bird unknown to the police,
And soar for a thousand miles and be carefully hidden
Modest and golden as one last corn grain,
Stored with the secrets of the wheat and the mysterious
    lives
Of the unnamed poor.

James Wright, "The Minneapolis Poem,"
Shall We Gather at the River

CONTENTS

ILLUSTRATIONS

AUTHOR'S NOTE

The stories recounted in this memoir are drawn from my work as a teacher between 2001 and 2004, and my subsequent visits and interviews with my former students between 2005 and 2008. Scenes from my childhood in a small mountain town fill in the layers of a narrative that begins with my experiences as a working-class girl and follows my journey as a teacher for other girls who lacked opportunity or access. Though I grew up in small-town Appalachia and my students were coming of age in an urban ghetto, we were connected through a twist of history. Their elders were largely migrants from Appalachia who, in the postwar decades, had left family farms and coal mines in eastern Kentucky and West Virginia to seek a better future for their children in the city.

The basic facts of this chronicle are this: I grew up in Appalachian North Carolina, the daughter of working-class parents. My childhood was tainted not just by economic distress but by the things that often go with such distress. My parents could never escape the traumas of their dirt-poor childhoods, and

I left through the only escape hatch available to a working-class girl: education. Later in life, I found myself in Cincinnati for a university job and decided to teach part time in an elementary school in one of the poorest neighborhoods in the city. I first worked as a volunteer in a second- and then third-grade class-room, teaching reading and writing. It was in these classrooms that I met the girls who would later become my students. I decided to form a unique class, just for girls, and we met each week during the school year and daily over the summer. Our curriculum was simple: literature and story, including these young girls' own life stories.

I have chosen to recount my journey in a way that portrays my students and my teaching work from the inside. In so doing, I have adapted the tools of a novelist to the task of reporting on my experiences as an educator. Readers are drawn into the inner worlds of my students, not only in my classes, but also in their homes and on the streets. Discerning readers might wonder how I could garner such intimate material, how I could know what a girl might be thinking or feeling at a given moment. The length of time I taught the same girls in our small class, four years, was one resource that allowed me to go deep, and most importantly, to garner the trust that allowed these girls to reveal their inner thoughts, feelings, dreams, and anxieties. Coupled with time were other tools. I pored over thousands of pages of detailed written notes, transcriptions from recordings of all our classes, and interview materials in order to recreate the scenes depicted in this memoir. Each moment of this narrative in which a reader is able to peer into the inward thoughts of my students is tied to an outward exchange during our classes, to my interviews, or to a girl's written journal.

This does not of course mean that the experiences recounted are without the overlay of my own way of seeing and understanding things. Though this book portrays eight lives, including my own, there is just one narrator. I hope that one day the girls portrayed in this book will write their own memoirs, and in so doing fill in the spaces where I could not see or hear with enough clarity to tell the complete story of another's life. And yet, I have not pulled back from the challenge of recounting my students' inner childhood worlds. I have portrayed their worlds more seamlessly than a purely sociological study would, with the intent of helping to bring readers inside the hidden lives of poor whites. This is not done merely for literary effect. I believe that more just actions and social policies, including our response to the crisis of education for the poor, can only come from deeper understandings of these still mysterious lives. It is my dream that readers of this chronicle will be moved to a different kind of thought and action, not by means of a new assortment of facts and statistics but through the intimacy of a story.

Chapel Hill, North Carolina
February 2012

A Teacher on a Mission

When I was a young girl growing up in a sleepy Appalachian paper mill town, I had a lot of dreams for a girl with limited opportunity. Probably the biggest of all my dreams was just to get away from where I was. I spent most of my girlhood in a perpetual state of roaming. The road in front of the wood-frame house we rented in my early years was paved but it soon turned to dirt, as it wound out of town and toward the hills and "hollers" nearby. At home were my parents and one brother, only ten years old but already trouble. He was a gangly, miserable kid who was as disturbed as he was smart; possibly he suffered some neurological damage from his difficult entry into the world, a city doctor would later surmise. My father donned his workman's clothes and packed his lunch pail, happy to get out of the house. My mother took Valium and Darvon and slept off her anxiety and depression. Off I would go, a plucky five-year-old in search of a little girl's dreams in the unlikely landscape of working-class Appalachia.

The dirt and gravel toughened my feet, but in my head I was more a princess than a scrawny little blonde girl with dirt between her toes. I could walk to the local general store down the road, where old men sat on benches outside, their cheeks bulging with tobacco. I could wander in the other direction to visit Mrs. White, a sweet older church lady who played piano and sang hymns in her scratchy country voice. But even a curious, enterprising young girl could go only so far. Often my journeys ended at a pasture next to our house, where I played with a small baby doll and some dimestore plastic animals: my kingdom. The days passed in this uneventful way until two things happened that changed my life forever. I discovered the world of books, and I began a twelve-year journey through some of America's poorest and worst public schools. It was an inauspicious start, but I can look back now and see my beginnings as a teacher.

Most people would agree that if there is a single ticket out of poverty and up the ladder of social mobility, it surely must be public school. Those of us who have struggled to climb that ladder would argue more than anyone that school was our hope. For me, school was probably more like my salvation. I went to school to find a place for my curious mind and shrunken heart to grow and flourish. But to succeed in school and beyond, an ill-prepared girl from an impoverished background needs some good luck: a teacher who spots her gifts and becomes her guide to the wider world, a good school that offers her a scholarship and a shot at success, one family member—perhaps an aunt or cousin—who has been a trailblazer and wants to help. As a typical girl of my background, I had none of these things.

My early childhood education was pretty much like that of any rural working-class girl in the 1960s. My mother had ordered some Little Golden Books from a mail-order source and stuck these on the same bookshelf that housed *Reader's Digest* magazines, a collection of Bible stories, and a few older, worn novels from her Arkansas childhood: *Little Women* and *The Five Little Peppers and How They Grew.* Men in my childhood didn't read and women did house chores, so it fell upon me to make sense of this odd reading curriculum. Always a child in search of adventure where I could find it, I took the thin Little Golden Books and found an inviting niche on the bank that separated our backyard from the pasture next door, its unruly grass rising to my knees. There I could hear an occasional car making its way up the narrow two-lane road leading past the general store toward the laundromat and single-wide trailers set on the hill. I could smell the sweet honeysuckle, and hear an occasional voice echoing.

I dreamed, as I read from the Little Golden Books, of worlds I would visit someday and adventures I would have. I would travel to Holland, with its pretty windmills and dikes; I would don wooden shoes like the brave little Dutch boy who held back the flooding waters of the sea with his finger. I would go off to Africa and sit among the animals like Jane Goodall—the lady I had seen on our small black-and-white RCA. Only I would study the lives of tigers. I would sit quietly and become their friend, just as Goodall had scooted up next to chimpanzees in the jungles of Tanzania. At night I would sleep in a large white tent staked into the rich African soil.

Then I went off to our local public school, and my dreams were put on hold for over a decade. I came out trained in rote skills but was completely unprepared for the kind of thinking, reading, and writing you need to do in a good college. So my journey from a naïve, poorly educated rural girl to a woman with an advanced degree from Harvard was full of detours that drained and derailed me.

At seventeen I went to a local college on a scholarship. I recall the six months I dropped out of that college to work in a warehouse. I needed money and a car, so I put my educational future on hold while I assembled and packed up boxes, like a contemporary version of the city factory girls trying to work their way out of poverty in the early 1900s. No longer a young woman with a promising educational future, I was there to fill mail-order boxes with items ranging from travel sewing kits to sex toys. Oddly, the experience felt more normal and ordinary than any college class. Part of me even enjoyed my time taping together boxes in my place on the packing line, because this was the kind of thing I had been educated to do: work hard and follow orders. Still, as soon as I had the money I needed, I went back to college and fumbled my way through a higher-education system I barely understood.

After college, I packed up and flew to France with some pocket money and a one-way ticket, not completely sure what I would do over there. I picked grapes (*les vendanges* in French) and did a stint as a nanny and housemaid, my best attempt at the study-abroad experience. I came back to live in the big city of Washington, finding an office job at Georgetown University so I could take free classes in language studies and teaching. A professor spotted my work, and my life changed again: I earned a graduate fellowship. At last, two years later, I landed at Harvard University to finish advanced study in the subject that was closest to my heart: education.

Out I came with my student loan debt and my books and theories about teaching. I had become a specialist in childhood literacy education and had learned how to conduct research. But the rebellious part of me sought out a curriculum of a different sort than a university could offer. I read novels and dreamed about how I would change the world. I drank strong coffee and even scribbled out a few poems and stories. Then, one day, I found myself in Cincinnati for a teaching post in the education department of a local university. It wasn't long before I discovered a neighborhood that made me feel I had entered a time machine and traveled back to my childhood.

The neighborhood was only minutes by car from downtown Cincinnati—nestled at the foot of one of Cincinnati's famous hills—but the drive felt like one into a rural West Virginia hamlet. The community was poor. Once a neighborhood of German and Irish workers, Lower Price Hill had become a haven for southern white migrants from Appalachia in the postwar decades. *Here,* I thought to myself. Here is where I want to teach.

This is how I met a young girl named Blair Rainey.[1]

I volunteered to teach reading in the local neighborhood elementary school, in the classroom of a second-grade teacher with a warm manner and a soft Kentucky accent. It was there I first spotted a tiny girl who looked even younger than her eight years. She looked sickly, more like a child from a coal-mining county in eastern Kentucky in the 1960s than a child growing up in a prosperous city at the turn of the new millennium. Her skin was pale and ashen. But her eyes expressed something else: toughness, spirit, and, most of all, precociousness. She had the same fiercely intelligent eyes as her grandmother, Grandma Lilly, brown with the mixed Cherokee heritage of their rural ancestors.

When Blair was born, too soon and with drugs in her system, she was so tiny that she fit into a shoebox. She shook at first from the effects of crack cocaine in her tiny body, until the drug worked its way out of her. Then Grandma Lilly, who had already determined that Blair was going to be her special baby and claimed child custody, put infant Blair in a crib. She was still so small that one morning she rolled over and fell out between the bars.

From that day, Blair slept in Grandma Lilly's bed. She began to grow up and walk and use language. Soon afterward, she started to speak and sit by her grandma's side in bed, and, as Grandma Lilly read books to her, it became apparent that Blair was no ordinary girl. This one was special, and she was going to be the one who made it out.

Now I was determined to be the teacher who made a difference in Blair's life. I wanted her to have what I never had: a first-rate public school education and a real shot at her grandmother's dreams for her. The next fall I decided to create my own after-school reading class for Blair and the other girls in her third-grade classroom. I located a classroom in Blair's elementary school that we could use once a week and during the summer. It was on the first floor of a three-story school building, with a large row of windows that peered out onto the school's blacktop playground, and beyond that, to one of the neighborhood's small side streets. During school hours, it was used for counseling and remedial tutoring. But for two hours each week and during the summer it became ours—a room of our own. The room at first looked sad. The gray carpet was frayed and soiled in spots. The walls that had once been white were yellowing, the corner paint peeling. To make the room feel like a place where girls would want to gather, I brought in wicker armchairs and a loveseat I bought on sale. I plumped colorful pillows on the makeshift furniture and began creating a library with books about girls' lives.

Every Monday after school during the regular school year, and every day during summer school, my students met to read and talk about books and to write stories of their own. The girls in my reading class moved into fourth grade, and still we continued to meet. In summer of 2002, our second summer together, with drippy Ohio Valley heat descending upon the neighborhood like a moistened blanket, Blair and I drew together our two armchairs and talked about fiction.

"Doesn't it keep you up at night when you read your book?" I asked.

"No," said Blair quickly.

Just weeks before she turned ten, Blair had recorded her preferences in a journal she kept for my class: "*Blair Rainey lives in Cincinnati. Blair likes to color and draw pictures of many things. Blair's favorite food is pizza and her favorite drink is Mountain Dew. Blair likes to go swimming in the summer time and get her dog off of the chain. Blair's favorite color is blue. She has blue folders, a blue swimming pool and blue teddy bears. Blair's favorite book is* Rose Madder *by Stephen King and she is reading it at home.*"

During that year I made the amazing discovery that Blair, a fragile-looking girl and barely ten years old, was a Stephen King fan. The heroine of her favorite book was a young woman named Rose. Rose's husband, Norman, is a monstrous ex-cop who, in one bloody and gruesome scene, beats her until she loses her unborn baby. Fleeing her husband, Rose escapes to a new city, but Norman uses his old skills as a cop to track her down.

"I wanted my name to be Rose," said Blair, clutching a blue Beanie Baby. Her small torso and spindly limbs barely filled the armchair.

"Does your grandma ever read Stephen King with you?" I asked curiously.

"Yeah, but my grandma don't like him. She thinks his writing is terrible and his stories are horrible." Grandma Lilly preferred old books, like *Black Beauty* and *The Little House on the Prairie.*

"What is it about Stephen King's books that you really enjoy?" I asked.

"The parts when *scary* things happen," said Blair. "And I like to read *long* books." *Rose Madder* was 420 pages long.

This story of one precocious young girl, her Stephen King book, and a hopelessly idealistic teacher helps to shed light on a big dilemma. How can education open doors for girls such as Blair, the daughter of poor whites, and a girl with dreams as big as any girl in America? Her small but important life story is part of a larger American narrative. She is the young heir to a labor history, a slice of our national life that is disappearing. The courageous southern migrants who fled Appalachian poverty had come to midwestern cities in search of manufacturing jobs and a better future for their children. Now young Blair had inherited a forgotten landscape, tormented by job loss and a growing street-drug problem. Dropout rates were high too, reflecting an intergenerational history—the earlier workers in Blair's neighborhood could find jobs without a high school diploma—but also a sense of detachment from school. What Blair most needed was a first-rate education that would allow her to create a new kind of future, leading her away from the streets and their torments and toward the life her Grandma Lilly envisioned for her. But when I set out to become an educational agent of hope and change for Blair, I discovered that the single thing that could have made the biggest difference in her life—public education— was itself part of the problem. In spite of the intentions of individuals at Blair's school, who were as hardworking as they were big-hearted, she was caught up in the same two-tiered system of schooling I had lived through. It's like John Dawson, an Appalachian migrant who moved to inner-city Chicago in the 1950s, remarked: "A poor kid don't get the same teachin' that a rich kid gets."[2]

Educational reformers who talk about making a difference in the lives of poor students often cite the need to teach basic skills that will one day translate into jobs. But mixed in with the facts of economic disadvantage are clichés about poor and working-class students: we lack basic skills, we don't have aspirations, maybe our parents or caretakers don't care as much. Yet here I was, a teacher confronting a girl who in many ways was more like me as a young girl. She was a precocious reader, but one without a sliver of the opportunity that her more privileged peers received. Her love of Stephen King books was puzzling and even troubling for me, but it also spoke to her gift. This was no remedial reader. How many girls her age could handle a 420-page novel?

Now I have always been a dreamer, so I set out to do something that was as naïve as it was promising. I wanted to offer Blair and the other girls who joined my class something different, a class that went far beyond the teaching of basic skills. Part of me was always a traditionalist. Like any serious English teacher, I knew that it didn't do my students any favors to ignore problems of reading fluency or writing mechanics. But I decided to focus on one of the oldest teaching tools—literature, stories—and create the kind of class that girls in elite schools in America might have: a class for the gifted. I turned to fiction, and especially to stories about girls with few resources but plenty of grit and intelligence. My students would read works of literature and use these as a basis for talking and writing about their own complex lives. We would read our way into a real education, and out of the hopelessness that Blair felt even as a young girl.

The stories that follow chronicle this odyssey, from its beginnings when Blair and her classmates were only eight and nine years old, through the years of middle girlhood and then into those of early adolescence. You will watch me as I struggle to gain a real understanding of my students' lives—and of their strange love of horror. For it turned out that Blair was not the only fan of Stephen King's gruesome stories. As I puzzled over the thought of girls so young reading horror fiction, I began to understand more fully the nature of their true lives and feelings. As this chronicle progresses, you will watch as these girls grow up and become young teens. Their dreams of better lives, their struggles, and at times their stumbles *back* into the streets that claimed so many of their mothers provide an intimate portrait of the grueling journey toward young womanhood faced by the daughters of America's poor whites. You will see me grapple with a question that haunted me: How can one teacher truly make a difference when everything else is working against her students, and her? And what role can books and literature play in such a worthy cause? Can they open doors for other students, the way they once did for me? Could they help provide, in Blair's case, a ticket to upward mobility and the things her grandmother wanted for her? This coming-of-age story is the story of one teacher's struggles to create change and opportunity for girls in the other America.

As our journey is revealed, so are the lives of my other six students. Adriana is one of them, a girl with big dreams. When she was a very young girl, Adriana traveled by Greyhound bus to Las Vegas with her mother. The trip left a strong impression, and Adriana wanted to do things that no one in her family had ever done. She wanted to be a biker, she wanted to see the world, and she wanted to go to college. Over time you will see Adriana contend with the bone-crushing loss of the thing that meant the most to her: her family. Her mother, Kelly, would be sucked into the destructive orbit of a street-drug culture, with the prescription painkiller OxyContin as the first step into an abyss ending in heroin. It is a story that tragically repeats itself across an eight-year journey.

Alicia, our group's tiniest member, a girl with a baby-doll face, soulful eyes, and a sweet, comic smile, would lose her mother at age ten. Her distant stepcousin, Mariah, who eventually joined our group, had faced a similar trauma at an even younger age in the East Tennessee hamlet where she was born. Adopted by a new family in the city, this troubled past haunted her, even as it drew her back to the sweet mountain land where she felt she belonged. My small class would, over time, become a gathering of sisters, orphans in one sense—victims of the reach of drugs such as OxyContin into the lives of the most vulnerable. This was a new chapter in the history of the resourceful but poor laborers who came to the city from Appalachia. It was also one that I knew could destroy a young girl's dreams.

You will follow the unexpected twists—the surprises, the disappointments, the moments of epiphany and change—in the lives of girls such as Shannon, Jessica, and Elizabeth. These three students struggled at first with their attachments to books, to education, and to me—the Teacher. Shannon was our group's self-proclaimed tomboy as a young girl, more interested in basketball than books or school at age nine. She found a voice as a journalist in my class and by the age of eleven was writing moving essays about the challenge of being a girl in such an unforgiving place. But as much as she found herself in an intimate gathering of girls, she lost herself in larger public school classrooms. She would give up on school at sixteen, shortly after losing her baby, who was born at just twenty-three weeks. Shannon's story of alienation in public school is one that repeats itself across time in individual girls' lives and in family histories.

Jessica struggled too. She was from the start of my class an academically weaker student. Still, in my special literature and creative writing class she blossomed. One year older than most of my students, Jessica became our outspoken leader and a poet in search of peace and a better world. But the closer Jessica got to adolescence the further she distanced herself from public school. "How do I help her change this?" I asked myself continually as I watched and worried.

The same was true of my concern about Elizabeth, a passionate girl in search of love. The holes in her heart would get too painful to bear when her family was torn apart and she was sent to foster care. She too became part of our sisterhood: a smart girl who struggled to hold on to her fragile connection to education when the world around her was changing so fast she couldn't understand things.

And Blair, our group's Stephen King fan? Like all of the girls in my class, and like me, Blair was a girl with big dreams. Grandma Lilly thought her gifted grandbaby might someday become a criminal lawyer, for Blair had a way with words. At age nine, Blair herself saw a lot of possibilities for her future. She could be a singer, or maybe someone who lived on a farm. By the time Blair turned sixteen, she would have fallen in love for the first time and become a poet, with a dream of publishing her first book of poems. This Stephen King fan and aspiring writer would also have dropped out of school.

The journey I undertook is based on the belief, indeed the conviction, that things can and *must* be different for girls such as Blair Rainey, and all of the girls who share her dreams and her crushing obstacles to opportunity. My own life journey, from a poorly educated girl in a small mountain town to a Harvard-educated writer, teacher, and social advocate is one message of hope. But then so are the stories of seven determined girls who were every bit as gifted and promising as I once was. Each different, but all steadfast in their desire for a better life than the one they had inherited. These daughters and granddaughters of southern Appalachian workers have grit and resolve, but they need much more if they are to succeed in our new unforgiving economy. The stories that follow provide a chronicle of one teacher's odyssey in poor America, and of the pitfalls and possibilities that arose along a road carved out of simple materials: literature, reading, and stories of childhood dreams.

PART I

Childhood Ghosts

CHAPTER ONE

Ghost Rose Speaks

For Blair Rainey, things began to change in the winter when she was nine years old. This was the time in her life when Blair began to find herself on the pages of her book.

Before then, she had listened and watched as her half sister, a girl in her teens, read aloud. Then things began to come together in a strange new mix: the scary movies Blair loved to watch on television; the book she was starting to read herself; the human drama in her family's social center, a front-facing bedroom. Blair loved to read there, sitting up in bed. Lying next to her was her Grandma Lilly, a heavyset woman with a bad hip and gray, braided hair pulled back tightly to reveal a weary face. For years, her grandma had struggled to hold things together with the thin trickle of funds from Social Security and child support. Blair had slept next to her grandma since she was an underweight newborn, tiny enough at first to fit in a shoebox. But she was growing up. Now everyone in her family knew that Blair was the smart girl who was going to make it out. On gray afternoons that winter, the world in her grandma's bedroom moved to its own rhythms.

Blair.

The television set blared drama and talk shows. A small, scrawny terrier danced in circles for attention. Blair's grandma lay in bed, answering the phone and barking out orders to her grandkids. The bedroom, with its view of the streets outside, smelled of pets and baby pee and musty warmth.

From outside, sounds from the streets drifted in. The crazies were out there, including Blair's mother, a sad and angry ex-addict. "Get your ASS off the sidewalk!" she would scream at some unlucky soul walking by. There was the lady who walked around all the time talking to the billboards. One day she was walking by, and she looked at the chain link fence and said hi to it. Then there was Kooky Old Joe, who had served in World War II. Kooky Joe said that a bomb had gone off right by his ear, and he went around talking to everything too. The streets outside were ugly and crazy and weird, Blair would think to herself, as she sank deeper and deeper into her book.

Blair was born in Lower Price Hill, a neighborhood of just over one thousand on Cincinnati's west side. Close by were the brown, slow-moving waters of the Ohio River. Her grandmother's people, migrants from Appalachia, had once crossed the river on their journey north from eastern Kentucky. They were part of one of the largest population shifts in America's history. Between 1940 and 1970, over three million Appalachian people packed their belongings and left the mountains, hoping to find work and a better future for their children in midwestern cities. They moved into neighborhoods close to old-industry centers, in cities such as Chicago, Dayton, Akron, and Cincinnati. As Janice Sheppard of Williamson, West Virginia, described her journey in the 1950s: "I sold everything we had within two days, made arrangements, and then on the day I decided to leave I had just enough clothes for [my] nine kids."[1] She put everything she could in the trunk of a car and headed north.

The migrants from the southern mountains were typically poor; few were landowning farmers. But up north, men and women could at least find work in warehouses and on the shop floor. In their new urban homelands, the southerners formed close-knit urban villages with ties to their rural points of origin in Kentucky and West Virginia. A stretch of highway, such as old Highway 25 in Kentucky, linked particular counties in Appalachia with particular city communities to the north.

In the summers, Blair visited her one relative who still lived in Kentucky, an aunt in Hazard. Down there, Blair got pushed in a creek by her two half brothers, who were wild and always looking for fun and trouble. She let the family dog off its chain. Sometimes she dreamed of living on a farm with two kids of her own, her dogs, and a horse. But the world that Blair knew in Cincinnati was the concrete universe of the streets. It was better for her inside, especially in late winter, when the purple-gray shadows of dusk came early to the neighborhood.

In March, curtains of early spring wind and rain brought odors from a nearby creek, now a putrid dark green from industrial sewage dumped into its waters—and into the air that Blair breathed. Her asthma kicked up then; out came the inhaler. As the spring afternoons warmed, children and young mothers with baby strollers spilled out from cramped rooms in rental units, onto narrow side streets lined with cigarette butts and trash. Older adults with weathered faces sat on stoops or in rainbow-colored folding chairs, enjoying a smoke. Grown men, most of them white, worked on cars. Their faces often had tired, stressed-out expressions. The factory and warehouse jobs that once beckoned workers from poor counties in Kentucky and West Virginia had begun leaving the neighborhood in the 1980s. The old-industry side of the neighborhood, near where Blair lived, was a ghost town. Warehouse windows were boarded up or gaping. Shards of glass were ground into sidewalks that had once known the human warmth of workers going to and from their jobs.

Then summer came. Blair attended my literature and creative writing class for girls over the summer; she had already been part of my afterschool class during the school year. From my work with her over that year—and the year before, when I volunteered in her classroom—I had learned a tough lesson for a naïve teacher: unless I drove Blair, now ten years old, to summer class myself, sleep often took priority over educational opportunity. And so on the morning of June 25, 2002, I set out for Blair's house.

It was early still, a teacher's start to the day. The light outside was soft, with a pale-gray cloud cover that would lift by midmorning.

It would be a hot day. I drove across one of the many bridges connecting Kentucky, where I lived near the river's edge, to downtown Cincinnati. The sights were familiar from each morning's drive. First there was the busy downtown area, with Starbucks on one corner and high rise banks on the right. Businesspeople in their two-piece suits and secretaries in their heels had begun to walk briskly on the sidewalks. Five stoplights further and I made a left turn, heading west. The road widened and the larger buildings disappeared. Then the road crossed a viaduct, with some old train tracks visible below and, scarcely visible from the road, the polluted creek where earlier generations had taken cool dips to escape the summer heat. Moments later the first of the old brick warehouses appeared to the right. I had arrived in the girls' neighborhood.

Finally there was the intersection—the community's geographic and emotional center. I came to a stop at the light. A few locals wandered into the Paradise Café for coffee and a smoke as I waited. A woman with a tired face and heavyset hips lit up a cigarette while she waited at the bus stop outside. It was an intersection that tended to give outsiders an uneasy feeling. As seventeen-year-old Bill Ferris, who grew up in the neighborhood, said to a reporter in the 1980s: "You're standing there on the corner by the light, and you hear all these doors locking—click, click, click—like you're going to come and pull them out of their cars and rob them."[2]

The light changed. I turned right onto Perry Avenue, the two-lane road where Blair lived. Most of the houses on her stretch of street were of modest size and in need of repairs to their clapboard frames. Her part of the neighborhood had been dubbed Little Appalachia for its resemblance to rural hamlets in West Virginia or Kentucky. The two-story wood-frame homes sat close together, their yards spilling over with bicycle parts, discarded car tires, wrappers and cigarette butts, and young bodies at play.

Grandma Lilly had bought their home years before. She had labored to completely pay off the house in only six years. Now, at least, her grandchildren would have a roof over their heads if anything ever happened to her. But Grandma Lilly's precarious health and the thin trickle of Social Security benefits didn't create the conditions for upkeep on an older two-story house. From the front, it appeared to sag, the front-facing porch weighing heavily on wooden beams. The house stood across from a tall yellow billboard with black lettering that shouted its message: WE BUY UGLY HOUSES.

Most mornings it was an ordeal to get Blair into my car and to the special reading and writing class I had created for her and five other girls. I walked to the side door, past two barking chows straining against their heavy chains, and up the concrete porch that was missing its handrail. From inside came a sleepy young adult voice: "*Who* is it?" The voice belonged to Blair's older half sister, still in her teens but already working the night shift at Taco Bell. Once inside, I found most of the household still in bed. Blair's toddler niece lay curled up next to Grandma Lilly in the front bedroom, where up to four generations slept on a given night. On one of the cardboard boxes stacked next to a dresser sat Blair, sleep-deprived and growling a feeble protest. She was a night person. But once she got to my reading class, Blair usually perked up. One of the reasons was that in the summers my class always began with breakfast.

By eight that morning, I sat with Blair, still looking crusty-eyed and cranky, and five more of my students at a makeshift breakfast table—the kind of round work table you could find in any public elementary school in America. Next to me sat Miss Susan, an instructional assistant at the school who often joined the girls and me for breakfast on summer mornings. On the table, covered with a cheap paper tablecloth, were the food offerings I had brought in this morning: blueberry muffins and raspberry jam, granola, yogurt, orange juice, and a bowl of hard-boiled eggs. I always fussed over my students, southern style, at our summer breakfasts, and Blair brought out my motherly instincts. She was a picky eater, and I nudged a couple of YoBaby fruit-flavored yogurts in her direction. Blair had taken home a point-and-shoot camera of mine to photograph some of the darker reaches of her house, including the attic. She was creating photographic images to go with a story she was writing.

"I live in a cave," said Blair, the crumbs from a blueberry muffin at the sides of her mouth. "And my house is hell."

"I've been to hell and your house ain't it," shot back Miss Susan, speaking quickly and glancing sideways at Blair. Her words were as much about delivery as content. Audience was important, and she aimed her remark at all of us around the table. Her lips parted in the faintest of smiles, revealing the gap from her two missing front teeth.

Blair snickered at Miss Susan's in-your-face reply. These mornings felt to her more like being with family than sitting through one of the dreaded summer school classes held in other parts of the school building, for the unlucky students who couldn't pass their end-of-year tests. She knew that here she could get in someone's face as well as Miss Susan—or anyone else she encountered on the little section of street she was allowed to roam—could. Blair's tiny frame made her look like a little girl, but the motor mouth on her was something altogether different. For a girl who came into the world as an underweight baby with drugs in her system, the physical world had to be subdued by verbal wit, intelligence, and bravery.

Miss Susan plopped a banana down on the table in front of me. She looked older than a woman in her late forties. Money was short, and Miss Susan had to work two jobs to make ends meet. Her black hair was pinned back, revealing the tired lines on her face. There were shadows under her steel gray eyes, though those same eyes betrayed a youthful, sassy feeling. She was a proud woman who could beat the shit out of anyone who messed with her.

"Eat this, it's good for you," she said in a voice made husky from smoking her Newport Lights.

"Did you work late last night?" I asked. Miss Susan worked her night job at United Dairy Farmers, serving up ice cream cones and floats. Some nights she didn't finish cleaning up until after one in the morning.

She nodded and muttered soberly, "Mmmmm."

"Miss Deborah, you know where I worked for ten years?" said Blair. "In *hell*."

"She's a little demon with two horns comin' out of her head," said Elizabeth.

"She's goin' down—*God*, I HATE to see her go that way!" said baby-faced Alicia, who sat next to Elizabeth.

"I'm a smart-mouth and evil *bitch!*" said Blair. She picked at the corner of her blueberry muffin carelessly, as though eating it were the last thing on her mind.

"And my attic is like Rose Red," she said, thinking once again of the house that she was photographing. Blair let the fingers of her right hand rest for a moment on the book she had brought from home. On its cover was an image of a bull and the title *Rose Madder*. On the inside page were accolades from reviews. "A work filled with terror from the very first page," read one. "Disturbing, haunting...King paints a vivid nightmare," read another.

"*Rose Red!*" said Adriana, her half-closed eyes coming alive with the thought. "I wanna read *Rose Red*—actually I wanna see the movie again because I like it when the ghost lady, she pulls that dude's *mom* into the closet."

Blair could picture in her head her own mother, who had been in and out of the household all summer, trying to hold things together after her latest round of rehab. There had been ten babies born to Blair's mother, and Grandma Lilly could keep only a few of them. Family came first, but there were limits to what even family could do in such desperate circumstances. The trouble for Blair's mother, I discovered, began with alcohol and drug abuse, things she had tried to correct in sporadic rounds of rehab. In between her stays in rehab and halfway houses, Blair's mother went around with different men. Blair had never met her biological father, but she knew he was a different man than the man she sometimes called her stepdad, a drunk. The changing cast of characters gave Blair a feeling of being in a crazy house. The only good thing about her mother being in the house was that Blair's half brothers didn't act out as much and hit her.

Sometimes her mother sat in the front bedroom, watching television along with everyone else. She was a large woman whose auburn hair fell upon her shoulders in a wild way, as though blown by a fierce wind. Her face was sallow and had a haggard, angry look. She was, Blair would say, *very* mean; if you saw her on the street, you would feel afraid. Sometimes when she was out of money, she would beg from Grandma Lilly, who struggled to keep food in the mouths of Blair and the other grandbabies left to her care. Other times she would go around and do things to get money from men. Blair didn't *like* people like that. As a matter of fact, she didn't like her mother. She wouldn't have minded if an evil house like Rose Red had sucked her mother into one of its shape-shifting walls.

"In *Rose Red* something happens to women," said Blair. "They end up *dead*."

"What's *Rose Red?*" I asked innocently. I had missed King's made-for-television movie when it aired over the winter.

"A haunted house," said Blair, turning the plastic spoon in her banana YoBaby yogurt like a stubborn three-year-old. When her mother was around the house, Blair wanted to be the baby. At those times, she would come into my class with a pacifier dangling from her mouth. She would crawl on the floor, cooing and making high whimpering sounds. She had acquired a nickname: Itty Bitty.

"And there's this girl," said Elizabeth. "She's magical, she's the only one that can wake up Rose Red."

Elizabeth sat next to Miss Susan, nearly opposite the round table from me. She was one of our group's heartiest eaters, but you wouldn't know it from her skinny arms that always seemed ready to flail at something. In front of her on the bright pink tablecloth was a tiny junkyard of the morning's feast: two empty yogurt containers, a banana peel, a pool of muffin crumbs. At the sides of her mouth were the vestiges of the raspberry jam she had smeared on her muffin. Elizabeth spoke in the same throaty tones as Miss Susan. She spit out her words as quickly as she ate:

"That-was-scary, man, when that hand popped out of the refrigerator. I didn't know that was gonna happen."

The movie had aired on television in late January. The most important character in the movie is the old mansion itself, a house named Rose Red and set on a hilltop in Seattle. The house is sinister, and has been from the day it was built in 1906 by an oil magnate, John Rimbauer, for his beautiful young wife, Ellen. The house snatched their little daughter, April, born with a withered arm. It added rooms like a metastasizing tumor, and these would shift constantly, with dire consequences for the unsuspecting visitor. But the house has been quiet, a "dead cell," since 1972, the year that a pocketbook-clutching lady on the Historical Society's tour had disappeared. All of this is of great interest to Professor Joyce Reardon, out to obtain scientific proof that paranormal phenomena actually exist. Into the house she goes with her strange cortege of hired psychics, including fifteen-year-old Annie, an autistic girl. Then the house begins to come alive. Roses and other plants bloom in the solarium, clocks start to tick, and the trouble begins. One by one, the members of Professor Reardon's band of psychic explorers are picked off by Rose Red. But sweet Annie is different. Rose Red's long-term occupants call out to her in barely audible spirit voices: "Annie, Aaaaanniee."

"She woke up the house," said Elizabeth, leaning forward on her bony elbows.

The conversation had woken up Adriana herself, and her oval eyes, half-shut before, now revealed their rich lavender tones.

"Okay, this is gonna take a while," she said. Adriana rarely took the floor for long, but when she did she expected the others to pay close attention. "Okay, in that Rose Red house, something happens to girl—women, and something different happens to—"

As will happen with any group of girls sitting together and eating, Elizabeth and Blair had begun whispering on the side, snickering at some secret joke. Shannon looked distracted. She wasn't a fan of *Rose Red,* or any of King's stories really. Little Alicia was giggling at Blair's latest bit of food play—crumbling your breakfast muffin into a tiny mound. Our two tiniest girls felt like sisters sometimes, and they were in cahoots this morning.

"Hel-LO RUDIES!" said Adriana, narrowing her long eyes into a look of preteen disgust.

It was my cue to suggest that we clear the table of breakfast and start our reading.

The ground-floor classroom that I borrowed for our class was divided into several sections. Near the front of the room, close to the blackboard, was an eclectic assortment of inexpensive wicker armchairs, old-fashioned wooden chairs, and more modern plastic chairs, all shuffled into a makeshift circle. It was our meeting area, a place to talk about books and the stories and journal entries written by the girls themselves. Against one wall was a pair of rectangular work tables, one of which held our gleaming new Mac computer. Against the other wall, below a row of large old-fashioned windows with wooden sashes, was the round table that doubled as our breakfast nook and, when class had started, as a desk for writing. Placed on the carpet near our meeting circle were two stacks of oversized pillows for plopping up against a wall or lying more comfortably on the thin carpet. Finally, at the far side of these work areas, but facing our meeting circle and blackboard, were some white bookshelves I had brought in myself—sale finds from an office supply store. Miss Susan had assembled them one morning, holding tiny nails in her lips, a hammer in her hand. In the bookshelves were the literary titles I had worked for over a year to acquire: writing grants had become the raison d'être of my weekend life ever since I began my literature class.

Those shelves might have looked like an ordinary collection of books, pretty humble compared to something you would find in a wealthier school. But to me they were special: I had searched everywhere—the Internet, local bookstores, libraries—to find just the right titles. Now there they sat, rows of novels and stories featuring girls as heroines. There was Cynthia Rylant's sentimental novel about a girl's coming of age in a poor family, *A Blue-Eyed Daisy.* There was Alice Hoffman's magical tale of girlhood friendship and summer love, *Aquamarine.* There was Frances O'Roark Dowell's novel *Dovey Coe,* about a working-class girl who could get in your face every bit as much as my girls in their finest moments. And there were even some literary classics, favorites of girls across the generations: *The Secret Garden, Anne of Green Gables.*

I stood back and soaked in the scene with a teacher's sense of well-being. The girls were well fed, the morning light was angling in from our east-facing windows, open to let in a thankfully cool morning breeze. The neighborhood outside was still quiet at this hour, not yet nine. I watched as the girls meandered toward the bookshelves. We had no hard and fast rules about which books the girls had to read. I pushed my literary titles, marketing these like a savvy sales rep. I read from them, displayed them in inviting ways on the shelves, put up attractive posters. But I also wanted the girls to make their final selections for themselves. It was summer, after all, a time for indulging ourselves a little even if we were in school. And some part of me was more curious learner than stern schoolteacher. I stood back to watch as the girls made their choices. That summer I had given in and set aside one shelf of our bookshelves for paperback books for the young connoisseur of scary fiction. The girls huddled excitedly around that shelf: they couldn't wait to get their hands on the three-book series, The House on Cherry Street, that was the summer's hottest read. It was a tale of a haunted house that began with *The Haunting,* moved on to *The Horror,* and reached its riotous conclusion in *The Final Nightmare.*[3]

That night I sat up in bed with a copy of the book Blair had brought to my class, confronting my misgivings about so young a girl reading horror. After I had finished teaching for the day and driven Blair home, I managed to find a copy of her King book at a local bookstore. Sleep didn't come easily that night, and it wasn't just because *Rose Madder* was a page-turner. The story scared the hell out of me. As I read, I felt more like a helpless little girl than a grown woman, a professional educator, living in a safe top-floor apartment.

In one scene, Rose's psychopath husband, Norman, goes after Pam, a sweet blonde hotel maid. Pam once lived at the home for abused women where Rose resides, and Norman thinks she can reveal Rose's whereabouts. Norman traps Pam in a hotel laundry room, trying to squeeze the information out of her. But his interrogation quickly turns gruesome. He grabs Pam by the throat; she slips out of his grasp and lunges for the door.

> She looked almost nailed to the door, and as Norman stepped forward, he saw that, in a way, she was. There was a coathook on the back of the damned thing. She'd torn free of his hand, plunged forward, and impaled herself. The coathook was buried in her left eye....
>
> [Norman] yanked Pam off the coathook. There was an unspeakable gristly sound as she came. Her one good eye—bluer than ever, it seemed to Norman—stared at him in wordless horror.
>
> Then she opened her mouth and shrieked.[4]

The next morning I sat at my kitchen table, nursing a soothing cup of coffee. My eyes were bloodshot and puffy. I still felt foggy from a sleep that started late and ended at six with the shrill sound of a digital alarm clock. But even so my mind was at work, trying to make sense of Blair's words. The parts of the story jammed against one another: a young girl, Stephen King, horror. This wasn't what I had in mind when I had created my literature class for girls. I thought I knew what Blair needed. She was growing up in a poor neighborhood. And public school wasn't exactly a sanctuary, not the uplifting school experience of the Hollywood cliché, with the wide-eyed children in their thrift-store clothing, discovering a slice of the American Dream. In a time when more and more seemed to hinge on single-shot yearly tests, girls attending public school in poor neighborhoods spent much of their school days in an endless rehearsal for the big March tests. I wanted my class to be about something different: the gift of literature, a chance to expand their minds through the world of books and to share stories and life dreams. I wanted to open the door to what Robert Coles once termed a literature of social reflection. We needed a place, I believed, to read and talk about fiction, and about all the real-world things that make life for a poor white girl so complicated and hard and beautiful—all at the same time.

But *Stephen King?*

When I was still a girl, about the same age as Blair, I had my own share of childhood ghosts. There was my family, as complicated as Blair's in its own way, though we were not as severely poor. And there was school, where I sat for years in a kind of quiet daze, a combination of boredom and acquiescence to my fate. A girl was not supposed to be outspoken, so I held my peace, without anyone realizing that here was a girl with a curious mind and dreams about the world. The mountain landscape was my closest friend in those days. Always a child in search of adventure, I would go off for long walks, during which my imagination was free to wander as well. And very early I began to form a sense of my destiny around the idea that I would leave. At home was my mother, lost in the fog of her depression; my brother, already on the miserable life course of a disturbed kid without the benefit of medical help or therapy; and my father, an angry man—the son of an alcoholic who had never recovered from his own dirt-poor childhood. In my walks, I created my own form of leaving until one day I had the chance to go off to college and become an educator.

And now here I was, like a woman who had traveled in a time machine. I was trying to be a teacher for a girl struggling to find her own way in a crazy world. I felt lost and confused about Blair's love for a kind of fiction that was gruesome and freakish—or at least, that freaked me out. But I didn't want to be the kind of teacher who just taught skills without trying to get to the heart of her students' stories. I felt that Blair was trying to tell me something with her fascination with Stephen King stories. So rather than closing the door to her version of childhood ghosts, I went in the other direction. I listened carefully, until I could almost hear the faint voice of a character she was beginning to create. *Rose.*

Later that morning, I sat with Blair, who was lounging comfortably in one of our armchairs. Blair's hair had earlier in the summer been cut into a sweet pageboy. It made her pale face look even more childlike, though her small gray eyes had an older-girl edginess. Something about her was different that morning, and I struggled to make sense of it. Her hair was slicked down with baby oil; it looked nearly wet. Later I learned why. Oil was a good antidote to lice. If you got nits or lice in your hair, the

Ghost Rose.

nasty things would slither right off. With so many little ones in the house just then, Blair didn't want to take chances. She herself looked small in the ample armchair. An oversized T-shirt, a thrift-store find, hung down nearly below her knees. The fan placed near an open window was rotating, making its whirring sounds, and we began to talk about fiction.

Blair had been putting the finishing touches on a story she was writing about a ghost in her attic, a girl named Rose, Ghost Rose. Rose does a terrible thing: she gets in a fight and beats up a girl she doesn't like. When Rose gets home, she tells her father what has happened. He tells Rose to go to her room, like he always did when she did something wrong. But then he takes her up to the attic and locks her in. He never lets her out for anything. When it is time for breakfast, lunch, or dinner, he always brings her food. She can drink only water or orange juice. After some years, Rose dies in the attic.

Rose was still in the attic, Blair assured me as we talked. In her hand was a copy of *The Final Nightmare,* the last of the books in the House on Cherry Street paperback series.

Life in the rooms below Blair's attic, where the spirit of Rose resided, had been crazy and unsettling that summer. Blair's half brothers were wired with a frenzied energy, their gangly adolescent limbs in constant motion as they ran hoodlum-like around the house and the street in search of trouble and entertainment. Both boys had been in trouble in school throughout the year; it was rumored that their behavior had been affected by the drugs in their systems at birth. With her smart mouth, Blair frequently found herself caught in the path of their blows. The real stability was in her grandma's bedroom, where Blair slept, the door locked to make sure one of the boys didn't come in and wake the younger ones. In spite of these precautions, Blair often complained of lack of sleep.

There were fights on the streets on hot summer evenings. An ordinary argument, with its shouting and cussing and stepping up to the brink of blows, would cross the line into a real brawl, with or without the benefit of knives or guns. There was trash, too; people just threw their trash on the ground. The gutters were filled with it, which Blair found disgusting. As a ten-year-old girl, Blair saw her neighborhood in shades of gray. The streets were dirty, crazy, and weird, she thought.

As a matter of fact, sometimes Blair felt crazy herself. And at night when things got quiet, she could hear Rose talking in a terrible, sweet voice.

"Rose only speaks to *me*," Blair said. Her small eyes seemed focused on some secret place, not visible to me. She was starting to speak in a high-pitched child voice, like Ghost Rose herself.

"What does Rose say to you?" I asked Blair.

"I *want out*," was Blair's sweetly uttered reply.

This was the summer when it began to dawn on me that Blair's ghost stories and horror novels were about more than things that go bump in the night. For Blair the stories were just as much about her place in a world that was frightening and troubling and beautiful. It was a world of sharp contrasts. The strength and resilience of female voices were present within and around all of my students. So was the backbone of extended family, the very center of life for girls in an Appalachian community.

But Blair and my other students also faced bone-crushing loss: their childhoods had been stolen from them. For the landscape in which they were coming of age was a haunted one. It was depressing, uncertain, sometimes fear-provoking. People fought on the streets, dealers worked their corners, the unemployed were listless and ashamed, the air was foul with pollutants that would never be tolerated by the more privileged. Inside their homes, girls had the warmth of family love, but even this couldn't shield them from harm. The earlier southern migrants had been poor at the start of their journeys to the city, but now, with the loss of jobs and a street-drug problem—the abuse of painkillers—the community's poverty was starting to spin out of control. The street's worst effects were tearing at the fabric of intimate family. Everywhere my girls turned they found reminders of the demons they had to stare down just to make it to the other side of adolescence.

In their improbable way, I was learning, the horror stories offered hope. Hapless heroines could outwit sinister spirits and crazies. Even the heroine of *Rose Madder* could find the inner strength to defeat the horrifying monster that Norman had become. Spirits such as Blair's Ghost Rose could speak out in angry voices, letting others know how trapped and alone they felt. I too was trying to create hope around the only form of transcendence I knew: an education rich in literature and reading.

All around me were the mantras about education for the poor. I was supposed to be getting the girls workforce ready, skilled enough at reading so they could at least finish high school. What the pundits and policymakers would have seen, if for a moment they could have peered at Blair as she talked about books, was a young girl with more than her share of reading skills. She was looking for something deeper in literature, maybe a small place for herself beyond the graying walls of a public school classroom. The road ahead for her would be a long and difficult one; that much I knew from my experience. But I was determined to help Blair find her own way.

It would not be the last time we heard about Ghost Rose. Nor was Rose the only ghost to make an appearance in my summer class. As the weeks wore on, I would learn that other girls were living haunted childhoods. There was Alicia's Ghost Howard—now he was a crazy one! Always up to no good. And there was the ghost of little Bobby in The House on Cherry Street paperbacks, Elizabeth's favorite literary ghost. A floodgate of stories had opened, and out the ghosts poured.

There is a tradition of storytelling among people of Appalachian heritage, and the culture is no stranger to dark tales or gore. But something different was going on, I suspected, something to do with the way in which these brave, resourceful girls—daughters and granddaughters of mountain soil—were coping with an urban neighborhood that had begun to turn into a ghetto, a ghost of itself. I couldn't have known at the time, for my students kept their secrets guarded at first, but the shadows of drug abuse, starting with painkillers but ending for some with heroin, were creeping even into their intimate families. Blair's mother was lost; she had done little more in the way of parenting than give birth to Blair. Alicia's mother was starting to slip, too, and experiment with weekend thrill rides. Adriana's mother would sometimes come home glassy-eyed from being high. We were becoming a sisterhood of girls with stolen childhoods. I wasn't conscious of these events at first, but one thing I did know: Blair had found a type of fiction that was speaking more powerfully as a teaching tool than any I could bring to her.

That night, in bed again with my copy of *Rose Madder,* I stayed up past midnight with my heart pounding, unable to stop reading the story.

CHAPTER TWO

Elizabeth Discovers Her Paperback

Even before our class began on a warm morning later that same week in June, our two floor fans were already working furiously. The sun's rays had begun to warm my ground-floor classroom past the comfort level. From the second floor came wafts of something that smelled toxic. The floors upstairs were being stripped, and it was of no consequence that the odors might be disturbing, or even unhealthy, for the children and teachers working on the floor below. An incident that generated anger and mistrust throughout the neighborhood crept into my thoughts. In the 1980s, several children had had to be carried out of the school on stretchers because of toxic fumes from a nearby paint shop. I wondered for a moment if the fumes we had to live with on this summer morning were safe for the girls, and for me. But I didn't have much time to linger on my latest source of anxiety. The girls would be coming in soon.

I pushed back my worries and looked around, admiring the handiwork of my teaching preparations. One thing I had quickly discovered was that compared to the increasingly regimented curriculum that teachers were compelled to offer during the year, summer school was like a tabula rasa. For four glorious hours each day, a resourceful teacher could offer the reading curriculum that she felt her students needed, not the prepackaged schemes marketed to desperate school districts as the latest fix for poorly performing students. All that spring and into the early weeks of summer, I had embarked on a hunt for the perfect summer reading for a class of girls, and not just any girls. Several of my students were still getting their feet on the ground as readers. Jessica and Alicia read haltingly, and either of them could give up easily if a book seemed too hard or too long. The landscape of the girls' lives made things different, too. How many novels for young readers feature young heroines who are poor and white, and who face anything close to the obstacles faced by my students? Today as I looked again at the bookshelves, I was sure I had finally found the book that would pull my students into its beautifully written story about a girl's life.

The novel was written by a woman with Appalachian roots and was set in West Virginia. Ellie Farley, the young heroine of Cynthia Rylant's *A Blue-Eyed Daisy,* is a pretty girl with long fair hair, blue eyes, and rotting teeth. At home, there are her four older sisters, ensconced in their teenage worlds. There is her hard-drinking father, Okey, out of work after a mining accident, and her stressed-out mother, who has shut the door on her feelings of rage and disappointment. Okey sometimes loses it in a bout of drinking. At those times, Ellie hides and cringes, while her mother absorbs Okey's verbal rantings and occasional punches. Most of the time, however, Ellie struggles for connection, even with her damaged father. The novel chronicles "some year," as Ellie inches closer toward her twelfth birthday.[1]

I felt a sense of anticipation that any book-loving teacher would recognize. For months, I had worked day and night to plan for our special summer class. For over a year, we had met after school each week, building trust and the ability to listen to one another. Now the day was ours and—even with the drippy Ohio heat and the fumes coming from upstairs—I was ready.

I straightened an old family quilt I used that summer as a cozy cushion for our meeting circle. Sometimes we sat right on the carpeted floor because the girls were so small—and so was our group. I couldn't get Jessica out of bed to come to my summer class every morning, so often we ended up with four students who had attended my Monday afterschool class that spring— Adriana, Alicia, Blair, and Shannon—and one who hadn't, Elizabeth. This was Elizabeth's first time in an intensive summer class devoted so strongly to reading and talking about literature, and she wasn't at all sure how she felt about things.

Elizabeth was the kind of girl who harbored secret feelings of anger and longing. She was a passionate girl, always in search of something. Elizabeth tended to throw herself into things head-first, the way that later in the summer she would jump into the deep end of the neighborhood pool without knowing how to swim. She had to be fished out by lifeguards. When she fell for something she loved, she fell hard and fast. All across the school year in our weekly afterschool class, I had struggled to find books that wouldn't provoke the word that Elizabeth hauled out for things she *didn't* love: *boring*. It had been a rocky year for Elizabeth and for me, but now I was hopeful that Elizabeth could find herself on the pages of a novel about a working-class girl's life. It was the very novel I would have wanted as a girl her age, a girl

Elizabeth.

without a teacher like me who would struggle with a choice so simple—the choice of a novel—and yet so important.

At 9:20 that morning, Elizabeth and I sat together on the colorful patchwork quilt, talking about the novel. We sat cross-legged on my old family quilt, and Elizabeth read a passage from the book's first section, Fall, about one season in a year of big changes for Ellie Farley.

"She was a nervous woman with a nervous laugh."

Elizabeth read aloud from a chapter entitled "At the Dinner Table." A narrator's voice conveys Ellie's anxious feelings as she sits at the family dinner table. On the one hand, there are the "silences and secrets of four teenage girls"—Ellie's sisters. Then there is Ellie's mother, full of hurt and angry resignation.

Elizabeth read aloud from the scene: "And though she had been welcoming with her warm arms when the girls were all small, she had withdrawn those arms more and more as the girls grew. Now Ellie couldn't remember the last time she had been hugged by her mother."[2]

Elizabeth paused for a moment. The story made her think of the house where she lived.

Elizabeth's family lived out Perry Avenue, past Blair's house. To get there, you turned down a small side street that dead-ended in a cul-de-sac. Beyond Elizabeth's home was an industrial park; to its right was a weedy, overgrown lot. Elizabeth's family owned the house, but the lot next door belonged to a slumlord who sometimes used it as a dump for old cars. Elizabeth's world the year she was ten was the small universe of a dead-end street and a rundown two-story house packed with nine young bodies. The only way in or out was by means of the green van that her dad drove, packing everyone in to drive to and from school or other required destinations. He was still working on and off, but the family was one of the poorer ones even in a neighborhood known for its hard living.

Elizabeth's mother had family in nearby rural Indiana, and her grandmother still lived down there. Most Sundays, the kids were packed into the green van and driven across the state border to a small country church. Elizabeth would listen to the Sunday preaching, taking careful note of how the minister was eyeing the breasts of the teenage girls. Her mother had left the country at fourteen and had gotten pregnant with her first child. Now everyone was kept under the stern, watchful eye of Elizabeth's father and—of course—the Lord Himself.

As she read, Elizabeth must have found herself connecting with many of the things happening to Ellie. Like Ellie, she shared a bedroom with four sisters. The youngest, little Julie, was still getting potty trained and sometimes wet their shared bed. As a matter of fact, Elizabeth thought that she herself smelled like pee this morning because of Julie. And like Ellie in the novel, Elizabeth could not remember the last time she had gotten a hug from her mother. Her mother, a woman in her thirties, was pregnant again and stressed out from trying to raise the nine children she already had.

Elizabeth looked to me, as if the realization had suddenly hit her.

"Hey, the girl in the book is just like me!" she said.

She seemed surprised at the threads of connection, but also excited—as though, I thought, she had stumbled upon an unexpected treasure, something that called to her as though it were meant to be hers, as she meandered through a junk store filled with dreary old relics.

Eureka! I thought. *This is it!*—the kind of moment I had dreamed about when I created a reading class for girls. Here was Elizabeth, a young reader who seemed to be in her literary element. She was making strong personal connections to a novel. She was engaged and active—reading the book with a questioning and curious spirit, going back and forth between the novel's fictional portrayal of a girl's life and her own life.

There was just one problem: Elizabeth didn't *like* the book.

"I'm sure you're *all* excited about reading," I offered hopefully as we sat on my quilt later that morning, having one of our first book group discussions that summer.

"I'm not!" shot back Elizabeth.

The idea of reading a novel about a girl like her was one big reason she didn't care for the book.

"It's kind of stupid," she remarked.

Elizabeth's observation stung a little, but I was determined to move ahead. The time felt right to dig into a character-driven novel.

"Can some of you talk about how your life connects with Ellie's life in *A Blue-Eyed Daisy?*"

In the meantime, Elizabeth had embarked on a different agenda: finding the few swear words that appeared on the novel's pages.

"And she said a cuss word that says h-e-l-l," Elizabeth said, thrilled with her discovery.

This was, I knew, a time in Elizabeth's life when the word *hell* had strong meaning. On their Sunday jaunts to the country church where her mother's cousin did his preaching, the girls in the family learned about being saved from going to Hell. Now it was hard to get her thoughts wrapped around the kinds of things I wanted to discuss.

"That is not a cuss word!" said Alicia.

"What about my question?" I said, with more firmness in my voice. I was starting to grow irritated, or maybe just a little hurt.

"There's this boy that kissed her," said Alicia. "Harold, his name was Harold."

"Oh, my gosh!" said Elizabeth, her long arms making a tiny movement upward, like a young sparrow about to flap its growing wings.

The thing that meant the most to Elizabeth that summer was the door of friendship that had been opened to her by our group's sweet-faced Alicia. Before this happened, Elizabeth didn't have a best friend in school. She felt alone and disconnected in the world. At home were her eight siblings, ranging in age from a toddler in diapers to a girl in her teens, and Elizabeth's stressed-out mother. But everything had changed with her discovery of a friendship that seemed fated to happen. One afternoon we had gone on a fieldtrip to a local bookstore so that each member of my class could pick out a book to call her own over the summer. Elizabeth chose an illustrated copy of *The Secret Garden,* and with the book came two necklaces with charms. It seemed only natural to her that one of the charms should go to Alicia.

"Like the book said, Ellie was getting kissed," said Alicia. "And a long time ago when I was little there was this stupid idiot boy that tried to kiss me. I smacked him and punched him and told my mom. But he kept on doing it, so I kicked him and I kept on beating him up, and he finally stopped."

Elizabeth said, "The only part that would've stopped him is to kick 'im where it hurts. That's what I say."

"No, you don't do that," said Alicia.

"*Uh huh,* I would do it," said Elizabeth.

"Are there other ways that Ellie's life experiences or her feelings connect with your life?" I asked.

Blair sat opposite Elizabeth and Alicia on our quilt. She thought about the bedroom she shared with her grandma, her little niece, and sometimes one of her half sisters. The teenage boys, her half brothers, came in and out of the room at night when they wanted to watch television, and this kept Blair awake. She could picture the room she wanted, with a big bed and Pooh Bears on the wall.

"Ellie's life is like mine because she is sad all the time," she said.

Alicia was still only nine, and she looked every bit the part of our group's little girl. She had worked herself into a serious case of the giggles over the kissing scene in *A Blue-Eyed Daisy*. But when Blair spoke, Alicia's face softened into an expression that seemed older.

"Why are you sad all the time?" she asked.

"Because I'm tired of sharing a room with my sisters," said Blair. "And my dad—like she has a father that drinks a lot—my dad's a drunk and a smart-aleck."

I thought about the word that Blair used: *dad*. I had a hard time attaching it to the factual details of her biological father. He had been little more than a passing moment in her mother's quest for alcohol, drugs, and, I suppose, love, to the extent that love could be distinguished from desperate need and desire. Every time Blair thought about the man she called Dad, she felt angry and confused.

"And he never stops drinking," she said.

"If I was Ellie, and I had a father that drank and a mother that argued," said Adriana, "I would call the police. Ellie needs better parents. Parents that are nice, that don't get drunk and argue with each other."

Adriana lowered her eyelids, as though her vision were turning inward. "I bet Ellie wants a nice house with absolute no parents and quiet and . . . and a big swimming pool. The reason I say that is that is what *I* need."

I thought of the novel and its story about a girl who struggled for a relationship with her damaged and defeated father. "Is what you want different from what Ellie wants?" I said.

"I want it to be no parents," Adriana replied. "And the reason is—I hardly get to see my real dad. He doesn't come to see me because he's too busy up his stepkids' butt. My mom and stepdad argue all the time in front of me, which they're not supposed to."

Adriana let out a small laugh. "This one time my mom and my stepdad were arguing, and my mom threw the coffeemaker on my stepdad. And it broke."

"My mom beats the crap out of my dad!" said Alicia in her young voice.

"My mom is like hers," said Blair, looking sideways at Adriana, seated to her left. "Because her mom breaks things over her stepdad's head, and *my* mom breaks telephones over my dad's head."

"What's it like for you to read a book with a character who reminds you of yourself in certain ways?" I said. "What does it feel like when you're reading?"

"Weird," Blair replied.

"What does *weird* mean?"

"Crazy," she said, as if this second word explained everything.

"Why do you want us to read all *boring* books?" said Elizabeth. She had been unusually quiet during our discussion. Now she seemed downright sulky. And there it was again, the word that Elizabeth loved to throw out at such moments.

"Well, they don't seem boring to me," I confessed.

"I know, that's the problem," shot back Elizabeth. She had come alive again within our group. Her hazel eyes flashed; her long, skinny torso straightened upward.

I started to explain: "It's hard for me to understand what you like because—"

"We don't want your kind," said Elizabeth, before I could finish my thought.

It was my kind of *book* she didn't want. And there was a reason for this: my sentimental novel about a girl's coming of age couldn't hold a candle to the paperback that Elizabeth and her best friend, Alicia, had discovered on their own.

It was found in a cardboard box of paperback giveaways, donated by someone from outside the girls' community. From the moment Elizabeth discovered the book, she knew it was meant to be hers. *The Final Nightmare* was an old-fashioned ghost story, the third in the House on Cherry Street series about a summer rental house with a dark past. In the stories—written by the husband-and-wife team, Rodman Philbrick and Lynn Harnett—eleven-year-old Jason, his mom and dad, and his four-year-old sister Sally moved into an old gabled house for the summer. Almost right away, the house began to assert its haunted nature.

The spirits haunting the house revealed themselves only to Jason and Sally—the children. This was in part because at the book's narrative center was the ghost of a child, Bobby, who had died when an evil nanny, Miss Everett, chased him with such malice that he crashed through a second-floor banister and fell to his death. The nanny's spirit still reigned as an evil witch. Little Bobby also roamed the house, his child-voice aimed mostly at young Sally.

The morning following my attempt to lead the book group, Elizabeth and Alicia lay sprawled on the carpet with pillows to cushion their elbows. In front of them on the floor was the paperback with its torn front cover. The two girls took turns reading pages, though Elizabeth read faster. She read aloud like she spoke—fast and with an edgy tone in her voice. Alicia listened closely. Young Jason had gone upstairs to the attic to investigate some inexplicable things about the summer house on Cherry Street.

> I stepped into the attic.
>
> I gasped in surprise. And instantly bent over coughing as the dust flowed down my throat. But I didn't care.
>
> The attic was a wreck!
>
> The walls were totally smashed in. There were big holes in the floor.
>
> And Bobby's rocking chair was still there!
>
> The little rocking chair was the only thing that wasn't smashed to bits—everything else was broken or damaged.
>
> Even my parents would have to believe the house was really haunted when they saw this!
>
> I was about to yell for my dad. Then I heard something move behind me. A rustling, sneaky sound in the shadows.
>
> The back of my neck tingled.
>
> I was slowly turning around to look when a horrible voice spoke right by my ear. A creaky, raspy voice of the undead.
>
> "*You!*" it shrieked. "*It's all your fault! I'll get you! I'll get you for good!*"[3]

It was not surprising to me that Alicia chose to read the paperback book that she and Elizabeth had discovered in the box of secondhand giveaways. Alicia had lost crucial ground in reading that year. Near the end of the summer before, just months before she was to enter fourth grade, Alicia moved across the river to

Kentucky. There was some hint of family trouble, but none of this was spelled out for teachers such as me. Later I would be able to fill in some of the pieces—the street drugs, her mother's falling out with an older churchgoing generation, the desperate need for housing. But mostly what I saw were their effects. In late spring of the school year, Alicia had moved back to Cincinnati, looking lost and reading far behind peers such as Elizabeth. *The Final Nightmare* was at just her reading level, and she read even its fast-paced action and campy dialogue slowly—word by word.

Elizabeth was in a different place. She was already a stronger reader, and she had been part of my weekly class during the school year. Across the school year she had changed so much as a reader that I knew that summer reading could be a turning point for her. Also, I felt a teacher's sense of urgency, because already Elizabeth was beginning to lose her attachment to school. This was strange and troubling to me, because earlier that same year she had started to find herself in the world of books.

The previous winter, when our ritual of talking about fiction was interrupted by the clang and hiss of an old radiator letting out its steamy heat, I had decided to introduce Kate DiCamillo's sweetly moving and sentimental novel *Because of Winn-Dixie*.[4] Set in a working-class locale in rural Florida, the novel featured themes familiar to Elizabeth. Its young heroine, India Opal, lived with her single dad in a trailer. India Opal was motherless and she felt alone, but her fate changed one day when she befriended a mangy dog in the local Winn Dixie grocery store.

Until then, Elizabeth had been all resistance to the strange notion of reading about a fictional character whose life echoed her own. But things changed for her with this new novel, and once she got into it she couldn't put the book down. She gave the book a rating of five stars, the highest number possible. Elizabeth was starting to feel differently about reading. She was beginning to realize that she could be a girl who enjoyed books.

"I'm the only one in my family who likes school," Elizabeth remarked one February afternoon in my afterschool class for the girls.

Once she knew what her heart wanted, Elizabeth was not a girl to be easily deterred.

But in Elizabeth's regular language arts classroom, another kind of change was stirring. Earlier that year the girls had spent up to an hour each day reading books that I helped acquire for their morning instruction. Now reading literature had been overshadowed by practice sessions for the end-of-grade test. In March, the students would take their yearly proficiency test; fourth grade was a benchmark year. Everything seemed to ride this one performance. Teachers would be judged on the results. Students would be deemed proficient or not, though no one seemed sure what this would mean in terms of retention. One thing was known: Failure to achieve a proficient score in reading would result in a recommendation for remedial summer school classes. None of the girls wanted to have the dreaded letter sent home.

Boredom was a feeling that Elizabeth knew well, but now her boredom seemed tethered to an even stronger feeling: anger. One morning in late February, Elizabeth sat fuming over the latest practice test. The theme for the morning's run-through was Johnny Appleseed, a topic that could just as easily have been plucked out of one of my schoolgirl workbooks. The story was stupid, Elizabeth felt. The students in her class had been given a reading selection about Johnny Appleseed. First they had been asked to compose a journal entry, "Your Day as Johnny

Appleseed." Now they were being asked to write a factual report based on the reading selection.

"This is *boring*," Elizabeth said as she confronted the paper in front of her. "This sucks," she added, her rage threatening to unhinge her. She found the whole thing maddening, but the exercise was still casting its shadows of uncertainty. Her worst fears were confirmed when she got her paper back, red-inked with the ominous words: *Not Passing*. Elizabeth exploded. She wrote *STUPID* in bold, oversized letters, leaving her own mark on the idiot report. Inwardly, she was beginning to have doubts that she could make it through the needle's eye of the March test.

In January 2002, the No Child Left Behind (NCLB) Act had been signed, cementing the effects of an accountability movement that was already sweeping through public schools across America. Nothing in the bill spoke to the role of literature in the teaching of reading. In fact, the language of NCLB made testing, not curriculum, the new mantra of education. "Measurement is the gateway to success," said President George W. Bush, of the bill he made a centerpiece of national educational reform. The narrowing of the curriculum was an unintended consequence, the effect of trying to reduce complex and imaginative thinking about books to a single-shot test with multiple-choice answers. Teachers in the poorer schools found themselves scrambling to get their students to bubble in the right choices, something that came naturally to students who had grown up with parents talking to them about books. Students such as Elizabeth were novices; they had more trouble figuring out the language game of the test. What Elizabeth truly needed was guidance in the basic process of finding herself in books that featured richly developed characters and literary themes. But this kind of teaching was becoming harder and harder to justify, because it was difficult to quantify in scientific terms.

"There's something wrong with me" was Elizabeth's understanding of the whole testing business.

A paradox was starting to reveal itself to me, and it had to do with the ways that reading was swept into the currents of the accountability movement. The rhetoric of the accountability movement in public schools was all about change. But from what I could see from my vantage point as a teacher, little had changed since my days in a school serving the children of North Carolina factory workers and farmers. The accountability movement had frozen into place the same inequalities that shaped my experiences in school. If anything, students like Elizabeth, those who could most benefit from reading novels and talking about literature, were now even *more* unlikely ever to get that kind of rich liberal arts education. For her, the pervasive focus on test preparation was squeezing out a nascent love for books and learning that could have helped her achieve the success that everyone wanted. It was not fair to Elizabeth, who had taken the first quivering steps toward becoming a real reader. So when summer came, I was even more determined to help her find her way into a work of fiction about a girl's life. It didn't occur to me that she had already found herself in a book, and that it wasn't my book—or my *kind* of book.

Again and again in the evenings of that summer, confused and exhausted after the day of teaching, I returned to the question of why Elizabeth, Alicia, Blair, and so many of my girls were so much in love with their stories of ghosts and horror. A small literary movement was occurring in my summer class, in subtle ways that, when added together, created a collective feeling for books. Adriana's mother still had the copy of *Pet Sematary* that her Grandma Fay had lent her, just before she died. On a slow, warm night that summer, Adriana had watched the movie with her mother—for the third time. Elizabeth got to watch the occasional scary movie in her crowded living room, after she helped put the youngest to bed. Blair sat up late into the night, listening to her half sister read from the Stephen King books she bought at Walmart. Adriana felt certain that the basement of her apartment building was haunted. A girl had been raped down there. And Alicia was sure that there was a real ghost in her grandmother's house, for the young man who had once lived there had shot himself.

The young girls in my reading class were not alone. Horror fiction had become rampant in popular culture, so much so that parents and teachers had begun to voice concern about the images of maiming and psychopathic mayhem flooding the popular book and movie market. These movies—*Final Destination, The House of 1,000 Corpses, Slash, 13 Ghosts*—were geared to a ravenous audience of horror fans, many of them still in their teens. Such trends had led to a flurry of writing about the subject by literary and film critics, cultural scholars, and even psychoanalysts.

One explanation offered for the feeling that my girls experienced when reading scary books is the notion of a psychic safety valve. Fans of horror and ghost stories can experience a thrilling read, and yet know that in the end *they* will be safe. This can be cathartic—like screaming bloody murder on a roller coaster ride, then walking off with tears of laughter streaming down your face.

But this wasn't the only explanation for the strange appeal of horror. Every reader of fiction searches for the threads that can connect her inner life to the landscape she inherits. And these threads of connections need not be real—or not something you can see or touch in the everyday world. Fiction's special appeal is that it can take us out of *this* world and help us connect with what can only be seen through the imagination's inner eye. Part of the beauty of ghost stories was that they were *not* real. *Crazy, weird,* and Elizabeth's favorite word, *boring*—this is how my students felt about reading a realistic novel. The gray world of ghosts and horror stories felt more familiar and strangely, more soothing, than the harsh light of a realistic novel.

Elizabeth wasn't yet ready for novel about a girl who was "just like her." Could I bring myself to enjoy the kind of book that she loved?

Later on the morning of June 27, I sat with Elizabeth on my family quilt, and we talked about books. By that time, the temperature inside our borrowed summer classroom had started to rise. The late morning air felt heavy and wet with humidity. The toxic-smelling fumes from upstairs were getting to me. By eleven that morning I was already feeling exhausted and confused about how I should work with Elizabeth. But curiosity—a desire to understand what I don't know—was always one of my strongest motivations as a teacher. So I tried to get to the bottom of Elizabeth's feelings about reading. Like everything else, she was passionate about her books.

"So do you like to read?" I asked Elizabeth, who was looking smug, like a young queen on a royal carpet.

"Heck, yeah. Whoo!" replied Elizabeth.

It wasn't exactly the response I had expected. Since our book group discussion earlier that morning, Elizabeth had seemed lost in a preteen sulk.

I probed a little further: "What books do you think we could read in our summer class?"

"The books you're going to order—NOW!"

I knew exactly which books Elizabeth meant: the House on Cherry Street series. Elizabeth was as stubbornly committed as any girl could be to reading the ghost stories.

"And what else?" I asked, still hoping to plant seeds for the kind of literature I preferred, such as *A Blue-Eyed Daisy*.

"Zip!" she replied.

The House on Cherry Street books were out of print but available on Amazon at cheap prices—as low as a dollar each. I sat down that night at my computer and ordered as many cheap copies as I could find. It was a small gesture on my part, but word spread quickly. Maybe summer reading wouldn't be so boring after all. It was clear what Elizabeth wanted to read, and engagement of any kind seemed more urgent than my concerns that the girls' paperbacks were less character-driven or literary than my novels. I was starting to lose Elizabeth, and she was only ten years old. Where would we be years from now, in adolescence, if she could not form a stronger attachment to school? It was time for Elizabeth to find herself once again in books, even if it was the improbable world of ghost stories and horror fiction that took her there.

CHAPTER THREE

We're Sisters!

A sickly-sweet odor prevailed in our classroom on the morning of June 28. On humid days and when it rained, the smell was always worse. Smells from a nearby industrial stripping company that burned off waste in the bottom of barrels and pumped it into the air mingled with those from a former creek, Mill Creek, that now doubled as an industrial sewer. In earlier times you could actually swim in the creek. Now the creek was so polluted from industrial waste that it had a rainbow of colors in its water: blue, green, orange. On warm sticky days it felt like you were living in a chemical factory, unable to escape the odors seeping into your skin.

At 8:45, I sat with the girls and Miss Susan at our makeshift breakfast table, lingering over food and talk. Sometimes our breakfasts stretched on past the nine o'clock hour, when my summer reading class officially began. And this promised to be one of those mornings. The neighborhood outside was quiet. Adults were still sleeping off the effects of second or third shifts.

Alicia.

Children were only beginning to emerge on the playground and the streets. Only the whirling fans in our ground-floor classroom, rotating in a helpless attempt to ward off the encroaching midmorning heat, interrupted the rhythms of talk at our table. Already I could feel pockets of moisture forming between my skin and the button-down cotton shirt I wore that morning.

Alicia sat next to Blair and across from Miss Susan and me at the table covered with a hot-pink paper tablecloth. She had a small face, with long oval eyes that had a soulful quality, like a mystical wood fairy or small elf. Her eyes could flash colors of gray or sea blue in her comical moments. But this morning she seemed more contemplative than normal. Changes were happening in her family, and Alicia seemed to be struggling to understand what it all meant. At first, her mother had begun staying out late at night. When this happened, Alicia and her brothers found themselves alone in the rental unit all night. Finally Alicia and her brothers had moved in with their grandma. Soon after that, strange events began to take place.

"You guys know what happened yesterday? I was sittin' on my bed and my window was open and a *bird* flew in."

"A bird? A bird?" said Elizabeth, suddenly looking up from the pile of bread and jam on the small paper plate in front of her.

Blair looked up too. Her thoughts had been elsewhere: all week long she had been hard at work on her own fictional story, set in the attic of her house. At night when the house went dark, she lay awake, half-dreaming about the attic and its invisible occupant, Rose. Sometimes at night she saw things. When she couldn't sleep she would stare at the dresser her Grandma Lilly had placed against one wall. She could see things on it, like Frankenstein or Freddy Krueger with his claws.

"One time my grandma seen a bird fly through her bedroom window," said Blair. She still looked sleepy at this early hour. On her plate was a half-eaten piece of French bread with jam and a cooked brown egg that was still in its shell.

What all of the girls knew about birds was this: When a bird flies through your window and goes out a *different* window, that means somebody is going to die. If it flies through your window and goes out the *same* window, that means somebody is going to be born.

One time a bird had flown through Alicia's bathroom window and then flew back out. That was the time her baby cousin Nathan was born. Alicia was nervous about this latest sighting of a bird. And there were other things about the house where she now lived that didn't seem right. For one thing, the house had a ghost. The ghost's name was Howard, and he was prone to misbehaving.

Earlier that week, Alicia had been holding her baby cousin while her Aunt Emily was doing her hair.

"And the *light* was flickering on and off," said Alicia. "My aunt said, '*Stop* it, Howard!'"

"Psycho!" said Shannon in a giddy voice. Her mother's people, down in West Virginia, liked to tell stories, and she perked up at the prospect of a good ghost story.

"And the light kept flickering on and off," said Alicia. "And my aunt didn't have 'nough light, so me and her went upstairs."

Ghost Howard's room was downstairs. It was the dining room now, but it used to be his bedroom. His mother was a woman named Dora who had worked at a nearby Boys and Girls Club. She had to retire because she was old and people were mean to her. One time someone put a banana peel on the floor and she slipped and broke her arm. Then her son, Howard, couldn't take it anymore and he shot himself in the head. Dora moved out, but Howard's spirit remained.

"My brother was downstairs, and he heard a big noise," said Alicia.

Elizabeth had for once fallen still. Even her restless arms seemed to be in a state of listening.

"My brother walked, he walked into the living room. And there it was! He saw the light had fell. And *busted* all over the floor. And if me and my cousin was still in there we would've been *cut up*."

My thoughts drifted back to my girlhood, when I used to sit outside at night with my friends and tell ghost stories. The mist that hung low over the mountains framing our small western North Carolina town seemed to give rise to spirits. Long summer evenings were our time for sitting outside for hours, imagining that a flickering light barely visible on one of the hills was a lantern, its owner a sad and tormented dead man. The ghosts of my childhood always lived elsewhere—on the hills—turned a luscious, nearly blue color by the rain—or on the back roads where lost souls and headless girls roamed at night. It had taken me by surprise, when I first began teaching my students, that the ghosts haunting their neighborhood were so close. You could hear them breathing at night, their voices speaking from the spirit world. And they were *real,* I had learned. The girls' stories made them come alive, and stories were what mattered anyway.

Adriana's voice interrupted my brief journey into the past. Her friend Alicia's story had made her think about the house closer to the bingo hall, where Miss Susan herself had once lived.

"Ain't there a ghost in that blue house down by the church?" she said.

Miss Susan shifted her broad shoulders and raised her head slightly, like a queen signaling her intent to speak. The girls hushed up and I listened too. Miss Susan had a story to tell.

Once, when she was only a young woman, Miss Susan had lived in a house not far from the school. There were some things about the house that were not right, she said. Miss Susan's eyes darted in Blair's direction, then stared straight ahead.

It started when Miss Susan, then a young mother of two little girls, began to notice freakish things. The vacuum cleaner would start up on its own. The family dog wouldn't come into one room where Miss Susan often read. Some parts of the house stayed mysteriously cold, no matter how high the heat was turned on.

One day, Miss Susan was taking a shower, and she saw a shadowy figure enter the bathroom. Assuming that it was one of her girls, she opened the shower door to speak to her. No one was there. On another occasion, Miss Susan was brushing her long hair in her bedroom, and she felt a presence behind her. She turned around to see a man wearing a 1920s suit and a fedora. The man reached out to her, but then he disappeared.

By the time Miss Susan finished her story, Alicia's long eyes had gotten even wider, with a look that melded fear and delight. She smacked her lips softly.

"I'll never go in there again!"

"I want to go in that house, man!" said Elizabeth. She shot Alicia a glance with her hazel eyes, and I could see the energy that I hoped some day could be channeled in the direction of books and learning.

I was mesmerized by the story, feeling like a girl again myself. But even so, the cogs of my teacher's brain were turning. I couldn't help but think of the paperback series that Alicia and Elizabeth were reading. The books had many parallels with the stories that came out of their own cultural lives. The two children living in the sinister house on Cherry Street in the series had to contend with ghosts every bit as unruly as Alicia's Ghost Howard, or the unseen spirit in Miss Susan's old rental house.

"Are you still working on *The Haunting* today?" I asked, looking in Alicia's direction.

Alicia nodded, though she had become distracted with more important things. She and Blair, looking like sisters with their fine blonde hair and porcelain complexions, were whispering some giggly secret. Putting their two heads closer together, they suddenly flat out erupted in giggles. Alicia had begun to turn red and was snorting from trying so hard not to squeal. Blair began to chant, and soon Alicia joined her. The two had their arms around each other:

"We're sisters!"

"We're sisters!"

I smiled with the two girls, but all of us at the table looked at them in a puzzled way.

"What makes you sisters?" I asked.

Soon we learned the story: *both* of their mothers were out on the streets. The trouble had come into Alicia's life in the form of a small white pill.

Only a few years before, a perfect storm—brewed of anxiety, despair, and the chronic health problems that afflict the poor in Appalachia—had gathered force in the neighborhood. It was a storm that had already cast its shadows upon poor white communities across the Appalachian region and in rural Maine. In 1996, the prescription painkiller OxyContin was released on the market by Purdue Pharma. The drug's active ingredient was a synthetic opiate—oxycodone—with a twelve-hour time release that was supposed to reduce the likelihood of addiction. But weekend drug users who were used to crushing milder painkillers—Vics (Vicodin), Percs (Percocet)—for a short-term buzz made a discovery: when crushed to disable the time-release function and either snorted or injected, OxyContin yielded an intense, warm rush, an opiate high. The journey from weekend user to addict could be as short as weeks. Suddenly whole communities of unsuspecting thrill seekers were finding themselves reeling from the impact of an addictive opiate. The difference was that this was a *prescription* drug, and the dealer could be anyone: a grandmother, a neighbor or friend, anyone with a prescription.[1] Someone on Medicaid with a chronic pain problem could get an OxyContin prescription for one dollar. By the time my class was in full swing, the drug had acquired a new name: hillbilly heroin. Entire families and communities were transformed. In one old-industry Appalachian town in Ohio, nearly one in ten babies would, before the decade's end, test positive for drugs, with painkillers in the lead.[2]

The cycle of addiction caught many by surprise. As Paul Tough wrote in a 2001 article in the *New York Times Magazine:*

"When you hold it in your hand, an OxyContin pill doesn't seem any different than a Tylox or a Percocet or any of the mild narcotic preparations that have for years seeped out of the pharmaceutical pipeline and into the lives of casual drug users. Despite appearances, OxyContin actually belongs to the other side of the drug drive; it might look like a casual Saturday-night drug, but it's a take-over-your-life drug."[3] As the medical community became increasingly aware of the drug's diversion, tighter safeguards were set up around its prescription, making the drug more costly on a street market. The going price by the early 2000s was one dollar per milligram, forty dollars for a forty-milligram pill.[4] Users could snort or inject four or more pills a day. People who would never have imagined themselves as hard drug users found themselves turning from OxyContin to a cheaper drug, heroin, that satisfied their need for opiates. Many of the new addicts were younger, people in their twenties or thirties. Some poor women who did the drugs turned to the one commodity they had in a cash market—their bodies—to raise the needed money for pills or powder.

The girls' small community, with one foot still in the history and culture of Appalachia and the other in an inner-city urban world, had weathered many storms over the decades. Poverty had been a fact of life since the arrival of the earlier southern white migrants in the 1950s and 1960s. The Appalachian workers came in poor, and many of them had been able to earn only a basic living with their factory or warehouse labor. Then came the loss of manufacturing jobs, and things got worse. Most remaining jobs were the undesirable kind, such as working in a barrel-stripping company that dealt with toxic waste. But even worse than these troubles was the prescription painkiller that dragged unsuspecting thrill seekers over the abyss of serious addiction. I wasn't especially aware of this problem at the time, but soon

I was to become a teacher for the orphans of OxyContin's devastating effects on the lives of women such as Alicia's mother.

Before she started doing the drugs, Alicia's mother used to be a force to be reckoned with. She was built solidly, with long chestnut hair and beautiful eyes with a striking oval shape. She could beat the crap out of Alicia's dad whenever the two got into it. She *always* won.

Then came her slide into the cycle that began with taking OxyContin and ended with shooting up heroin. Since then, everything had changed. Her lovely chestnut-red hair lost its color and faded. Her face took on a sunken and gray look. She lost weight and wore ripped-up shirts and baggy pants. And she started hanging out with a dude who beat her and gave her drugs. One day Alicia had been out walking in the neighborhood with her aunt, not long after she and her brothers moved in with their grandma. Alicia noticed a group of women, talking and sharing a smoke. Standing among them was Tiffany's mom; everybody knew she was a prostitute. Then Alicia was surprised to see *her* mother among the women. Her mother turned only long enough to catch Alicia's startled look, then she followed the other women to a storefront where girls and women sold their bodies for drugs.

Alicia stood up from the breakfast table and wiped away her tears of laughter. From the playground outside our windows could be heard the clear high voice of a child. The neighborhood was starting to come to life.

"Hey, you guys! There's this little boy named Bobby in my book, and he's always comin' into Sally's bedroom at night."

"Ain't Bobby the ghost?" said Elizabeth. She had felt strangely alone when Alicia and Blair had hugged each other. And something in the girls' words had disturbed her. They made her think of the stuff going around the neighborhood about *her* mother. Sometimes she would hear fragments of the story, like finding a torn piece of fabric and trying to imagine the shape of the garment that someone once wore. There was the part about a pregnant girl, only fourteen and away from home. There was the question of other men before Elizabeth's stern, controlling father came along. But she pushed these thoughts out of her head as quickly as they came, because she wanted to live in the moment. And on this summer morning, there was our reading group, her friend Alicia—still red-faced from the giggles—and the book they were reading, *The Haunting.*

"Yeah, and the part about the thing in the attic was so freakin' weird!" said Alicia. "And I was like, 'Jason—*don't go* up there!' An' he was like, 'There's something creepy going up my spine.' Then that little rocking chair start rocking—"

"Was that the part that freaked you out yesterday?" said Shannon. Only yesterday Alicia had let out a high scream, like a single note at the highest point on a scale, when she and Elizabeth were reading together. What Shannon had not realized was that the scream was part of the story. One of the invisible occupants of the house was always letting out bloodcurdling screams.

"Tryin' to say *I* was scared, you little *punks!*" said Alicia, who sat back down to finish her raspberry yogurt.

Blair thought about the story she was writing, and the attic where it took place. All week long she had thought about both, and especially about the little girl, Rose, who lived in her attic. Sometimes Blair could hear her voice up there.

"Are you finished using the camera?" I said. I had given the girls a point-and-shoot camera so they could photograph images to go with their own short fiction and true stories about their lives. Since we had the luxury of four hours together each morning, we had time for both reading fiction and working on the girls' writing. Blair had kept the camera for days, photographing the old double mattress on the floor, lit by a single bulb hanging from the attic ceiling. For one photograph, Blair sat on the mattress looking up at the camera held by her brother. Her mouth was partly open, as though she were trying to speak.

"No—I'm still going to take a picture of the attic with *some food* in the room where she is locked up."

"What does Rose look like?" asked Shannon. My students had by this time become accustomed to helping one another flesh out the details of their written stories. In that sense they had begun to echo me, for I had asked similar questions many times over the past year.

"She has short blonde hair," said Blair.

I glanced upward at the clock on the wall, aware that the first hour of our class was slipping by. The girls could have gone on and on with their stories, but it seemed like the right moment to clear the table and start our hour of reading. I spoke firmly, in a teacher's voice.

"Okay, girls—let's clear things off the table. And Shannon, can you take the juice and leftover yogurts back to the teachers' lounge?"

Elizabeth stretched her long arms over her head and stood up stiffly. Adriana offered to help Shannon carry the remaining food and juice to the refrigerator. Alicia began throwing away paper plates and cups, yogurt containers, and plastic spoons. Blair sat stubbornly at first, her legs crossed, looking like a sleepy young princess surrounded by the movements of her court. Then she slowly rose to begin helping, before I had to adopt a motherly tone of tough love. Our long breakfast was finally over.

Alicia plumped up a pillow and created a cozy reading niche for herself in one of our armchairs. She wore jean shorts and a white T-shirt with short sleeves trimmed in elastic. One of her pale, skinny legs was thrown over the arm of the chair. During the hour we devoted to reading, I often circulated among the girls to take notes about their progress with different books. My concern about Alicia's struggles to catch up with the other girls after a bad year in another school drew me to her, and I scooted up a chair to listen to her read a scene from *The Haunting*. Alicia had come to a chapter in which eleven-year-old Jason survives a harrowing experience.

Jason has gone into the downstairs bathroom to wash up for a morning breakfast of some of his mom's pancakes. As he turns on the rickety water faucet, hot water comes gushing out. The water pipes in the walls break, sending scalding hot water in every direction. When Jason tries to open the bathroom door to escape, the doorknob comes off in his hand. Trapped in a tiny bathroom with dangerously hot water coming from all directions, Jason hears cackling laughter, "a mean, cruel laugh that echoed through the steam-filled bathroom."[5]

Reflecting later on his near-death experience, Jason ponders why all the freakish things keep happening to him. "A guy could get paranoid around here, that was for sure!"[6]

When she got to the word *paranoid*, Alicia's eyes stopped. She looked up at me with a puzzled expression.

I began to offer an explanation about what *paranoid* means. From outside we could hear hollering, probably a teenager calling to someone in an upstairs rental unit in one of the small brick townhouses. Alicia's eyes looked momentarily in the direction of our windows, then back to her book as she took a second to soak in my explanation. Then she began to offer her own.

One time, an aunt of hers, heavy with pregnancy, got *paranoid*. A bird kept trying to come through her window, and Alicia's mother had explained to Alicia what this meant. Later, Alicia had been sitting in bed, reading, in her grandma's house. And the window was open. A sparrow came to her window, then flew in. Alicia and her brother tried to make the bird fly back out the window from which it came, but instead it flew out another open window. Soon after, Alicia's uncle called and he was crying: her aunt's baby had been born dead.

"We was *upset*," Alicia said.

And she was nervous, too—*paranoid*—that more bad things could happen. A sparrow had recently been lingering at the window of the bedroom she shared with her little brother, in her grandma's house not far from school. Alicia hoped this did not mean her grandma or grandpa would die. Right now they were all she had.

Later that day, I went on a long neighborhood walk with Alicia.

The occasion was this: for months I had wanted to learn more about the neighborhood's labor history. Finally I had been introduced to a neighborhood elder, Mr. Floyd Taulbee, who was more than happy to take me around the blocks where people used to work. Only ten minutes from the school was a nearly deserted landscape of old warehouses and factories. The old buildings were large and made of brick. Most were five or six stories with windows that were boarded up or gaping. On the sides of the buildings, large lettering told the stories of their past: Serta Mattresses, Kay Furniture Warehouse, MY-NEIL Import Co. That day I received the call on my cellphone: Mr. Taulbee could

Industrial landscape.

take us for a walking tour of the area after class was over. I made some phone calls to the homes of the girls who walked to my program. We would go together on the walking tour with Mr. Taulbee, then I would walk the girls home. Alicia was able to go along, and so was Shannon. On the way out to meet Mr. Taulbee, we also had the good fortune of running into Jessica, who had been skipping my class that week. She eagerly joined our small group and we were off—across a main artery and onto the sad and silent streets beyond.

Jessica knew the area toward which we were headed well. She occasionally slipped down there to have a smoke with her girlfriends under a viaduct, talking and giggling for hours. But these blocks were unknown to Alicia, and forbidden to children. She gripped my hand tightly, her eyes darting from building to building as if she expected something monstrous to jump out from their shadows. The area was creepy enough, but we were armed. Besides Mr. Taulbee, our experienced guide, we had my cellphone and a tape recorder and camera to record our walk. A drug dealer would have taken one look at our little procession and retreated into the shadows, terrified of being documented. Our group made its way past the old warehouse buildings, with Mr. Taulbee doing one of the things he did best: telling stories.

Mr. Taulbee had first come to the city in the 1930s, before the largest flush of postwar southern migrants. He was from eastern Kentucky, but he had never known the cruel poverty of coal mining towns. His people were farmers—tobacco among other things—and they had earned an honest living. Now he was one of his community's longest residents, happy to share the story of the neighborhood's labor history.

We came to an empty lot, located near one of the only functioning industries: a barrel-stripping company that cleaned and refurbished barrels containing industrial waste, some of it toxic. About the only companies remaining in the neighborhood were those dealing with waste. The city's largest municipal sewage treatment facility was only a few minutes' walking distance from the barrel-stripping company.

Mr. Taulbee looked out over the deserted lot before us, but what he saw was the old way of life that had once graced the area.

"Set right here on this corner was the most *beautiful* tavern you ever seen," he said. "What they did was, you go in there and sit down for a meal. They had so much on your plate that you couldn't eat it. Big café. And it was the most beautiful place you ever seen. And the owner got shot," said Mr. Taulbee, his storytelling momentarily turning a dark corner. "He got killed.

"And I'll tell you another little story 'bout like that one down on that corner," he said, picking up an earlier thread. "I used to come from where I used to work to here, to cash mah check and eat supper. Those people was the most beautiful people you ever wanna meet."

Beautiful, Mr. Taulbee said many times over, his memories filling in the frame of the ghost town that lay before us.

Our group moved on until we were in front of the stripping company, with its stacked barrels, asphalt, and smokestacks spitting out billowy gray clouds of industrial residue into the air we were breathing.

"Stinkyville," said Shannon as we approached the site. The stripping company was a notorious polluter that had been cited for breaches of environmental pollution standards.[7]

Mr. Taulbee's voice became somber as he took in the scene. "You can see there's nuthin' here no more," he said. "Absolutely nuthin'."

The availability of manufacturing and warehouse jobs in the neighborhood peaked in the 1960s, the last decade of large-scale migration of rural southern whites into the inner city. The neighborhood's population in 1970 was close to three thousand. By the year 2000, the number was just over one thousand residents, with 56 percent of them living below the poverty line.[8] With the downsizing of older manufacturing and shop-floor jobs, the prospects had become bleak for the neighborhood's young people. High school dropout rates were miserable, officially listed at 57.9 percent but believed by grassroots activists such as Michael Maloney, founder of Cincinnati's Urban Appalachian Council, to be even higher. The social demographics of dropping out and poverty reflected the community's history as a haven for Appalachian migrants who were poor to begin with and didn't always see the need for school completion. But they also reflected a growing sense of hopelessness. The expanding street-drug culture had only worsened prospects for the young. Nearly everyone had a family member who was using diverted painkillers—or worse. Most people viewed the streets as unsafe. The prevailing sense, even among students as young as my girls, was one of wanting to get out. In fact and feeling, the neighborhood had become a ghetto.

Suddenly Jessica, who was prone to bladder problems, declared that she had a bathroom emergency. We were by then nearing the end of our walk, but she couldn't wait. There were few inhabited buildings of any kind on this side of the neighborhood, but we were in luck. Mr. Taulbee knew of one place that was still functioning as a bar, and he skillfully led our group in its direction. The building was old brick, built saloon fashion, and inside its darkly lit main room we found a female bartender and her lone customer—a woman who looked to be in her late thirties sitting at the bar. Jessica and Shannon went together to the back, in search of the toilet. The rest of us stayed up front, Alicia still gripping my hand as we learned about the tavern's history. Looking glassy-eyed, a cigarette dangling from her lips, the woman sitting on a barstool began to share stories from the tavern's past.

"This place was put up in 1876," she said. "An' the riverboat people would come up. And there were about thirty rooms that you could rent upstairs. So when they got off the riverboats for a stop in Cincinnati, they'd come in and they'd have a drink. And maybe they'd rent them a little girl for the evening."

The woman glanced in the direction of Alicia, listening quietly. "Well, not a little girl—a woman in the trade. An' they would rent a room upstairs."

Jessica and Shannon emerged from the back of the tavern. We said our thank-yous and good-byes; the women at the bar had been kind to us. As soon as we were out of earshot, Jessica blurted out, "That bathroom was *nasty*." The word was drawled out with traces of a soft rural accent: NAH-sty. We made our way back across Eighth Street, where the sight of familiar homes and kids playing on the streets felt like a warm serving of comfort food after being in a chilling wintry climate.

On the way to her house, I asked Alicia to share what she had learned about her neighborhood.

"That it was *NAH-sty*," she replied quickly.

Alicia and my other students wanted no part of this educational journey into the past, for me a teaching text, but for them only a reminder. Their neighborhood may have once been the hope of a generation of laborers from the southern mountains. That was gone now, and my students wanted one thing. Like Blair's Ghost Rose and Blair herself—and like me when I was a girl their age—they just wanted to leave.

Over time I would learn to take note when I heard a word spoken with a certain cadence and inflection. *NAH-sty*. Alicia spoke the word with a hint of a rural accent, though she had lived all of her nine years in the city. It was a word that bound her life with those of the other girls in my class. Looking back on our walk with Mr. Taulbee, the most powerful thing for the girls themselves was probably not the history lesson I wanted, but a growing sisterhood that might someday even include a teacher like me. Young Alicia was afraid, but she was not alone. Even I was starting to learn how to listen to her stories, shaped by a neighborhood that was filled with ghosts.

Later that afternoon, the midday June sun now heating the neighborhood as if it were under a glass tent, I walked Alicia home. She lived just minutes from the school but was never allowed on the streets alone. There was always the fear that her mother, now banned from the family, might show up and try to talk to Alicia. And that was no longer allowed. Alicia's older stepcousin, Mariah, joined us for the journey. She had been on the playground as we descended from the school, and she wanted company. The three of us walked slowly, taking in the boisterous scene: young boys flying by on bicycles, and girls walking together in groups of two or three. We passed a narrow three-story townhouse, made of brick and weathered by time, air pollutants, and the creative work of young graffiti artists. It could have been any building, with its floors of rental units. But suddenly Alicia stopped and looked up.

"You guys see that house right here?" she said. "It's *haunted.* That house right there is haunted."

It was, Alicia went on to say, the house where she had once lived with her mother in a top-floor rental.

I looked up at the run-down brick townhouse that seemed pretty much like all the others on the narrow inner-city street. As I glanced at its windows, I felt that I could almost see the shadowy face with its terrible eyes staring down at us.

PART II

My Life as a Girl

CHAPTER FOUR

Girl Talk

Alicia took out the pacifier she had in her mouth. Even though the girls in my literature class were now in fifth grade, some of them occasionally brought a pacifier into our classroom. I wasn't really sure if this was some kind of symbolic clinging to early childhood, or a new preteen mode of expression. Maybe a little of each, I thought, as Alicia began to speak.

"You guys want to know a secret?" she said.

It was our first meeting of February 2003, months into the new school year, and the late winter day was cold and bright. Alicia sat in one of our two wicker armchairs. She glanced quickly around the circle of six girls and me, their teacher, that made up her audience. Then she drew in a breath and began her story in the fast neighborhood style.

"I got to talk to my daddy and he might be getting out of jail."

Elizabeth studied Alicia with a soft, intent expression. Mariah, who had joined my literature class that fall, shifted in her place on the loveseat, settling in for the story. From outside our classroom

Alicia.

windows, tightly shut on this late winter afternoon, came the distant calls and laughter of children on the playground.

"Wanna know how he got in there?" said Alicia, looking briefly in my direction. The girls in my class already knew the story, I suspected, but their heads nodded along with mine.

"He got charges pressed against him because when he was living with us down here, one night he was drunk and he started coming up the steps and he started beating on the door 'cause he was wanting his clothes." Alicia drew a breath.

"'Cause he was gonna go live with his sister. And my mom wouldn't give him his clothes. She said, 'Come back tomorrow and get your clothes because you're drunk right now and I don't want to deal with you.' And he said, 'No, I want my clothes now.' So my mom opened up the door and she gave him a basket of his clothes. But he still had two baskets and a bag left of his clothes, and she wouldn't give it to him until tomorrow. So she shut the door, she locked it, she put a knife so he couldn't get in. And then she took the knife out so if he tried to kick the door in, it wouldn't fly and hit one of us. And she took it out and put it away. And all the sudden, a few minutes later, the door just fell down. My dad came in and got his clothes and my mom and them started arguing, and we had to split them up and my dad left.

"And then the next day, come to find out, he had charges pressed against him. And my mom pressed charges against Isaac Thomas too because she's got a knot on her eye right here and it's black and blue and different colors. And she's got a black eye."

"'Cause Isaac Thomas beat her up," chimed in Mariah, speaking like a voice in a Greek chorus. Mariah was Alicia's stepcousin through Mariah's adoptive family. She was one year older than most of the other girls because, like Jessica, Mariah had once repeated a grade in school. Mariah relished being in the know about the darker edges of neighborhood life, and she was coming alive for the conversation.

"He always beats her up; she's so stupid!" Alicia said. "She pressed charges on him before, an' she took the charges off when they went to court. And now she's pressing charges against him again for what he did to her again. But we don't believe that she really pressed charges against him."

The cycle that Alicia described was familiar to all of the girls sitting around the circle, and many knew the details of her mother's fall from family grace. All of us had also known Alicia's mother before her heavy drug-using years, and Shannon spoke aloud a question that hung in the air.

"Your mom used to be really smart and really nice," she remarked. "But I don't know what happened to her."

"Huh!" Alicia said. "You don't want to know about the other things!"

There was a momentary lull in the talk around our circle. Then Shannon probed further: "What happened to your mom?"

"She got on drugs," Mariah said, speaking for her younger stepcousin.

Alicia went on to fill in more of the details: the drug dealer her mother met, the fighting and bruises, the nights when Alicia was left alone in the house. She still looked like a young girl—Alicia was only ten, and tiny for her age—but the neighborhood was growing her up fast.

I have always been a romantic, and a sucker for a good love story. So with Valentine's Day near, I decided to screen a romantic film for my girls. I thought a literary movie could have the same kind of teaching impact as a good book. But it had to be the right film: fun, safe, and engaging, while also offering complexity and intellectual challenge. I ended up with George Roy Hill's film *A Little Romance,* a charming study of a twelve-year-old American girl in Paris who falls for a French boy. The film's heroine, Lauren, could not in one sense be more different from our girls. She lives with her glamorous film-industry mother and her rich stepfather. But Lauren falls for Daniel, the son of a ruddy-faced, loose-tongued cab driver. "I'm going to beat his ass!" rants Daniel's father after Lauren and Daniel run off to Italy, aided by an aging con man named Julius (Lawrence Olivier). There, in Venice, they fulfill the fantasy that fueled their youthful adventure: at sunset, with bells clanging overhead, the two kiss as their gondola passes under the Bridge of Sighs.

Romance was in the air as my students, excited about the prospect of a movie afternoon, turned to the subject of love.

"What Valentine's means to me is love, peace, and joy," said Jessica.

On Jessica's lap was the literary world she preferred to the official one of school: a fluffy pink diary with the words *My Crush Book* emblazoned on the front cover. On one page was space for a boy's picture. On the facing page were spaces for the girl to answer short questions about the boy. Jessica and Alicia took turns filling in information, for Alicia knew Jessica's boyfriend. His name was Justin. Justin had a sexy body and he kissed good, Jessica thought. Jessica glowed with the newness of romance, but sometimes she came into my class looking tired and out of it. With her new circle of friends, Jessica was out late at night, smoking and making out with her boyfriend. She sat next to Alicia, to whom she confided her stories and secrets. Always a loyal and discreet friend, Alicia soaked up this world that was both familiar and out of bounds.

"Valentine's is really, like, for someone special, and for love," said Adriana, whose long violet-blue eyes, accentuated with eyeliner, had a sly expression.

"But what does love *mean?*" asked Blair.

"Shut up! That's what I think it means!" said Alicia.

Then Jessica shared the really big news. Her brother had found out he was going to be a father.

"He is?" said Mariah.

"Whose baby?" said Blair.

"Jeremy, my brother," replied Jessica. "Brittany Fields is pregnant now."

"I seen Brittany, like, five times and she does *not* look like she's pregnant," said Mariah.

"She's only three weeks."

"That's why she's been *puking* at the Club," said Blair.

"Yep, don't say I said anything," warned Jessica.

"You can't do nothing around here," said Mariah. "'Cause every time you try to do something, people always snitch on you and turn your story around. If I find out who lied and told Scott Dixon I was pregnant, it's gonna be a *whole* lot of drama started. If they have something to say, they better come say it to my face."

It was hard not to notice Mariah in the girls' fifth-grade homeroom. She was a year older than my other students—she had already turned twelve—and she was frequently in trouble. She had a serious mouth on her, from which cuss words and angry taunts flowed easily. Mariah could get in your face at a moment's notice; her fuse was short. At those times, she could talk and act more "street." Her hazel eyes would flash, her throaty voice would go lower and louder, her upper torso would tilt forward in a fighting posture. Early that year she had gotten in serious trouble for calling the visiting student teacher a bitch. That had won Mariah her teachers' disfavor. Right away, she was on probation, under close scrutiny by a team of seasoned fifth-grade teachers with traditional values. Mariah was looking for trouble, and she was looking for attention, especially from boys. Her teachers knew it and clamped down on her.

Mariah herself aimed for an uneasy truce. "I mean, like, if she don't get smart with me or anything I will not say one word to her," Mariah said later, speaking of her homeroom teacher, who taught language arts and social studies. "We can be friends, or I can be her worst nightmare." Mariah's homeroom classroom was bulging with books, packed into white bookcases lining an entire wall. Of that library's many offerings, her eyes had been drawn to Cynthia Voigt's novel *Bad Girls*. She wanted to read the book, but it was challenging for her in the early months of school. Mariah identified with the title because, she said, when she was little *she* used to be bad. Fighting and cussing were two things that she felt made girls get a reputation for being bad.

Beauty was a thread drawing together the frayed edges of Mariah's complicated life story. "I'm beautiful, I'm beautiful," was how she described herself. "Beautiful, funny, don't like to work." An olive-complexioned girl with dark chestnut hair and a swagger to her walk, Mariah found boys' eyes drawn to her as she sauntered by on the street or lowered her lids flirtatiously in the classroom. It was a mixed blessing, for adults sometimes judged this behavior as too "fast" for a girl not yet in her teens. Mariah herself felt she was in control of things. She could throw back one-liners as fast as boys could toss out their nasty remarks. There was an edge, however, to Mariah's attraction to the wild side of life. She was a thrill-seeker who relished jumping off cliffs into deep mountain water. A beautiful girl with a willful spirit could find trouble on the street, and her adoptive family imposed strict curfews and constraints on her freedom.

Her history was unique among her peers, for Mariah was first generation, having traveled the road from Appalachia to the inner city at the age of two. Her birthplace was the beautiful Cumberland region. She was the daughter of a woman who had fallen prey to drugs. Her mother had lost most of her children, and Mariah was adopted by a family from the city up north. She had suffered cruel abuse at the hands of her young, unstable birth father. Her father had raped another girl. He "nearly lost it," said Mariah, one day when she was a sick little girl and wouldn't stop crying. But Mariah still felt the call of her blood kin and of the lush rural landscape where she felt she belonged. In the summer, she was sometimes able to visit her kin in Kentucky and Tennessee, and she dreamed of returning to the land of her birth. She saw love as her ticket out.

"Love just means, I don't know—it just gives me things to do," said Mariah. Her hazel eyes flashed, and she shifted on the loveseat where she sat next to Alicia. "And I'm already *in love*, but I gotta wait until I turn eighteen." She crossed her legs and tilted her head to one side, like a young woman about to enjoy a smoke and share her secrets.

"Who are you in love with?" I asked.

"Scott Dixon. I'm getting married to him when I turn eighteen. But I won't be living down here. One of my dreams is to hurry *up* and be eighteen so I can get married and move to Tennessee and get away from this hellhole down here."

"What makes it a hellhole for you?" I asked.

"People doing drugs," Mariah replied bitterly.

One week later, I was confronted by an unexpected set of images as I walked through the cafeteria of the 1930s-era building where the girls spent their schooldays. The easiest way into the school was through the back door, after crossing the blacktop playground where the most potent medley of community and school voices was heard. By midafternoon, family members would be clustered there, waiting for their youngest to emerge through the cafeteria door. Entering through that door on the second Monday of February, I expected to find the usual mix of familiar sights: lunchroom ladies readying themselves for the first onslaught of late morning, kids walking single-file from one classroom to another, a student getting bawled out for unruly behavior. Instead, a confusing medley of military images awaited me inside the building. Some of the lunchroom servers, who typically donned hairnets for their work, wore headscarves with army camouflage patterns.

More military images appeared further inside. Teachers dressed in army fatigue pants or an army shirt passed me in the faculty lounge as I checked my mailbox. Inside, lying among the usual announcements, educational catalogues, and notes from teachers, was a peculiar artifact: a photocopy of an old 1940s military poster. *Keep Up the Great Work in the Field of Battle!* said the handwritten note scribbled next to an image lifted from a poster of United States Marines raising the flag at Iwo Jima. Beside the original caption of the photocopied World War II poster (NOW— ALL TOGETHER) someone had written *All together and as a team we will raise our scores.*

What could be going on here? I asked myself, feeling at the same time stirrings of the familiar. In public schools in poor neighborhoods, *themes* are an all too familiar aspect of everyday life. Kids and teachers roll from one set of inspirational messages to the next—like being in a theme park that every six months or so gets a fresh retooling of its rides, amusement stands, neon signs, and garish displays. This time, I was to discover, the theme was Proficiency Boot Camp.

It was a confusing choice of metaphors, because America was about to go to war. President George W. Bush had only recently announced his intention to invade Iraq, and military talk (ranging from speculations about possible war plans, to bold assertions of military might, to vehement antiwar protests) was pervasive. In such a time of military pumping-up, mixed with anxiety about America's involvement on foreign soil, it would have been tempting to draw dotted lines from Proficiency Boot Camp to the build-up for war. This seemed to be Elizabeth's reaction; she decided she would skip school if it turned into the boot camp she knew from movies and television. Though the hoopla surrounding America's war on terror may have provided inspiration, the bigger impetus for Proficiency Boot Camp was the March tests that were just around the corner. The message was loud, in the military tradition: *We are going to whip you into shape for the big tests!*

The choice of themes for the buildup to the March tests also struck me as particularly ironic. Historically, it has been mostly from the poor and working classes that the ranks of military boot camps are filled. Was a new generation—the daughters of America's working poor—truly receiving their birthright, equal educational opportunity, a ticket to full participation in a democratic society? Or were these same girls being groomed for a working-class life, boot camp and all?

Americans like to hold on to the hopeful vision that anyone can transcend poverty with hard work, good skills and training, and a little luck—it never hurts to have native intelligence. A recurrent theme in our national consciousness, that America is a classless society with opportunity for all, has received a caffeinated jolt from changes in the economy and labor market. Gone are the days of an industrial past, many would argue, the days of educating poor and working-class children to be laborers on the shop floor or factory. What we now have, the story goes, is a meritocracy, where testing and the mastery of skills can assure any young American her foothold in the global marketplace.

What is harder for prosperous Americans to understand is the real story about public education for the poor. All too often, the stagnant differences in educational curriculum, opportunity, and methodology—such as the rote learning I endured as a schoolgirl—have only been blacktopped with the language and ideology of a meritocracy. Beneath the veneer of access and opportunity are the older layers of an industrial past, like a geological formation with its older strata still intact. And so—voilà!—we have Proficiency Boot Camp. The layers making up this odd pastiche include the skill-and-drill curriculum I once received, the never-ending regime of test preparation associated with No Child Left Behind, and a kind of military symbolism so blatant that it wouldn't be tolerated for one day in an upper-middle-class school. The hope that students could actually pass the big yearly test and gain even a sliver of the opportunity enjoyed by the privileged is like a safety valve keeping everyone on message.

I had arrived at the girls' elementary school early that morning to set up things for my afternoon literature class and help out in their fifth-grade language arts class. A quick glance around their classroom was all I needed to realize Blair was again not in school. Often on Fridays and sometimes on Mondays she stayed home, always with a different excuse. I exchanged a knowing look with Mrs. Stevenson, the girls' language arts teacher. She pulled me aside while her fifth-graders read one of their reading passages. Grandma Lilly had phoned, saying Blair had some kind of stomach ailment. Off I went, on what had become an all too familiar mission, to see if I could get Blair back in school. It was a role I had begun to share with the school's community liaison, who had by then referred Blair's case to the truancy officer, a local policeman. None of this had much of an effect on Blair. Grandma Lilly, who had hardly missed a day of school when she was a girl, threatened to haul her smart but stubborn grandbaby into school herself if she had to. But everyone knew this would never happen. Grandma Lilly was bedridden, nursing her bad hip and knee and barking out orders to the youngest children, her great-grandbabies, left in her care. Blair slept late and was prone to missing the early-morning schoolbus. Once that happened, getting her out of the house and down Perry Avenue to school was an ordeal, even for an adult with a car and healthy knees, who could negotiate the side porch stairs with their missing handrail.

At ten o'clock I drove to the house where Blair lived with her Grandma Lilly. The sky was a pale silver-blue. The day was wintry and raw. A bitter wind blew against my car windows, and

I cranked up the heat even for the short distance from the school to Blair's house. Perry Avenue was nearly deserted, with the exception of two locals waiting in huddled anticipation at the bus stop. Soon I reached Blair's house and parked my car out front. Between the street and the sidewalk was a muddy patch that I always stepped over gingerly, trying not to get mud all over my shoes. Today the mud made a crunching sound as I made my way to the side entrance. Even the big hairy chow chained to his doghouse in back was more subdued than usual. The amber colored dog let out a couple of low grunts as he watched me climb the stairs, his exhaled breath visible in tiny puffs. I arrived at the side door and knocked, drawing my wool coat more tightly around me.

My eye was drawn to one of the side windows on the clap-board frame house. It was missing its glass pane, and someone had covered the gap with a sheet of clear plastic taped up with duct tape. From inside the house someone yelled: *"Grandma!"* I thought momentarily about how I could help the family get the window replaced, but my thoughts were soon interrupted. A teenage boy opened the door, and I walked inside to the warmth created by a cacophony of electric space heaters and an open kitchen stove. Turning into Grandma Lilly's bedroom, I found Blair on her usual perch, on her grandma's bed.

It was hard for me to fake the tough love and annoyance—the stern voice of a schoolteacher—I knew I was supposed to express. Blair looked watery-eyed and thin, with her inhaler in one hand. Her stomach was still hurting a little too. It turned out that the whole household, from the babies to Grandma Lilly, was suffering from a low-grade viral infection. If Blair hadn't missed so many Fridays and Mondays since the beginning of school in the fall, I would have backed off and returned to school without her. But Grandma Lilly and I talked and agreed that Blair needed to be in school, even if she did take an occasional hit from her inhaler.

"What could be an incentive plan to get Blair in school every single day?" I asked Grandma Lilly, glancing sideways at Blair. We were all by this time perched on the king-sized bed: Grandma Lilly reclining on her pillows, Blair sitting cross-legged in the middle, and me on the outer edge. In spite of the cold outside, Blair wore jean shorts and an oversized white T-shirt that hung sheetlike from her narrow shoulders. She looked sheepish, though distant, her small brown eyes determined to avoid me.

Grandma Lilly offered her motherly insight. What Blair most wanted were clothes, like a pair of flared jeans and a 1960s-style peasant shirt, the latest fashion for the preteen age group. I glanced at some cardboard boxes stacked near the wall and an old chest of drawers. Did any of these contain warmer clothes for Blair, I wondered. Over the fall and winter the family had been short of food. Someone had brought over a Thanksgiving turkey, but it was touch and go most of the time. Grandma Lilly couldn't work anymore, and her Social Security payments didn't cover the bills. No one else of working age was bringing in a regular paycheck.

Suddenly the somber mood in the bedroom shifted. We hardly ever got in more than a few minutes of quiet talk before something changed: The phone would ring with more bad news, or a new cast of kids would come in and turn up the television set that was nearly always left on. This time the force that interrupted our talk was the gangly teenage boy who had let me into the house, Blair's half brother. He came into the bedroom with the quickness of an actor entering the stage and, *whoosh!*, sprang onto the bed and began jumping trampoline style. Not far behind was Blair's three-year-old niece, who bravely tried to come through the door that the boy had shut on his way in. Blair came to life herself with all the commotion. She jumped out of bed, shoved little Angie out of the bedroom, and slammed the door hard. I winced involuntarily.

"*Don't push that baby!*" cried Grandma Lilly from her bed.

Blair smirked, then resumed her place on her grandma's bed. Her half brother moved over to the couch, close to the television set, where he started channel surfing for something more interesting than late-morning talk shows. I wondered why he wasn't in school, but put the thought just as quickly out of my head. I was there to get Blair.

On the way out, with a reluctant Blair in tow—she had managed to dig out some warmer clothes from the chest of drawers—I noticed a slight girl, about fifteen or sixteen years old, who had Blair's small, intelligent eyes and pale, pretty face. In her right hand was a lit cigarette that had created a visible layer of smoke near the low wall where the girl stood at the sidewalk. Her belly was bulging, heavy with pregnancy—six or seven months at least. There had been talk of Blair's older half sister running away from her juvenile detention facility and living at home for a while. Could this be her, I wondered, thinking it best not to ask right now. Blair was cranky enough as it was, and when she was in one of her dark moods she didn't care for idle talk. Inwardly I asked myself if I was looking at a reel of film projecting Blair's own future onto the frozen sidewalk before me. The thought was an unsettling residue from a morning that had been stressful enough as it was.

Back in Blair's third-floor language arts classroom, I looked at the model she and her classmates had been given for the day's language arts lesson. She and the other students were getting ready for the kinds of tasks everyone expected to see on the writing part of the proficiency test, just over one month away. One writing task they would face was to compose a personal narrative. Mrs. Stevenson had passed out a model that appeared in a language arts resource book. Blair scanned the model quickly, her inhaler placed on her desk, just in case she needed it. Her eyes betrayed little in the way of feeling as she read the words designed to teach young Americans how to write a personal narrative.

> Today was one of those days to remember. It was a day filled with life's simple pleasures. Awakening, I peeked out from under my soft comforter.... A warm, mouthwatering aroma led me down to the kitchen, and there it was, a breakfast like no other: three pieces of golden French toast oozing with syrup next to crisp strips of bacon.... Mom stood over the stove flipping more French toast. She was so excited to have a day off; she celebrated by preparing a morning feast.

A breakfast like no other? Golden French toast oozing with syrup, prepared by a mother who was fortunate enough to have the day off from work? This seemed like a cruel joke for a girl such as Blair. Her mother had abandoned her, and her beloved Grandma Lilly was bedridden. Her family was severely poor, and food was scarce. Blair's dinner was typically a frozen meal from Walmart. And breakfast? Blair slept until noon on the weekends, and on schooldays—when she *was* at school—she picked at the free breakfast served at her public school: cold cereal and a small carton of milk. Holidays were no different. On Thanksgiving I had brought over two freshly baked pumpkin pies, to supplement the free turkey Grandma Lilly had received. The world evoked in the writing model was hardly one that Blair knew. She was by then a month shy of her eleventh birthday, and a strong writer and gifted reader. But we were starting to lose her, and every day, and every teaching decision, mattered. It wasn't just Blair who might feel lost and alienated when she confronted this kind of writing. Many of my students, like Alicia with her family troubles, were facing the loss of their childhoods at far too young an age. Most of my students were growing up poor. How could they not feel detached or even angry when *this* was the model of a personal narrative?

At 2:45 that afternoon, just after a rousing rendition of "The Caissons Go Rolling Along" was broadcast on the loudspeaker system to mark the day's end, Blair sat in my literature class, looking up at Elizabeth with disgust. Elizabeth was queen for the day: our group's leader in charge of an opening greeting, one of our weekly rituals. One of her perks as leader was to choose where she wanted to sit, and she had chosen one of our coveted armchairs with its bright, comfy pillows. Elizabeth sat like young royalty on her throne. She had grown two inches during the fall and winter, and she was nearly as tall as I was. Blair was furious, for *she* had wanted to sit in one of the armchairs with its inviting cushions. She sat on the floor stubbornly next to the armchair, her hardened eyes trained on Elizabeth. I came within an inch of snapping at Blair to get off the floor and take another seat, but I thought better of it. Today might not be the day to wage a weary battle with a cranky student. And soon Blair's mood shifted anyway, because Elizabeth caved in to our group's stubborn Itty Bitty. On her way to one of the less desirable plastic chairs, Elizabeth threw out a jab in my direction, as if to assure me that she was still in charge.

"Why you always spending money on us?" she said.

She particularly enjoyed making fun of the snacks I brought in each Monday. Today's afterschool snack was over the top: steamy hot chocolate, a fresh baguette with little Mirabel cheeses, and cut-out cookies shaped like hearts in celebration of Valentine's Day. Elizabeth felt a slight buzz from the sugar and chocolate.

"I care about you all, and I like spoiling you," I admitted.

"Your food is weird, man," said Elizabeth.

"At least she isn't *poor* like you!" Blair snapped as she scooted back into the armchair and settled against a pillow.

Elizabeth said nothing.

"I think girls should be romantic."

It was Adriana speaking in our discussion circle, reading from the place where she felt safest to share her thoughts and feelings: her journal. On the inside of her journal was a large yellow Post-It note with a stern message to intruders: *Whoever gets in this note book is going to get their ass beat. So stay out!!!* Her journal was a place where Adriana could write about stuff that was private. And her mother, Kelly, had warned her about letting others get into your personal business.

Adriana had assumed a quiet kind of leadership in my class. Often she sat back in her chair when we convened our circle, soaking in the other girls' stories and their chatter with only her wide lavender-blue eyes betraying emotion. But when it came time for the girls to share their journal writing, Adriana easily slipped into the lead. Her journal was the place she could share her secret dreams, such as the one she had since she was six years old: to get out of the neighborhood and move to Georgia with her best friend, Denise. Mostly Adriana didn't want to live anywhere near Perry Avenue, the long street that cut through the neighborhood, winding its way past Blair's house and up one of Cincinnati's hills. Adriana didn't want *her* kids to grow up in a place that she thought was horrible.

Adriana.

Adriana lived on a narrow side street in the heart of the neighborhood. Nearby was a Catholic church that served free spaghetti dinners in a large basement that doubled as a bingo hall. Adriana sometimes went there with her mother, because— like Blair's Grandma Lilly—Kelly Turner was severely poor. Adriana rarely saw her biological father, who had left when she was still a baby and taken up with another woman. He provided no child support for his two children, and Adriana thought of her mother's boyfriend as her stepfather. The apartment unit that Adriana called home was on the ground floor of a three-story brick building. There, Adriana lived a quiet life with her mother and a tabby cat they called Patches. She had little to call her own except her mother's love, but that was enough. Kelly Turner was a short and stocky woman still in her early thirties, with striking blue eyes. She was resourceful in finding ways to make ends meet, even when she couldn't find work—which was most of the time.

To spark a more critical discussion about *A Little Romance,* our film from the week before, I asked the girls to reflect in their journals about how the film portrayed Lauren's romance, and how this story might connect to their lives and the lives of other girls in their community. Adriana had a lot to say about the subject of romance and, as I quickly learned, so did everyone else in my class.

She continued reading.

If not they should act like they do at least have a little romance in their life. Well, girls should like boys. Well that would be okay if they don't like boys. If they just like girls that means they are kind of gay. All I care is that they are nice and kind to me. Like I was getting ready to say girls could be sluts or hoes. Or they could be bitches or do tricks. They could do what they want to do. Like I said "Bitches and sluts should have the same respete as other girls do!" Some people say that

*you shouldn't juge somebody by the way they look all that matters is that they
have respete for you and others. Some hores and sluts have respete for people. But
some don't. Some sluts and hores are disrepeteful for their elders.*

I'll have to admit I was a little taken aback when I heard
such a raw and yet honest response to *A Little Romance* from
such a young film critic. The story in the film was charming
and bore little resemblance to the female world that Adriana
invoked. But she was finding her own connections to a movie
about young romance. Before I had a chance to look for something meaningful to say in response to all of this, Adriana
spoke.

"Any questions?" she said.

One of the rituals we adopted for the writing activities in my
class was to always invite questions and talk after a girl shared
her writing. This was critical for helping girls build a sense of
community around the sharing of literature. At home they didn't
participate in this kind of conversation, and it had taken me
years to make this strange way of talking seem more familiar.
But two years into our weekly literature class, Adriana and Blair
were hungry for such discussions. They were ready to tease
things apart, whether the subject was a work of fiction or a story
from another girl's real life, and look at them with a critical,
discerning eye. Blair lifted up her hand eagerly as soon as Adriana
had finished reading.

Adriana called on Elizabeth instead; her skinny arm had shot
up at the same moment as Blair's.

"I forgot what I was going to say," admitted Elizabeth sheepishly. Inwardly I wondered if the topic unsettled her, though she
had seemed to love the film. Adriana was nonplussed and pointed
her finger, freshly painted with black nail polish, in Blair's
direction.

"I think that girls can be what they want and do what they want when they want to do it." She spoke quickly, spitting out her words in a breathless stream. She had become as perky and engaged as I had ever seen her.

"They could even be strippers," continued Blair. "Just because they do that stuff doesn't mean they enjoy it. It just means they want the money for it."

"Yeah! They need the money," echoed Alicia, looking every bit the part of the young, blond heroine she admired in *A Little Romance*.

"Do they need the money to eat?" I asked. Suddenly I had become more student than teacher, trying to understand for myself the complex female world of a neighborhood that had turned into a ghetto.

"*Nah*, they go around and get *OxyContin*," replied Mariah, nearly coming off the loveseat with the force of her words.

"Ooh, I got somethin'!" said Adriana.

"No, wait, wait, wait!" said Blair, bouncing in her armchair. Itty Bitty had the floor, but I looked protectively at Adriana. Her feelings bruised easily when she felt the other girls were not giving her their full attention. This hurt because, Adriana thought, nobody in her whole damn apartment ever listened to her either. But this time Adriana had a patient look, like an indulgent older sister, even though she was in fact younger than Blair by five months. She let Blair continue.

"I think they go around and get money so they can get drugs," said Blair. "Cause my mom used to have a drug problem."

"Same thing—" began Alicia, but Blair quickly spoke over her.

"And she used to go around and beg my grandma for money. And then if my grandma didn't have any, she'd go around and get money from other men."

"How did you feel about that?" I said. Elizabeth shifted in her seat and leaned forward on her elbows. Mariah muttered something too low to hear. Alicia looked depressed, which was strange, for she was more often than not our group's comedienne, always ready for girlish fun and improvisation.

Blair spoke even faster. "I didn't like it because I don't like people like that. I don't like her. My mom's *mean*. If you guys knew her, you'd run from my house."

The thought of seeing Blair's mom come out of the house yelling, her long amber hair wild, gave Elizabeth a slight chill. But she snickered, and so did Alicia, sitting next to Elizabeth in the circle.

Finally Adriana saw her chance to speak. "Some girls, they do all that stuff, but not just to enjoy it. Like what Blair said—they like to buy drugs. And some girls have *kids*. But they don't care about their kids. They try to buy theirself something, 'cause all they want is that pill."

I listened carefully as Adriana spoke and puzzled over the possible meaning of her words. By this time, nearly all the girls' families had been touched in one way or another by the problem with prescription painkillers. The girls' neighborhood had gone in half a decade from a relatively stable, if working poor, neighborhood to one where users and dealers were now a common sight on the street. I wondered now how close to home this all was for Adriana. Was the story she was telling a warning based upon her own experience?

"I want to say something!" Blair's excited voice interrupted my thoughts. "Some girls go down to the Mexicans and they get money to have sex with 'em."

The men that Blair called Mexicans were the latest immigrant arrivals to the neighborhood. In fact they came from different countries, and many were from Central America, particularly

Guatemala. These disparate workers of varying Hispanic origins had settled in a cluster of apartment buildings along Perry Avenue, on the way to Blair's house. They created their own grocery store and shared living spaces in the cramped apartments. Many of these new immigrants were young men, the first in their families to arrive. They worked long hours each day and pocketed their earnings. Most did not yet use banks. In the mornings, the short olive-skinned men could be seen waiting at the bus stop. The white locals did not speak to or acknowledge them.

"Why would some girls go down to the Mexicans to get money?" I asked.

"Because they're *rich*," said Blair. "They're rich and they don't have to pay rent or anything."

Jessica, who was sitting across from Blair, looked briefly in my direction and then straight ahead. She spoke with her gentle rural twang. "And why they go down there is because—they, like, when they're doing it with the Mexicans or something like that, and the Mexicans leave their pants in the bathroom or something like that, the girl—she'll go in there and she'll check their pants for money and she'll rob 'em."

"That's what people say," said Alicia, nodding from her perch on the loveseat, and still looking unusually sullen.

"There's this girl—I think it was Nichole and Tiffany—they were walkin' down the street, and this Mexican asked them to get in the car. Nichole dipped in the Paradise Café. She said, 'FUCK you! HELL NO!'" Mariah was off on one of her stories. Her head was tilted forward, her eyes were flashing, her olive skin deepened in color. I listened but knew it was probably at least half fiction. The girls' most dramatic storytelling often featured dark-skinned men as stock characters, ready to drag young white girls into their cars or down dark alleys.

I glanced quickly at my watch. The light from the windows facing the playground had turned to dusky gray. It was getting close to three thirty, and only thirty minutes remained in our class. I knew Jessica had decided to write about a theme that she chose herself, some sad moments in her life, and I knew that she wanted to share her thoughts before the afternoon was over. I turned to Jessica and asked her to share the reflections in her journal.

"I've got two sad moments," said Jessica. "One of my sad moments is that my mom might be going into the hospital. And my second sad moment is that my uncle died."

Jessica's uncle had been the one she loved most, and she felt especially sad speaking of him. Her deep blue eyes looked moist, and she sniffled once. Alicia reached down to the low table in front of her and handed Jessica the box of tissues I kept around for moments like this. Sure that Jessica was in good hands—for Alicia could be as motherly as she was comic and goofy—I took a moment to go to the supply closet to get some cameras so the girls could take them home that afternoon to create photographs about their everyday lives. From the closet I could still hear the girls' low whispers. The official word was that Jessica's uncle, a man in his forties, had died of a heart attack. But the unofficial story was worse. After the medical community had begun its big crackdown on prescription painkillers, the street price of Oxy-Contin had shot up. Now heroin was cheaper, and it gave drug users a similar kind of opiate high. The story had begun to circulate that the uncle's death was heroin-related.

When I turned around with a box of cameras under one arm, I saw something odd. Mariah and Alicia had gotten up from the circle and were sitting on the carpet, their backs to the wall nearest the blackboard. Alicia had been strangely quiet while Blair talked about her mother, lost to drugs and alcohol and the streets, and when Jessica talked about her uncle. Now she had begun to sob, and Mariah started crying too. I put down the cameras and rushed over, kneeling next to them. The other girls followed and knelt beside me.

"It's my fault! It's my fault! It's my fault!" cried Mariah.

"What do you mean?" I asked, looking desperately from one girl to the other and trying to piece things together.

"I said some terrible things to my real mom and now I can't take it back!" cried Mariah.

"I want my *mom* back," said Alicia, nearly choking on the tears that were by now streaming down her face. "My mom's a—*prostitute.*" She let out a helpless sob.

Mariah emerged long enough from the cocoon of her own grief to give Alicia a gentle kiss on her forehead.

Afterward, things moved slowly in my class. Blair crawled on the floor with a pacifier in her mouth, making cooing sounds. Alicia found among our bookshelves an old Halloween picture book with no printed words but pictures of skeletons and ghosts. She looked through the book once, wiping away her tears. Then she got giddy. She twirled and twirled around and around and around until she was red-faced and wide-eyed. Mariah settled on one final writing activity in her journal. She wrote down some of the words that people in her neighborhood used to describe girls: *hos, sluts, whores, prostitutes.* She had been inspired by Adriana's honesty in sharing her journal writing.

I went home drained and exhausted that evening. Like Alicia one week earlier, and Adriana, Blair, and Mariah this week, I knew my students were soaking in the tough, in-your-face voices of the women around them. They inhaled their words and their fast-paced manner of speaking, just as many would soon inhale the harsh but soothing smoke of Marlboros and Newport Lights. But they were fragile, too, even though the streets were growing them up too fast and hard. How can I really help them achieve their dreams? I asked myself as I made the journey across the Ohio River and to my comfortable top-floor apartment. The girls were trying to shape their lives against impossible odds. The grueling nature of the climb out of poverty and away from the trouble that touched everything they loved, even their intimate families, made the steps forward harder than most Americans could ever imagine. All I had to offer them was the gift of our class. I could only give them novels and writing and a place to share their stories and their dreams. But I knew that our small class each week was special to the girls because they were starting to share something so raw and rich that it could never fit into a teacher's manual. They were starting to share their own lives.

What is it like to be girl in this neighborhood, with one foot in Appalachia and the other in the world of the street? I puzzled over this question as I unlocked the door to my apartment. "My Life as a Girl." It was hardly the kind of writing theme you would find in a teacher's model aimed at getting kids ready for the proficiency test. But the girls seemed to want to tell their life stories. After two years of work together in the intimacy of my class, they were ready for a literature of their own.

I felt an odd mix of relief and guilt as I walked into my carpeted middle-class sanctuary.

CHAPTER FIVE

A Magazine Is Born

A raw winter wind rattled the old window frames in our borrowed ground-floor classroom on the third Monday of February. The girls' nerves were rattled too. There were a lot of things for the girls in my literature class to be miserable about. The late winter weather was cold and bleak. The time for their big March proficiency testing was near, and that morning they had taken one of the long practice tests, for writing. Blair's mother was at home, too, fresh out of a halfway house and acting crazy. Finally, over the weekend, Jessica and Mariah had gotten into a fight. The two girls sat opposite one another in our makeshift circle of chairs and a loveseat. Jessica had chosen an armchair, and Mariah sat on the loveseat, next to Blair. Mariah gave Jessica and Alicia a long mean look: Alicia had taken sides with Jessica. Jessica let her fingers touch the scabs on her shoulder.

"Nobody actually won because my Aunt Ellie—she had to pull us off each other," said Mariah in her throaty voice. She stretched out every vowel with the last remnants of her childhood East Tennessee drawl. Her voice rose and fell rhythmically.

"And she called me a bitch," Mariah said, glancing sheepishly at Jessica. "An' tried to spit on me. So I called *her* a bitch and I spit on her. And it made it on Jessie's coat an' she was like, 'Now you can go *home* for what you just did.'"

The room was quiet. Each girl was in that moment lost in her own thoughts about fights she had known. Elizabeth thought of the one time, down in Indiana, when it took six people to pull her and another girl apart. The girl was about fifteen, and she had called Elizabeth a slut. She was supposed to be a friend. "People ain't got *no right* to talk about other people," Elizabeth said.

Every single girl in my class knew what Elizabeth meant; secrets were hard to keep in such a neighborhood, where everyone knew everyone else's business. The fight between Mariah and Jessica had started with rumors that escalated with each retelling. Each girl had spread lies claiming that the other was acting like a "ho."

Elizabeth had listened intently as Mariah shared the story. Elizabeth sat in one of our plastic chairs, and her legs had grown so long that her feet touched the floor. She gently rocked the chair, lifting its front legs off the carpet and then tilting it forward again. She thought about mentioning the time that she got so mad at one of her cousins that she took her grandpa's gun off its rack and nearly shot the boy. But something warned her not to reveal this story. Instead she shared another secret about her life.

"I got some scars on my legs from cutting myself."

"What made you upset enough to cut yourself?" I asked, with worry in my voice.

"'Cause I get blamed for everything in the house. If something goes wrong, my dad goes like this"—Elizabeth lowered her voice to a throaty growl—"'Look what the *fuck* they did 'cause you're not watchin' 'em!' My dad says I need to get violence out of my mind."

Elizabeth's eyes darted in my direction. The corners of her lips moved in the faintest of smiles. "I don't have no violence on my mind, do I?"

I let Elizabeth's question settle uneasily into my thoughts for a moment, then I asked all of the girls curiously: "How did reading go for you today?" The girls had brought copies of the books they were reading to our circle gathering.

"Be honest," I said.

Things hadn't been going that well for many during our time set aside for reading novels, after we finished our afternoon snack. Shannon looked bored and out of it. Alicia and Mariah were in a tiff after Mariah's fight with Jessica. Mariah's antics could sometimes grate on Alicia's sensitive nature, and this was one day when Alicia had had enough.

"It didn't go well for me," said Alicia, speaking fast and with an air of moral outrage. "Because nobody would listen to me when I asked 'em to, and then I couldn't read, and I gave 'em a smart remark."

"It didn't go very good at all," concurred Shannon. "Because I read for a minute and then I fell straight to sleep. It was a deep sleep," she added. A few grins and soft snickers emerged from around the circle.

Mariah and Shannon had placed their chairs side by side during our reading time, both perched in front of one of the big windows facing the school playground. On the two girls' laps were copies of Angela Johnson's novel *Heaven*, about a fourteen-year-old girl confronting questions about her identity after discovering that the mother and father who raised her were not her true biological parents. But the girls' eyes were hardly focused on their novels. Their gazes were locked instead on a boy of about thirteen who was out on the playground with some of his friends. Shannon thought the boy was hot. Mariah remembered the time he flirted with her when she was with her friend, Tiffany. She had exchanged giggles and knowing glances with Shannon, occasionally peering down at her book when I shot the girls an annoyed look.

"What's making it so hard for you to get into your books?" I asked the girls seated around me, trying not to allow my frustration to overcome my clear-headed thinking. Sometimes on days like this it could feel personal, because the girls were resisting me, not just the novels I had worked so hard to bring them.

Mariah was the first to speak. "I ain't never liked reading," she said boldly, without a grain of guilt. She felt no shame about telling it like it was. "I don't even read upstairs," she added, lifting her head up a little higher. "And I probably won't read none this year or next."

I struggled for the right words. I mean, how does a teacher reply to a brick wall of resistance? Inwardly I asked myself if Mariah's fortress was one part drama and one part reality. The truth was probably a lot more complex than her explanation revealed. Our resident tough girl, or *one* of our resident tough girls, was probably also terrified of failure. She couldn't fathom the loss of face if she tried to immerse herself in a book but it didn't work for her. I had once seen her shed tears because the short novel she had been assigned in her fifth-grade classroom felt too difficult.

"Would you be willing to think about being different?" I said. "To think about changing?"

"Nope," she replied, the other girls' eyes following her closely. "No? Why?"

"I am the way I am. There ain't no changing me."

As teachers, it is all too easy to forget that we are constantly asking students such as Mariah to change not just what they do, but who they are. Over the twelve years of her life, Mariah had honed a repertoire of repartee, swagger, and savvy that some might call street smarts. She could hold her own anywhere in the neighborhood. She could mesmerize you with her dramatic stories. But I was asking her to do something so unfamiliar that it must have felt like being thrust into a foreign setting where she didn't even speak the language.

Rather than sugarcoat things, I decided to level with the girls.

It isn't always easy, I explained to them, to immerse yourself in a novel. This doesn't just happen, as it sometimes *seemed* to with the familiar language and narrative plots of the horror paperbacks. Sometimes you have to hang in there for a while until a book starts to grab you with its story and characters.

"Some of you might be giving up on your books before you ever reach that point," I said.

Mariah's hazel eyes softened. Perhaps she recognized some part of herself in what I was saying.

The old steam radiator that heated our room hissed once, then clanged three times. A few voices could be heard from the streets outside, but most sounds were muffled by a late winter wind. It was a bleak afternoon, and the girls in my class were just as bitter. But I had something new up my sleeve, and I had been waiting for the right moment to share wonderful news about a grant that had come through for us. First, I decided to test the waters of a literary theme that seem to flow out of my girls' stories about their neighborhood lives.

"What is it like to be a girl in your neighborhood?" It was my first attempt to delve into a topic I saw as something my students might find more engaging than the narratives they were given as writing models. As a class, we were ready for a question that had the potential to bring up things even scarier than the girls' beloved ghost stories.

I sat back in my plastic chair—I always let the girls have the coveted armchairs and loveseat—and waited a little anxiously for the talk that might come.

"I hate my life as a girl because my brother gets all the attention," said Mariah. "And every time my big sister and her baby comes over I never get no attention."

"I understand where you're coming from," said Shannon. "'Cause when my brother and his girlfriend come down to our house with Alexis—"

"—Yup, you get laid off with the kid," said Mariah. "Yeah, that's the problem. It's always all the attention going to them. An' I just want to scream out that I hate the fucking place."

"You cuss too much, Mariah!" said Alicia, who still had her baby face and sweet, soulful eyes. As a distant relative of Mariah, Alicia never hesitated to call her out at times when she got out of line.

"If you do cuss, God won't get mad at you 'cause it's a part of life an' it's just a word," said Blair. She let out a small raspy cough. But she was perking up with our discussion, or maybe it was the frothy hot chocolate I had served for our snack earlier. A faint glow had appeared on her cheeks.

"My life as a girl stinks because my brothers get all the *damn* attention, like going to the country with my papaw," said Alicia. Suddenly she felt giddy with the thrill of uttering a cuss word herself.

"Wanna know what I got from my brother at Christmas?" said Mariah. "*Jack shit.*"

Mariah looked at Elizabeth in a knowing way. "I once called my brother a big fat pimple bitch," she said. "'Cause he made me so mad."

"I ain't got a brother," said Blair in her scratchy voice. She had another upper-respiratory ailment.

Our eyes turned to Blair, even though I could tell that each girl had by then begun to enter an inner place where she stored all the angry and hurt feelings that had accumulated across eleven years. Blair's words brought everyone back to the present, because we all knew that she *did* have a brother. Three of them, in fact—all of whom shared a mother with Blair, though each had a different biological father. Our puzzled looks signaled to Blair that we were waiting for her to explain.

"You know what I called my brother last night?" she said in a voice that sounded bigger than the thin, sickly girl it came from. "I said I didn't like him. And I said I wish I never had a brother and I said I wish he were dead. And I said to myself I never really had a brother—he was always dead. That's what I said. An' my mom was like, 'That ain't true.' And I was like, 'It *is* true because all he does is beat me up.'"

Grandma Lilly could explain the bruises on her granddaughter's tiny frame. Blair often started things with her smart mouth. One day she had thrown a shoe at one of her brothers and he had thrown one back at her, giving Blair a black eye. Every time I tried to push, to get to the bottom of the frequency of these events, I bumped up against the reality of being a teacher in a neighborhood of Appalachian migrants and their descendants. In a world of Us versus Them, I could be many things as a teacher, but I would always be Them.[1] In fact it was rare for Blair to share some of the ways she was vulnerable at home to the excesses of boys who had never completely recovered from the drugs in their systems at birth. I sat quietly, glad at least that Blair felt comfortable enough to share her stories in my class.

"When my brother beats me up and stuff," she said, "I always say I wish I had a little sister because she would always play with me and everything."

"Amen," said Shannon appreciatively. She had two brothers herself, and she secretly wished for a sister.

"But my grandma always says, 'You're fine because you got me right here and I'm a girl too.' And that's why I always stay with my grandma—the only thing I do is braid my grandma's hair and I fix my hair and stuff."

There was a long pause while we let Blair's words sink in. Then Mariah, never a girl to let an opportunity to have the floor go to waste, spoke. "And there's one more thing I gotta say. My birthday is in October and I didn't get nothing but a bear. My little niece—she's only three years old—that's the only person that got me somethin'."

I knew the stories could go on and on, but the afternoon was slipping by and there was still work to do. I handed Jessica, our group leader for the day, a copy of a single piece of paper, which I asked her to read aloud. She stumbled over some of the unfamiliar words and the dollar figures connected with them.

iMac computer	$1,275
Magazine publishing consultant	$500
Printing costs	$500

The other girls were growing more restless and irritated by the minute. "We don't know what you're talking about," said Elizabeth, always willing to blurt out what everyone was thinking.

I stayed quiet, grinning mischievously. Jessica continued her labored reading.

Cameras	$300
Film	$200

Suddenly it was as if a light bulb had switched on. This was *their* budget for *their* publishing project. Jessica was the first to sing out the words.

"We're going to have our own magazine!" she shrieked, rising out of her chair. Alicia covered her mouth with one hand, as if in disbelief.

Over the past months I had devoted nights and weekends to the endless search for funding for our small but important afterschool class. Now a local funding source had finally come through for my latest educational idea. Ever since I had created my special class for girls in this neighborhood of working poor people, I had dreamed of creating a literary magazine with their stories and photographs. The idea was one that reached far back, into a time in my girlhood when I would have loved this kind of special opportunity. I can remember writing stories as a girl and stuffing them quietly into my notebook. There was no place then, in a public school for working-class kids, for something that I would now see as part of a liberal arts tradition, the kind of education you might receive in a language arts class for the gifted or later on a college-prep English class. But now things were starting to look different for these young daughters of warehouse and factory workers. A grant had come through, and we had enough money to buy an Apple computer, pay a publishing consultant, and buy new point-and-shoot cameras and film for the girls' photography. The opportunity was suddenly there, and we were headed into uncharted territory. I wasn't really sure how to create a magazine, but I knew I wanted to try.

"The girls in our group can dress up like models and photograph one another!" blurted out Blair, thrilled that she would finally get the clothes she desperately wanted.

It didn't dampen the girls' spirits too much when they learned that this would be a literary magazine, with their stories, poems, and photography. A literary magazine was a foreign concept among the girls; for them, magazines were part of a popular culture world. But they were by then used to the strange ways of a teacher who loved literature and creative writing. A title had to be chosen, and the girls momentarily forgot the day's grudges and weary struggles as they searched for just the right words.

Blair flipped through some of the models I passed around so girls could get a feel for literary magazines. There were copies of the *New Yorker*, the *New York Times Magazine*, and a more age-appropriate magazine called *Dream Girl*. Ours was to be a magazine about girls who could get as tough and sassy as the street demanded, and Blair had some creative design ideas. The magazine could be called *Booty-Shaking Girls in Greater Cincinnati*, she suggested. She was miffed when other girls challenged the concept.

"They'll think that we're trying to write a porno magazine and stuff," remarked Shannon.

"Just because you shake your butt doesn't mean you gotta show it!" argued Blair. Gone was Itty Bitty; she had grown in an hour's time into a sassy preteen.

I had been impressed with the title for a new magazine founded by Tina Brown: *Talk*. "What about *Girls' Talk?*" I asked, hoping to move our deliberations into a realm that wouldn't send shock waves through the school.

A litany of permutations followed: *Girls Speak, Girls' Voices,* and finally the title that seemed to grab everyone's interest: *A Girl's Word.* I had given Adriana the tough mandate to help us narrow down the choices. Like anyone in the hot seat, she used the best decision-making devices she could muster, in this case, crossing out some of the titles getting the least play.

Blair got angry. "Maybe that's my opinion—you don't have to mark my opinion out."

"I marked mine out," countered Adriana.

"Well, it's my opinion," insisted Blair, her foul mood threatening the newfound happiness that had settled over us that afternoon.

"Why you actin' like a little bitch?" asked Adriana in sisterly fashion.

"'Cause you are," snapped Blair.

"I know I'm the biggest bitch around here an' I can whoop your ass," replied Adriana.

It was female leadership in the local tradition, but we needed to move on. Later Adriana would share her sentiment that she liked *A Girl's Word* because that's what the girls would really be writing about—what *they* had to say.

So began the life of *A Girl's Word,* a unique literary magazine. It was to have essays about life as a girl, journalistic stories about things such as the drug crisis gripping the neighborhood, narratives about family and friends, and poetry, all supported by photography.

"I want to stay in this group until I'm eighteen!" exclaimed Jessica. It was a momentous change for a girl whose academic struggles were painfully predictive of future dropout. In our intimate class, something was changing for Jessica.

Most of my students preferred fiction to literary realism. But Shannon liked to tell things the way they really were, like a young journalist. When it came time for her to settle on a piece of writing she could contribute to our new magazine, Shannon knew the kind of feature story she would write. Topics had flowed through her mind: drugs, life on the streets, rape. As was her custom, when Shannon felt unsure of what to do or say, she stalled and did nothing. At such times, she took on an air of laziness, seeming not to want to work. But I persisted. Later that afternoon, I pulled up a chair next to Shannon's, near one of the windows facing the playground. Patiently and carefully, I helped Shannon develop topic sentences for a three-paragraph essay. A piece about being a girl had emerged. It would become the lead creative essay in our inaugural issue of the magazine. She ended up calling her essay "A Girl's Power."

> *Girls have power over what they wear and do and how they act. Girls also have power over themselves. When they do drugs they lose power and give it to men. When some men have power, it gives them the authority to rape. Girls can keep power by not dressing like a ho, not doing drugs or alcohol, and not trusting strangers. Girls can gain power by having a future and a career and by keeping their minds focused on school. Girls should be respected, and men should not disrespect girls' power. Girls should not disrespect their own power. To get respect you have to give and earn respect.*

The past few months in school had been rough for Shannon. It was not easy being a girl who wasn't boy crazy and didn't enjoy putting up her hair and painting her nails. Other people in her classroom saw her as weird, Shannon shared privately. She

Shannon.

didn't care what anybody said; all that mattered was that *she* was happy with herself. But the small-minded kids in her classroom still worked their effects on her. I could see that physically, Shannon had shut down, scrunching herself into back corners of the room, wearing loose-fitting T-shirts that concealed the changing curves of her body. Something different was happening for Shannon in our smaller, all-girls class.

"You can't trust boys," Shannon observed as we discussed her emerging essay with the other girls at the end of our class meeting that afternoon.

Mariah concurred. "They're only good in two ways, okay? Two ways."

"Kissing and getting penis," said Shannon, finishing Mariah's thoughts.

"That's all boys are good for—kissing and penises?" I asked.

"No," replied Shannon. "Boys are good for playing basketball and wrestling and having kids by."

"Ewwhh," moaned Alicia.

Shannon grinned mischievously. She loved the idea of playing with the boys, I knew, even if she hated some of their stupid, nasty ways.

"Down here," said Shannon as we talked about her essay, "I can be myself, and I know the girls. I just know that they're true and that if they really want to be your friend, they don't lie about something just to get someone to beat you up and stuff."

"Do you feel safe in our group?" I asked. I knew that there was more than one way to get beat up, and that Shannon was particularly vulnerable to the sharp-tongued jabs of the viragos among our group.

"Yeah, I do," she replied. "It's safe for me to be myself and let my feelings out."

Shannon often struggled to explain her complicated feelings, and she struggled with her commitment to our group. It was like a dance where sometimes she moved in close, and other times she pulled away. She would not stay with our group the following year, in sixth grade. Too many things called to her: her family, playground sports, band practice. But our literature class was a special moment for her, an interlude between childhood and early adolescence.

It only took one week for some of the girls in my class to conclude that they didn't *want* to produce a magazine anymore. Things changed for Mariah with the realization that she would be putting her stories out there for others to read.

"I ain't never writin' about my feelings ever again," she said in a loud, husky voice from her writing niche on the loveseat. *Slam!* went her journal as she flung it onto the low table in front of her. From around the classroom, heads turned to soak in the moment of drama.

"Why you spendin' all this money on us?" asked Elizabeth, asking a favorite question and giving voice to a rising tide of resistance.

All of my words about *choice*—you could choose what you wanted to publish and edit out anything you didn't want others to know—fell on deaf ears. No teacher had ever offered the girls such special things before, and suddenly they were more suspicious than grateful and eager. It was as if they were putting up a collective middle finger to the idea of creating their *own* literature. I called all the girls back into our circle.

For once, I was honest about how much the girls' words and their actions were hurtful to *me*. I had been so happy when we got the grant for the magazine project, I said. This is something I would have given anything to have when I was a girl your age. When I shared the news, you girls were jumping up and down with excitement. Now you are trashing the whole project.

There was a stunned silence in the circle. It was as if the girls had been oblivious to the ways in which their sharp tongues could sometimes lash out at the messenger of hope—me, the *teacher*. It was easier to strike out at me and to bitch than it was to confront the risk involved in putting words and life stories out there for others to read. Up until now, the girls' raw stories had been protected by the intimacy of our small class. Now, each girl would be edging her way farther along a road that was as fearful as it was inviting. I was simply the easiest target.

Rather than play the usual role of moderator of conflicts, I left the room. Alicia, an able facilitator, was our group's leader for the day. I want you to develop a way of working through this, I told the girls, now bleary-eyed. You need to decide how to move forward and if you even want to produce a magazine of your own. I left the downstairs classroom, shutting the door quietly behind me.

Long minutes passed. I sat, waiting, on the steps just outside the classroom. Inside, through the door's single window, there was a flurry of activity: girls running to and fro, construction paper passing hand to hand. Then Alicia came to the door, saying that the girls were ready. What awaited me inside was a construction-paper book of notes, adorned with Magic Marker tears descending like raindrops, and the message: *We are sorry*. Teddy bear, heart, and rainbow stickers dotted the pages, filled with individual variations on the "I'm sorry" theme. "I know we almost made you cry!!!" read Elizabeth's personalized page in the book. "We love U" was the final message on the inside back cover.

On that afternoon the girls and I talked with a new kind of honesty from both sides. I was still the teacher; there was no questioning of my role or my responsibility. But by the time I walked back into the classroom, something had shifted. We were girls, all of us, with voices that could lash out hurtfully but that could also reach out to a world beyond our small, nurturing group. When I suggested that the girls use the time remaining in our meeting to write in their journals, there were no theatrical displays or smart, in-your-face remarks. Mariah, who could be our group's barometer of angry feeling, sat next to Alicia on the loveseat and began writing a story about her life as a young girl in East Tennessee.

Her life as a girl was once very bad, Mariah wrote in her journal. She was left alone in the house because her mom was always gone, so she was left with her dad. One night Mariah was sick, and her dad tried to kill her with a knife because she wouldn't stop crying. Another night her mom had to go to work, and when Mariah went to sleep her dad came into her room with a gun. "Lay on the bed," he told Mariah, so she laid on the bed. "Close your eyes." She closed her eyes. He started touching her in places he was not supposed to. He tried to rape her. Now Mariah lived with a girl named Evelyn because her real mom could not handle her. She loved where she lived, but she never got to see her real mom. She hadn't seen her real mom for ten years, and now she didn't even know what her real mom looked like.

It was real literature, from the heart, and in writing it Mariah was getting ready to share her stories with others. Mariah would end up publishing her childhood experiences as fiction, in short-story form. That story would become, for Mariah, the strongest piece of writing she ever produced. She loved writing, Mariah later decided. Writing and photography were the *best* things she ever liked.

Adriana spent the rest of the afternoon sketching out an essay about the true story of her life as a girl. In spite of everything, she was a girl with big dreams, and she was starting to find the courage to express her thoughts and feelings in a new way. Her title was simple and honest: "Life Is Hard." "My life as a girl is hard," her personal narrative began.

Life is so complicated when your growing up. If you lived in my house you would go crazy. Any way if you would even live in my neighborhood you would get mad. Because there is people yelling and screaming because the people are always mad. Some people that live on my street buy pills. And they cant pay there rent.

When I turn 18 it will be hard. I'll be in college with a job. I would have to work all the time so I could help my Mom. And some of my family. So when I was 16 I would first get a job and when I got my paychecks I would put half of it up to save for college.

Adriana would face many trials and troubles as she got closer to adolescence. I wasn't aware of this at the time, but her mother, Kelly, was beginning to slide into an abyss that started with Oxy-Contin and would end with heroin. Adriana would soon join Alicia and Blair in a painful sisterhood of girls who suffered the loss of their mothers to drugs and the street. But here we were, starting to put all of these experiences into stories that had a special beauty because they were *real*. It could be, the girls decided, good after all to produce a magazine of your own, to carve something special out of the troubled world you had inherited.

CHAPTER SIX

Mrs. Bush Visits
(But Not Our Class)

Our conversation at the breakfast table on the morning of June 23 turned to the subject of politics. "The president isn't doing nothing for our country," said Shannon. She peeled a shell from one of the hard-boiled eggs I had cooked earlier that morning. The eggs were brown instead of white, and their unfamiliar color had drawn a few snickers.

"The president ain't doing a thing for poor people," said Miss Susan, who joined us for breakfast just as she had the summer before. Now that the fifth-grade school year had ended, I could hold my special class every day during the six weeks when the building was open for summer school.

It was only 8:15, an early hour for Miss Susan. At this hour, the neighborhood had the drowsy feeling of someone stretching her arms after a long sleep. Younger children were out on the sidewalks, barefoot and tousle-haired. Adults were still inside the cramped apartment units, sleeping off the effects of working second or third shifts. A boy of about ten rode by on his bicycle, standing up on the pedals and coasting down the street. A few

Jessica.

elders were up and outside already, like Jessica's grandpa. He sat on the stoop in front of his apartment, enjoying his first smoke of the day, perhaps thinking about the new part he was going to put into his 1979 station wagon. Along the sides of the streets and in the gutters was the residue from a summer night that had stretched on until two in the morning: cigarette butts, soda pop cans, a broken beer bottle, plastic wrappers, a condom, some crinkled receipts from the local store.

Miss Susan had again worked the evening shift at UDF the night before, serving up ice cream cones, sundaes, and floats. The purple-gray shadows under her eyes were as visible as they had been the summer before. The lines at their corners had deepened slightly. But her expression was the same, and the message it conveyed just as clear. She was not a woman you could mess with. Miss Susan had strong opinions about what was soon to happen at the school. The first lady, Laura Bush, would be visiting the school on Wednesday of the following week. The official story was that the first lady was going to read a picture book to a fortunate group of children from summer school. But everyone in my literature class also knew about the other reason for the first lady's visit to Cincinnati. She was coming to raise money for her husband's campaign coffer. A big fundraising event in an affluent neighborhood was scheduled for the day of her visit.

The visit had created a frenzy of new activity around the school building. Custodial workers were washing down the old rock walls on the outside of the school. Cleaning ladies were polishing the floors. Every so often you could spot men in black casing the place. Our breakfast table felt like the calm eye of this gathering storm of human bustle. This summer, I set up our breakfast on one of the round tables in the school cafeteria. The table on this morning was covered with a pretty lavender covering of crinkly paper, and on it were our breakfast offerings: banana muffins, hard-boiled eggs, granola, yogurt, orange juice, and—as a special surprise—some fresh bakery croissants.

The summer sky outside the cafeteria doors that opened onto the playground was a clear blue. It was breezy and cool for late June: the day would be a lovely one. And we were doubly fortunate that the downstairs classroom we had used during the year and the summer before was ours once again. Five of my students were committed to coming every day—no small feat for the summer. And this summer we would publish the inaugural issue of our magazine, *A Girl's Word*. In the classroom that I had painstakingly rearranged for our summer class sat a gleaming new iMac and bookshelves filled with novels, poetry, and short stories. Next to the computer sat a vase of freshly cut peonies, small roses, and daisies. A feminine space awaited us, but it was also serious in design. We did, after all, have a magazine to produce.

I had issued a blitz of reminders to get the girls to my summer class: flyers sent home, reminder phone calls, invitations to mothers. *Come in and join us for breakfast!* Dragging yourself out of bed for an 8 AM educational program was not easy when you had been out past midnight, pushing the limits of whatever curfew had been imposed. But of our earlier group only Adriana was missing, and only Elizabeth was not allowed to attend. The poor girl was forbidden to come by her gruff dad. He had always been a little wary of our small gathering of female voices, and his word was final. No amount of tears or begging would change his mind. He had determined after giving the matter some thought that Elizabeth would go to vacation Bible school instead. Alicia was incensed about this.

"I'm going to get on my knees and beg her dad to let her come," she said as she mixed some strawberry-banana yogurt, her favorite, with granola. Alicia's fine blonde hair had been braided into tight little cornrows, and with her new hairdo and pretty oval eyes, she looked like a fairy child. She stirred her yogurt and granola with a plastic spoon.

"I'm gonna get on my knees and beg her dad to let her come," she said. "I'm going to that Bible thing and while Elizabeth's asleep and everybody's asleep, I'm going to wake Elizabeth up and I'm going to bring her in here."

Elizabeth may have been shedding tears at the injustice of it all, but back in our group she had the friendship and support she so wanted. She would be missed—one of our beloved motor-mouth girls.

Our small group had not been selected to attend Mrs. Bush's read-aloud. As if to rub salt in the wound, we were told by the custodian not to let a single crumb from our breakfast fall to the newly polished cafeteria floors. The negative sentiment was flowing around our group at the breakfast table, and Miss Susan was among those who were miffed. Maybe it was this that led her to go off on one of her stories in her low, throaty voice. Miss Susan looked weary this morning. But her voice was strong and gripping. She never smoked at our breakfasts, but her right fingers moved restlessly on the table, as if in search for the cigarette that should have been there.

It was a story from her youth, when she was still a girl in her teens. Miss Susan was dating an attractive high school boy—a jock. As a young girl, she had it all: boobs, brains, and long flowing hair. The boy she was dating dared to tell his friends that she had "done something to him." Miss Susan hit the roof. She got some of his male friends to hold him down, and then *pow! pow!*— she beat the shit out of him. After that she spread the word that this pretty boy had himself been sucking dicks.

When she finished her story, Miss Susan leaned back in her cafeteria chair, satisfied. Jessica, who sat next to Miss Susan, snickered and then directed her large blue eyes back to the delicacy she was enjoying. Our Jessica was a hearty eater and a confirmed chocoholic. This morning I had brought in something new in honor of our scheduled fieldtrip, later that morning, to a French café in downtown Cincinnati. To help girls get in the mood for an imaginative trip to Paris, I had brought in some fresh croissants from a local bakery, including some *croissants au chocolat* with those delicious bittersweet pieces of chocolate in the center. This was my latest attempt to get the girls invested in something outside their everyday experience, and for this teaching lesson I had turned inward.

When I was growing up, I used to love learning bits of foreign languages—a fairly unusual passion for a small-town working-class girl. Even as a child, I would pick up fragments of languages—Spanish, French, German, whatever—and mumble random, make-believe sentences. I think it was an early attempt at leaving, which had been my secret dream, as it was now the dream of my students. When I got to college, one of the first things I did was seek out language classes and learn about other cultures. I always had a feeling that you could be anything you wanted in a foreign language, but there was always for me the constraint of reality. I couldn't afford the usual study-abroad experience that has become a staple of the middle-class college experience. Instead, after college, I packed up and flew to France with two hundred dollars in pocket money and a one-way ticket. I ended up picking grapes and strawberries and doing a stint as a domestic worker, a nanny. Even so, my French got better and my love for French culture grew stronger. I had become an odd mix of a minimum-wage worker and a Francophile. This gift that I had labored for, the gift of learning a language and losing yourself in a foreign culture, was something I wanted the girls to experience now, while they were young. And so I found a local café with an owner who would be in cahoots with me. For our visit, he would speak only French.

Jessica took a bite of the flaky croissant, savoring the small luxury of the dark chocolate in the center, and she thought about fighting. She could picture the moment when she had tried to kick Mariah's ass, but the memory from early spring had already begun to fade. That was months ago, and now the trees were green with summer growth. Jessica had a new best girlfriend, an older girl named Anna, and she had met a boy, Kyle. The two didn't get to see each other much, except when they went to the movies, but they talked on the telephone for long periods— Jessica didn't even *know* how long. On the phone, they shared personal things, such as all they wanted for their lifetimes. Jessica had liked Kyle for a couple years now. Being around him made her feel happy. She felt comfortable when they were together, and she thought he might be The One.

Jessica sometimes got to hang out past dark with Kyle and other friends. The night before, Kyle and some of his sidekicks had thrown live catfish into the community swimming pool. The same night, Jessica's uncle had drawn a heart with a flame on her shoulder, using a black ink pen. Outside the heart were written the words *Jessica & Kyle*.

"I'm not lying," said Alicia. "I was on sixty-three and it was like—it was just in a snap of a finger I was already on eighty."

Alicia, Mariah, and Shannon had settled on a new book, Alice Hoffman's magical tale of summer, *Aquamarine*. The girls may have chosen the book for its less daunting length—only 105 pages—but I was thrilled with the selection. It was an allegorical tale of friendship and a strange romantic love, unfolding around a club swimming pool: two best girlfriends spending their last summer together (one would soon be moving); a luminous teenage mermaid trapped in the club's pool; and an improbable love between the young mermaid, Aquamarine, and Raymond, a bookish snack-bar attendant. Later that morning, Mariah admitted that she had gotten into the novel. "I liked that book," she remarked. It was something that she and Alicia shared, this new experience of summer reading.

Alicia was soon in love with her book too. This morning she had been reading for nearly an hour, a landmark achievement for a girl who was still a struggling reader. The room had been quiet except for occasional sounds from outside: a child's voice from the playground, a car door shutting, some construction work being done not far from the community pool. Our classroom felt cheerful and bright. Alicia sat in an armchair with a copy of *Aquamarine* in her lap.

"What was it that made you get into your book?" I asked. I wanted the other girls to hear what had helped Alicia immerse herself in her novel.

"Well—" she began in her usual thoughtful manner, "I started getting into my book when they started getting Aquamarine out of the pool thing and taking her on that date with Raymond. And when they did I started getting into it because I wanted to know what they was doing and everything. And then after that I started *really* getting into it because that's when there was a little boy named Arthur. He fell in, and Aquamarine *and* Raymond both saved him at the same time. They said it was like *Raymond* and her didn't want to let go of each other."

Alicia seemed both excited and surprised by the way she had sunk into the novel's quirky but sentimental story.

"What was it like for you as a reader to get *engaged?*" I asked, curious.

"I don't know what you mean," she replied. Some of the terms we used to discuss novels were still at this point relatively foreign to Alicia and the others.

"It sounds like you really got into this book today," I clarified, using familiar language. "What did that feel like?"

"It felt *good,*" Alicia replied. "And I made a connection. Because it said"—and she began reading a passage near the end of the novel—"Hailey and her mom stood in the parking lot to watch. Before long, the entranceway was crushed, the patio was leveled, and the fence around the pool was shoved aside."[1]

"And it's just like outside right now," Alicia explained. "Because as I was reading it was like the bulldozer and stuff was tearing it down and I didn't know which one was louder. Yep, it was like I could really hear it. It was like I was really there."

All through that summer I had been stressing the importance of drawing lines of connection between your own life and the life stories and feelings of characters. Such threads of connection lie at the heart of what most would consider deep and personal engagements with literature. But for the girls, these were also unfamiliar ways of having a reading experience, almost like their awkward attempts to speak French. For Alicia, the experience of finding herself in the pages of a novel was concrete and literal. She could hear the construction work being done near the pool outside, but the bulldozer in the story seemed just as *real.* It was a huge step for her into the world of reading a novel.

Jessica also knew she had accomplished something special on this June day. "For my reading workshop, it went great," Jessica said. "*Per*-fect! *Great!* I read from page ten to twenty three and a half."

"Talk to us about how you got engaged in the book," I urged, hoping to turn Jessica's ebullient moment into something from which we could all learn. She began telling us what it felt like to immerse herself in a novel.

"What I did was that I thought about the front of the book— the beginning of it. And then I just kept on thinking of it. And then I got so interested in it that I just wanted to read it and read it and read it." Jessica's full, rosy cheeks were flushed with pride. She was ready to sing out her progress to the world.

The book she was reading was one she had picked out herself on a trip to a local bookstore. Francine Prose's novel *After* recounts the experiences of some high school youth in a post-Columbine world. In the story, there has been a terrible shooting at a nearby high school, Pleasant Valley. The result is a crackdown on everyday freedoms in a world transformed by the fear of violence. In a macabre twist, things start going too far, with the youth's own school, Central High, turning into a frightening totalitarian state. The novel concludes with the inner voice of its protagonist, fifteen-year-old Tom Bishop, longing for a return to peace and a normal life. "We had to find a place where we could live, where we could still be happy. Somewhere that hadn't been ruined yet. Someplace where there was peace. Somewhere where no one had ever heard about Pleasant Valley, or about what happened after."[2]

The novel had touched Jessica greatly, for she too dreamed of a place where there was peace and love and happiness. In my class, Jessica had become the spokesperson for creating the world of her dreams: a world of peace and love. She had become a leader.

On Friday the week before I had taken the girls on a fieldtrip to a local arthouse movie theater to see Niki Caro's poetic, visually beautiful film *Whale Rider*, set in a coastal New Zealand village.[3] The film's heroine, Pai, has been given the ancient name Paikea, traditionally reserved for firstborn sons. It is the name of Maori warrior leaders who in ancient times rode on the backs of whales. The film recounts Pai's struggles to learn the warrior arts denied to her as a girl, as she seeks the approval of her grandfather Koro, who is blind to his granddaughter's gifts. A stranded whale on the village beach triggers a chain of events that reveals Pai's destiny. Like the *paikea* of ancient times, she climbs on the back of the massive creature, reviving him with her touch, and rides the whale out to sea.

Jessica identified with the girl in *Whale Rider*. "I think in *Whale Rider*, she really stood out. She didn't think anybody loved her. And then when she saved that whale, they came up to her, like she was really life-saving and everything." In our small class, something was changing for Jessica. In her larger classrooms, she often looked "out of it," off in her own dreamy world of thoughts about boys and life outside in the teeming drama of the neighborhood. But in our small gathering of girls, Jessica came alive. She didn't care as much now about what others might think of what she had to say. In our group, she had found the strong voice that, in her church, she used to sing songs to Jesus.

"This is the part that communicates with my life," she said as she read aloud the closing words of *After*. "The reason why I think that it communicates with my life is because I would find someplace where there's no guys. Where there's peace and everything else there."

If boys and romance made life on the street fun and meaningful for Jessica, they had the opposite effect on her in the classroom. She couldn't concentrate on books and learning when there were distractions involving boys, and also girls who were as boy-crazy as Jessica herself. Once other girls began talking about boys and the thoughts got into Jessica's head, she stopped thinking about her work. When she got home, she felt horrible, as if *she* were terrible because she had been thinking about boys all day and not doing her work. But in our smaller literature class, she was able to put boys out of her head and focus on her own progress with books and writing. "It's peacefuller," Jessica said of our class, invoking the motif that drew her eyes to the pages of *After*. She could share her personal stories in an intimate group of friends. She could talk about personal things, such as her life as a girl.

Now the time had come for our French lessons. To get ready for our trip to the café we practiced some words and expressions from a one-page French dictionary I created for the girls' fieldtrip. *Bonjour, merci,* and a favorite with the girls—*j'aime le chocolat!*—provoked squeals of laughter as they tried out the phrases and performed a few short role-plays. Jessica's French kept coming out with remnants of her soft southern accent. "*Mur*-cy," she said, trying to wrap her tongue around the strange-sounding word for "thank you." The whole experience felt curious and fun and a little exotic. With most of the week behind us—and after a lot of hard work—we were ready for a summer adventure.

Off we went to the Café de Paris, where we would enjoy an unusual snack. The girls were armed and ready with their printed dictionaries of key words and phrases. We parked near the café and walked the short distance. We were little more than fifteen minutes from the small urban enclave where the girls lived, but it felt as though we had traveled to a different country. Around us were the gleaming, tall buildings of banks and major businesses, a landscape of affluence. Most of the girls were dressed in the usual preteen uniform of frayed jeans and T-shirts, but Mariah had worked on her outfit. She had on a pair of white shorts and a white tank top with thin straps. A pink acrylic sweater completed a charming, feminine look. The sweater came off as soon as we hit the downtown streets. Mariah walked with a swagger, like a female version of John Travolta in his opening scene from *Saturday Night Fever*. Male heads turned. Some of the girls rolled their eyes at Mariah's antics, but nothing could dampen anyone's mood. Once at the café, we sat outside. The owner had graciously put out some traditional green bistro tables for our group. The girls practiced their French: *Merci. Oui. J'aime le chocolat!*

We enjoyed our delicacies: croissants filled with warm, drizzly chocolate; frothy cappuccinos. *Decaffiné*, I insisted: the last thing I wanted was to have a group of eleven-year-old girls wired on caffeine. Midway through our snack, Jessica raised her cup. "I want to make a toast," she proclaimed, "to the best summer of our lives."

Jessica struggled to wrap herself around the new French words. She couldn't sing them out with the same rhythm and phrasing as her own language. It was not unlike the experience of reading literature, at least with the kind of novels and the close readings we were doing. There was so much about language in all these new journeys—about trying to speak and read in curious new ways, about putting your own words and stories into a remarkable new written form. In her memoir *French Lessons*, Alice Kaplan, a professor of literature, depicts the struggle entailed in learning a foreign idiom. "It's violent being thrown into a new language and having to make your way," she writes. "Violent and vulnerable: in a new language, you are unbuttoned, opened up."[4]

After three years of work together, it seemed as if Jessica, Alicia, and the other girls in my literature class were willing to risk that kind of vulnerability.

The sensation was a thrilling one for Jessica. "I feel like I done somethin' that I never did before," she said at the end of the morning, when we had our final discussion about the day's learning and events. For the first time in her life, Jessica was finding herself in novels. She was going to contribute her writing to a literary magazine.

"What does all this feel like to you?" I asked curiously.

Jessica replied: "It feels *great*, 'cause when I get out of here I just want to go home and just tell everybody what I've done for the day and everythan' else."

By Thursday morning we were exiles. Men dressed in black could now be seen throughout the building. A bomb-sniffing dog was due to arrive, and my students could not walk to the bathroom without adult supervision. We could no longer enjoy our breakfast in the school cafeteria: the first lady's visit was nearing, and the cafeteria floor had to be kept spotless. I set out our breakfast food on a metal picnic table in the playground not far from the cafeteria doors. A summer dew made things feel damp and chilly for late June, and the moisture had turned the sky a pale gray. In the air was the sour, musty smell of the pollutants you could always detect more strongly on such mornings. The barrel-stripping company, the nearby creek polluted with industrial waste, and the municipal sewage treatment plant were all within walking distance of the elementary school. These odors mixed with the smell of summer grass trying vainly to peek through the playground's blacktop edges. Our breakfast was more somber than usual, and Blair struggled to make sense of the changes.

"Why are we eating outside?" she said. Blair's hair had been slicked down again with baby oil—another go-around with lice for the little ones at home. With her summer pageboy flattened against her face, Blair's small brown eyes looked more deeply set, her cheeks sharp and pale. Her frame was still tiny but her face betrayed her age. She was eleven years old.

Miss Susan scowled and threw back her head. *"Hmmpf!"*

Shannon played with her food, dipping slices of fresh baguette into her hot cocoa, letting them soak up the chocolate before eating them. She replied to Blair's question. "Mrs. Bush's visit."

Somewhere on the narrow side street that dead-ended at the school playground, a dog barked. Blair settled at one of the picnic tables with her usual grumpy demeanor. She reached for a banana-strawberry yogurt and a plastic spoon, a choice that was becoming a new ritual for her. She crossed her legs and drew in her shoulders, shivering once.

"Mrs. Bush needs to stay in Washington," said Blair, hunched over the table.

"I'm gonna get smart with her if she ever talks to me," said Shannon, who sat directly across from Miss Susan.

"She puts on her pantyhose the same as you and me—one leg at a time," said Miss Susan with a faint lisp. She rose stiffly to leave and do some laundry before her evening shift at UDF.

The summer night before had been a long one for Blair. At ten o'clock she had begun reading the novel she had brought home from my literature class. Settling on a novel had not been easy at first for Blair. She could see in her mind a Stephen King book as she scanned my offerings of novels featuring girls as heroines, looking for something that seemed interesting. Finally she had settled on a novel by an acclaimed author of fiction for young readers: Patricia Reilly Giff. Her novel *Pictures of Hollis Woods* recounts the story of a girl who is abandoned as a baby and then sent to a string of foster homes, none of them suited to her wild, angry nature. As a last-ditch effort, the artistically gifted twelve-year-old is sent to live with an aging, eccentric artist, Josie. The story focuses on a young girl's struggles for love, belonging, and identity in the face of a fractured family life.

Once she got into a book, Blair inhaled it. She read until past midnight, sitting up in her Grandma Lilly's bed until the sounds from the movie on the television set and the sharp chatter and cussing of her half sister blurred, and she fell asleep.

"Everybody says Hollis is a mountain of trouble," said Blair. She was reading aloud from a review she was writing about the book. One of the publication options I offered for our magazine was to write a book or film review, like the ones you could find in any literary magazine. Blair had scribbled out her draft quickly and furiously. I thought back to Blair's demon-girl fantasies from the summer before as she read her words. Is she seeing some part of herself in the novel's angry young heroine, I wondered as she read aloud?

"The story is about an orphan girl who is a very wonderful artist. The main conflict of the story is about Hollis's looking for her true family to adopt her. But when the Regan family wanted to adopt her she ran away because she thought she did a terrible thing wrong. When they found Hollis they sent her to a woman named Josie. Josie was an artist so they thought Josie and her would get along real well."

"Any comments or questions?" she said smugly when she reached the conclusion of her smart-sounding review.

Blair was accustomed to wowing teachers with her academic gifts. She had an uncanny ability to hear a genre of writing, like a review of books or films, and replicate its language and stylistic features. Blair was a gifted artist herself, like Hollis Woods, but her talents lay with the written word.

I indicated that I had something to say. "I wondered if you could talk about how *your* life as a girl connects to Hollis's life as a girl?"

"It *doesn't*," said Blair sharply.

"No?" I said. "Doesn't have any connections for you?"

Blair seemed to rethink things. "'Cause she likes to draw and so do I. But I can't draw like her. She draws people's heads!"

I thought back to the novel's twelve-year-old heroine. "One of the things that I felt maybe connected with your life was: Hollis sometimes gets very angry. And she doesn't—"

"—I don't what?" Blair sensed I was going personal on her and she didn't like it.

"I noticed that *she* gets angry at people, at adults that she's living with. Does that connect with your life as a girl?"

"No," replied Blair, quickly and firmly.

I didn't believe her.

At first our new breakfast ritual—eating outside—had felt crazy and weird to Blair. We sat at our picnic table in the early morning, nursing our cups of hot chocolate before the dewy cloud cover had lifted and the sun had warmed things up. The old stone school building had by Friday become a sea of human labor. Members of the Secret Service roamed the hallways. Office workers spruced up the bulletin boards with red, white, and blue loops and flowers made from stapled strips of construction paper. All of this seemed strange to Blair, but by Friday it didn't matter anymore. The day was going to be a special one for her and all the girls in my class. For one thing, there was Alicia's surprise birthday party. She was finally, after all these months of being our only ten year old, turning eleven. I always did things up for birthdays. Today there would be fresh bakery cake, chocolate ice cream, and fizzy pink lemonade. Then there was our shopping trip. We had decided to leave the building for much of the morning: after Alicia's cake and ice cream, we would head across the river to a local bookstore that specialized in children's literature. Each of the girls would have twenty-five dollars in spending money for books—a pretty hefty sum for eleven-year-olds. Blair thought about the day ahead as she finished her breakfast. She could picture the bookstore and imagine the new shelves of books, as she polished off a blueberry muffin with some soothing warm chocolate. She had a feeling that was strange for eight in the morning: She was going to have fun, and she felt happy.

At the bookstore, Blair went wild. It was a small but crowded shop that had three rooms packed with literature. One of these was an enclosed back porch with sale books displayed on a large center table and stuffed into low bookshelves. Blair piled up as many of these sale finds as she could carry in her small arms. She had been pleased to no end to find a signed copy of a novel by one of her new favorite authors: Sharon Draper. *The Battle of Jericho* was the latest in Draper's chronicles of the lives of urban youth. Blair could do the mental calculations, for she was a savvy shopper. If she spent $15.50 on Draper's hardcover book, that would still leave her $9.50 for sale books. Some of those cost only a dollar. Her grandma would love this. She walked out of the sale room, leaning backward with books piled up to her chin, and made her way, smiling, to the cash register.

As I watched Blair make her way, like a child in a candy store, a question began to germinate in my mind. What if, I wondered, the special literature class we had created could be *the* reading curriculum for Blair and other girls? Blair herself was viewed as a successful student: she got high scores each year at proficiency testing time. But the three years I had spent working with her had unearthed unsettling truths lying just beneath this rosy veneer. For all her successes, Blair was at risk of slipping out of the enveloping arms of the public school system. Everyday anxiety and anger, or *hell* as she had described it the summer before, made sticking with school as challenging for her as it was for struggling students like Jessica. And yet here they were—Blair, Jessica, Alicia, and all the rest of my students—seemingly thriving in a setting where the focus was on reading novels, and on the girls' own literary writings. As a nation, we place so much emphasis on reading as the ladder to social mobility and opportunity. But one of the key functions of reading—to engage in critical and imaginative thought by immersing yourself in works of fiction—is being lost for those in greatest need. For the girls in this literature class, summer was a special time of discovery and learning. Why did this have to end with their return to school?

On our way back to school, Blair shared a small epiphany. Maybe next time around, she proposed, the girls could write their own books instead of just publishing a short story or poem in the magazine. Blair was starting to find doors that opened for her, in a way that was different from how she sometimes felt about the neighborhood. There were so many books to read and stories to write. Suddenly the world seemed full of possibility. The summer nights that lay ahead would be long, as Blair read books and watched television until she drifted off to sleep in her Grandma Lilly's bed.

Jessica also saw her world differently that summer. For the first time, she was finding herself in books. She was becoming a poet, too, the author of poems about the peaceful world she envisioned for herself and others. The following year would bring many changes. Jessica would find Jesus and get saved, and she would get arrested for the first time. She would cut school with her best friend, Anna, and she would read the verse of another poet, Shakespeare. She would dream of moving to Florida, where she could get away from all the trouble in the neighborhood—Jessica was afraid that trouble would drag her down too. All of these things lay ahead for her, but for one summer in the year she was twelve, Jessica experienced the simple joy of summer reading.

I felt differently about things, too, for I could see my educational vision taking shape—not the exact shape I had had in mind when we first started, but still something promising. My students had begun to read novels, and my eyes were opening along with theirs. I was starting to understand their lives outside our small class. During these precious hot months, I became a real teacher, able to bring the girls' worlds into our lessons, even as I brought aspects of my world—such as my beloved French lessons—to my students.

These summer memories remained with us as the days wore on, as the first lady's visit came and then passed, as our class ended in July, and as the neighborhood's troubles worsened with the arrival of the terrible August heat.

CHAPTER SEVEN

A Saturday at the Bookstore

Around Halloween and her thirteenth birthday, something strange and unexpected happened to Mariah during my after-school class. She fell in love with a novel.

Mariah began her sixth-grade year with a big chip on her shoulder. She didn't feel that her sixth-grade teachers liked her. She, in turn, didn't give a damn about them. If it were allowed, one of her teachers would call her a bitch, Mariah felt. Every time someone said that she had done something in the classroom, *Mariah* got in trouble. Her teacher didn't come to her and say, "Did you do this?" She simply assumed that Mariah had done these things, even though somebody else was telling the story. Mariah sulked at her desk, trying to stay out of her seasoned teachers' radar as she looked for ways to infuse fun and excitement into what seemed to her to be the dreary routine of schoolwork.

But when Mariah discovered the novel that fall, something seemed to shift inside her. She decided there could be a place for her in school, for here was a book that called to her. Once Mariah knew she liked something, she could throw herself into it, the

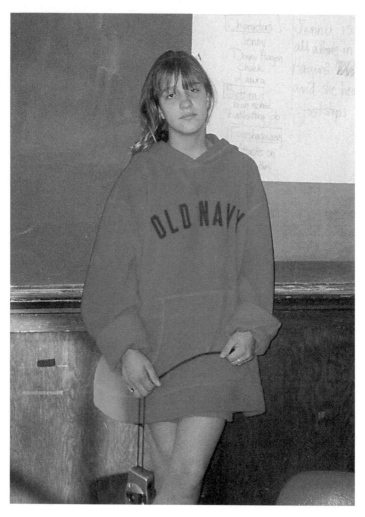

Mariah.

way she gave her heart to boys. She had just turned thirteen, change was in the air, and for once Mariah felt the sensation of finding in a work of fiction the excitement she so desired.

I had discovered the book on one of my regular weekend jaunts to a local bookstore in an upscale neighborhood. It had become a weekend ritual for me to browse the youth fiction section of this well-stocked store, looking for titles that might appeal to my students and enjoying an afternoon coffee in its café. From the minute I saw the cover of *Vampire Kisses* on a special display shelf, I was drawn by this book's clever and fun play on teen reader themes.[1] On its cover: a moonlit mansion framed by a gothic iron gate, bats flying overhead. Inside the book's jacket, the young reader finds a beguiling narrative synopsis: "In her small town, dubbed 'Dullsville,' sixteen-year-old Raven—a vampire-crazed goth girl—is an outcast. But not for long...."

There was a reason that I fell for the novel myself when I settled down to read it in an oversized leather armchair at the bookstore: Raven's strange tale is a story of love. The first cue comes with the book's opening inscription, a quote from Alexander Sterling, the goth guy with whom Raven falls head over heels in love: "I want a relationship I can finally sink my teeth into." Raven, the book's spirited goth heroine, finds herself in a budding romance with Alexander, a pale, dark-haired prince who inhabits the lonely mansion on Benson Hill, for Raven the only landmark in Dullsville with a glimmer of the edgy excitement she covets. Since early childhood, Raven has longed for one thing: to be a vampire. Her dark desires are at odds with the socially stagnant world of Dullsville, where she is ostracized by most of her peers in school and viewed by adults as a trouble-making oddball. "At school, instead of singing the songs of Mary Poppins," we learn from this heroine's inner voice, "I whistled to the theme to the *Exorcist*."[2]

I felt only a tinge of guilt at my complicity: I had fallen myself for this quirky story of outsiders in love. My enthusiasm must have been contagious, or maybe it was savvy book design. No sooner had I held up this popular novel than Alicia and Jessica *begged* me to set aside copies for them. Mariah joined the pair in sisterly fashion, at first sharing a copy with Jessica until I could get back to the bookstore and buy more. As she read the novel with Jessica, Mariah discovered a connection with its heroine, Raven. Raven was an outsider, just like Mariah herself. And Jessica thought the novel was well written and interesting. If Ellen Schreiber wrote another book, Jessica decided, she would definitely want to read it.

These girls were not alone in their love of vampire stories. As they inched closer toward adolescence, the other girls in my afternoon literature class seemed to live and breathe such tales.

Besides the gothic love story that Mariah, Alicia, and Jessica were practically inhaling, there was R. L. Stine's *Dangerous Girls,* enjoyed by Adriana, Blair, and Elizabeth. This latest release in the Stine collection for readers who had moved beyond *Goosebumps* paperbacks featured two sisters who got themselves in a mess by falling for fang-toothed boys. The three girls read the book quickly—all were fast readers—and moved on to *Vampire Kisses.* Then there was *Cirque du Freak,* the saga of Darren Shan, a teenage boy who has a life-altering experience when he sneaks into a traveling freak circus. When Darren goes back to the circus later that night to steal the pet spider of a vampire, the course of his life is forever altered.

The author of the series is also Darren Shan, the nom de plume of the Irish writer Darren O'Shaughnessy. Though he has written some adult fiction, O'Shaughnessy's *Cirque du Freak* series has catapulted him to celebrity status in the market for young readers. Among younger readers, the saga of Darren Shan has a literary status not unlike that of Stephen King's books among older ones. O'Shaughnessy's books are often frowned upon by parents and school professionals but are ravished by a youthful audience hungry for horror. With its coming-of-age story focused on a boy's life, Shan's series always struck me as having an implied male audience, but Blair fell for it. Maybe it was the gruesome prose that drew her eye to the book's pages: "While the crowd [at Cirque du Freak] hesitated, the woman with the bitten-off hand went on screaming. Blood was pumping out of the end of her wrist, covering the ground and other people."[3]

My students were hardly the only eleven- and twelve-year-old girls falling in love with their vampire stories. The vampire fiction craze has a history that starts with Bram Stoker's classic novel *Dracula,* and has resurfaced not only in Shan's books but also in the *Twilight* series. At a time in a girl's life when she enjoys retreating with a book, when reading is part of a secret emotional life, the stories offer a titillating mix of danger and constraint. "You are attracted to it because it is dangerous," said one thirteen-year-old girl, interviewed for an article in the *Guardian.*[4] Literary critics and psychoanalysts have attempted explanations of why so many adolescent girls are drawn by the genre. Vampire stories provide a metaphor for unspeakable desire; they present girl readers with gorgeous, if dangerous, monsters, the ultimate bad boys; they speak to the teenage girl's desire to be an outsider, like the dark creatures confined to nighttime blood gorgings.[5] Concerned teachers such as me face a dilemma: do we give in to the vampire craze and, like me reading *Vampire Kisses,* secretly enjoy the books ourselves? Do we worry about the sexually tinged images and metaphors or just give in to our inability to control the adolescent stirrings that are happening anyway?

I felt this mix of conflicting thoughts and feelings, but some part of me—maybe the wide-eyed, spirited girl I once was—wanted to grab my copies and read along with the girls. I finally gave in to this literary passion, or at least enough to allow the girls to read vampire stories written for the middle-school age group. Then one moonlit night in late October 2003, I decided to take Adriana and Mariah to a theater production of Bram Stoker's *Dracula.*

The occasion was Mariah's thirteenth birthday. She was the first of the girls in my literature class, now in its fourth year, to officially become a teenager, and we agreed that the occasion demanded something big. I had heard about the local theater production on my car radio, and I acted quickly. Tickets were selling fast. I could only take two of the girls this time—the tickets were pricey—and Mariah and I agreed that Adriana should accompany us. Adriana always felt left out because she was an August birthday girl and never got the chance to celebrate her birthday in my class. I spoke with the two girls' mothers, who happily gave their approval, and I phoned the theater box office.

The woman at the other end of the line when I called the box office warned me *twice:* "This is *not* a performance for children under twelve!" I thought for a moment about Adriana—she was one of the youngest in my class, still only eleven years old—but decided to go with my instincts. What could be worse than the gruesome stuff that scared the crap out of me, but that the girls had been watching and reading since they were nine years old? I also knew Adriana was mature for her age. The neighborhood, and her life at home with a single mom barely able to make ends meet, had grown her up fast. On the evening of the performance, I picked up the two girls at their homes, and off we went to the small local theater.

It was nearly 7:45 when we walked the short distance from my car to the theater. The moon was yellow and full—a luminous harvest moon. The October air was chilly, and the theater felt warm and comforting after our brisk walk. The feeling of excitement was palpable as we made our way from the lobby into the theater itself. Our seats were right off the stage, on benches that rose up on either side, perfectly suited for the young and the die-hard. The tightly packed audience, murmuring in anticipation, fell silent as the lights went down and the theater became completely dark. And then—*AAAAAAAH!*—a blood-curdling scream rose from the stage.

It was only the beginning. More screams would be heard as young Victorian ladies found themselves violated by Dracula's fangs and stakes were driven into the hearts of the hapless souls who entered his shadowy world.

Even I was a little awed by the amount of gore and screaming coming from the stage. Near our seats stood the crazed servant Renfield, pulling at his chains and screaming madly as he fed on a rat whose blood sprayed everywhere, including on Adriana's new white sneakers. The only other young people in an audience of adults were seated near us. A father had brought along his three daughters, one about the age of the girls in my class. The youngest was starting to whimper and cover her ears as Renfield lunged against his chains and spewed spit and fake blood. I glanced protectively at my two girls, ready to offer a reassuring hand. I shouldn't have worried: The two were laughing, loving the performance! They had found an imaginative nirvana in this turn-of-the-century tale of *bloooood*—as Dracula said in his Transylvanian accent.

The following Monday afternoon we gathered for our usual afterschool class. Adriana wore her new white shoes.

"I got scared because I got *blood* on my shoes," she said with a glimmer in her eye. Sure enough, the snowy white sneakers had some tiny red specks on them. The other girls sat around her spellbound, hungry for details.

Adriana and Mariah had been taken with a scene involving Lucy, one of the play's young Victorian ladies who had succumbed to Dracula and entered his dark world. In one memorable scene, she walked onto stage with a child's bloodied shoes hanging around her neck, fangs visible in her mouth, chanting with sardonic sweetness: "*Little* boy, *little* boy!"

"This girl named Lucy," Mariah said excitedly, "she had three people who wanted to marry her. At first there were only two guys that proposed to her. And the next day it was her doctor who proposed to her. And she didn't know what to say. Then Dracula came at night through her window and bit her in the neck and then, and then"—Mariah drew in a breath—"in the middle of it she came out with a white gown on her with blood and everything and baby shoes wrapped around her and she still had the markings on her neck and they put this wooden thing through her heart to where she would die and she was screamin'. Those people got *lungs!*"

Mariah paused briefly, long enough for Adriana and a couple other girls to practice their theatrical screams. Then Mariah went on, speaking in her breathless, excited style. She rose half out of her seat as she held the other girls captive with a second maiden's story.

"Mina—she turns into a vampire because Dracula bites her. And then, when Dracula bites her she thought she was gonna die. And Dracula made her drink some blood from his chest and she bit his chest. And then Dracula bit her twice in her arm and bit her in her neck and everything. And then that's when the feeding was over."

It was Mariah's favorite scene in the play. Dracula slips into Mina's bedroom, first biting her, then entreating her to bite his own bared chest. The two work themselves into an orgasmic frenzy in a scene that paints the sexual with a grotesque hue.

"It was *nasty*, though," said Mariah, uttering one of the girls' most potent words.

"They had a dream too," remarked Adriana.

"Yeah, they were having dreams an' everything and she was going, '*Ooh ooh ooh*' in the bed an' everything. It sounded *nasty*."

Mariah looked pleased with herself, for she certainly had her audience. She lowered herself back into her armchair—she had by that time gone fully upright for dramatic effect. Her eyes were still glistening, her skin flushed.

"Why are you touching yourself?" asked Jessica slyly. She had perceived a brush of Mariah's hand toward her crotch. Other girls squealed at the thought.

"No, it's NOT...—that's *nasty!*" said Mariah to the rude girls listening to her, but she laughed anyway at the crazy corner our discussion had turned.

Shortly after *Vampire Kisses* became the latest literary sensation in my class, I learned that the book's author, Ellen Schreiber, would be speaking at the bookstore where I had first spotted the book. That explained the special book display.

For me, going to hear an author read from her book has an intoxicating quality—experiencing this was another of the educational gifts I wanted my students to have. I wondered if they connected the words they read in their assigned readings to the voices of real, speaking people. Often I got the feeling that most of what my students read in school felt deeply removed from who they were or what they most cared about. This had been true for me as a girl. Sure—I had a gift for stories and a vivid imagination. But it took many years of reading novels on my own before I was able to read a work of fiction and perceive the real speaking voice of its writer, as vivid as the southern voices all around me. In large part, this was because of the way in which fiction was used in a crowded classroom of kids destined for the farm and the factory. There certainly wasn't any talk about literature, and no one would have cared about my opinion of the books I enjoyed. It wasn't until I was an adult that I discovered the rich, melodic voices of southern storytellers such as Flannery O'Connor, Carson McCullers, and Lee Smith. So when I did later on have the occasion to go to readings, I felt a sense of magic at actually hearing the voice behind the written page.

One time I had been fortunate enough to be in New York visiting some friends on an evening when Michael Ondaatje read from *The English Patient.* The 92nd Street Y where he read was packed; there must have been thousands of us, with not an empty seat in sight. When he began to read, the huge auditorium became still and yet profoundly alive. How simple was this voice speaking, *reading,* and yet how moving it was to hear a work of fiction read in this way. So when I discovered that there was going to be a Saturday afternoon reading of *Vampire Kisses,* I quickly seized the opportunity. What could be better, I thought, than going to hear the author? Besides, we had some October birthdays, so as a special incentive I threw in a visit to the bookstore's sit-down café.

First there was the important question of what to wear for an afternoon at the bookstore. The girls in my class decided they wanted to go dressed in black, fitting couture for a goth girl like Raven. After a little digging around, I discovered that a local Goodwill store was having a half-price sale on all its clothing.

So with two of the girls, Alicia and Blair, accompanying me after our class, I drove to the store, and we filled a shopping cart with enough black separates to clothe our entire group. From the new collection of pants, skirts, and tops, each girl created a look that was either goth or like something you might see in an artsy urban café. Elizabeth chose for her outfit a flowing knee-length black rayon jacket that, with her tall lanky frame, gave her a bohemian look. Alicia chose some black stretch pants and a black T-shirt. With a pair of clunky thick-soled black shoes she had at home, she would create a chic urban look, suited to her long blond hair and thin torso. Blair chose for herself a black silk jacket that fit loosely. With her porcelain skin and piercing eyes, she could easily pass for a heroine who might inhabit a dark fictional world. Mariah selected a shiny fake leather skirt that fit snugly around her hips. She fancied herself becoming a singer someday, and she thought the skirt suited her. And Jessica selected a fitted knit top with a pretty floral design in the center and tiny sparkles sewn into its soft black fabric.

Only Adriana decided that she would take a fashion detour by wearing her green sweater and a pair of jeans. She liked to do things her way, and she didn't give a damn what the other girls would decide to do.

On a Saturday afternoon in late fall, we drove to the bookstore in two cars. Mariah's adoptive mother drove one group, and I drove another. You could feel the excitement as we drove across town. Adriana felt as though she were going on a journey, like the road trip she had taken to Las Vegas when she was only a little girl. She watched as the houses changed from modest to upscale; the bookstore was located in a trendy district, further away from her neighborhood than our usual downtown haunts.

Someday, Adriana would later reveal to our group, she wanted to travel to London.

Elizabeth was in top form, for she was one of our fall birthday girls. Going out with us on a Saturday was something of a novelty for Elizabeth. Her gruff father usually wouldn't let her join us for special outings unless they were during our regular weekly class time after school. But this time he had given in. Maybe it was the fact of her birthday that softened his stern heart. Secretly I felt relieved, for I had begun to hear disturbing stories that the family was running out of food at the end of each month. I was all too pleased to be spoiling Elizabeth with birthday food. Some of our happiest moments were around shared meals, and this promised to be yet another of those experiences.

Only Jessica appeared to be cranky and out of sorts. It turned out that she had only gotten a few hours of sleep the night before.

As soon as we arrived at the bookstore and found the area reserved for the reading, we grabbed front-row seats like hungry music fans at a concert. Our payoff for getting there early was to get a luxurious brown leather couch and two old-fashioned wood rockers with cushy pillows. Girls crammed themselves onto the couch, but Blair and Elizabeth couldn't sit just yet. A frenzied mood had overtaken them, and they slunk like paparazzi between some nearby bookshelves, hoping for a sneak preview of our very own literary celeb. Then out she walked, dressed for the occasion in black: a black Hello Kitty tee, a shiny black miniskirt, black-and-red-striped stockings, and heeled go-go boots in black leather. Jessica, sitting in one of the two rockers, had a stunned expression on her face. The other girls looked giddy with excitement. Schreiber had an easy air—she had once done stand-up comedy—and a laugh that reminded some of the girls of Fran Drescher on the television show *The Nanny*. She began to speak to the audience, which—except for one other girl there with her mother, and a few of the author's family members—was mostly made up of our group.

Not all of her characters in the novel, Schreiber shared, were inspired by people she knew. Some were invented characters who were completely unlike her intimate friends and family. But she felt that many people could also identify with the heroine's central dilemma: a feeling of not fitting in, something many felt during adolescence and even adulthood. Raven, the novel's heroine, was strong and not afraid of her individuality.

Schreiber depicted Raven as the popular culture heir to a long tradition of gothic heroines, unafraid to assert their passions and eccentricities in a sometimes indifferent or even hostile world. She read a short excerpt from her novel, then there was time for questions. Adriana was the first girl to raise her hand.

"Does *Vampire Kisses* relate to you—like when you was a teenager?" said Adriana.

"As a teenager?" Schreiber said. Then she went on to explain how her interest in goth styles of dress had emerged later for her, when she began to do acting and stand-up comedy.

Blair had puzzled over the sad ending to *Vampire Kisses,* in which Alexander left both the mansion and the girl who so longed to join him in his shadowy world. In Blair's lap was a copy of her own short novella, *Vampires Together Forever.* Blair's story had a little bit of *Vampire Kisses* in it, and a little bit of R. L. Stine's *Dangerous Girls.* In her story, two sisters, Blair and Adriana, went to summer camp. There they met two boys, Charles and Chaz. Blair thought at first that Charles liked Adriana, but soon Charles revealed his feelings for Blair.

She wanted to share *all* of her chapters with Ellen Schreiber. But we had talked about how busy Ms. Schreiber would be on the day of her book signing. So Blair had carefully highlighted two chapters with colorful Post-It notes. One was chapter 6, "Bitten."

> While we were out in the woods talking, Charles started kissing me. He said he loved me. I'm not sure that he loves me. I really didn't care because I didn't want to stop. Then he came up for air, we stood up, he pushed me against a tree and started to kiss me again. I thought we made a good couple because we were both gothic. About that time I pushed him away because he was licking my neck. Then we started kissing again, then he jumped down and sank his sharp fangs into my throat and drunk.

"My question is, at the end—why'd you make Alexander *leave?*" Blair asked. "Why didn't he stay?"

Blair's voice was raspy again. She had missed school on Friday and stayed home with another respiratory ailment and its usual aftermath, asthma. But today everything was different: She had *begged* her grandma, crying and cussing up a mean streak, to let her come to the bookstore with us. Finally Grandma Lilly had relented; she couldn't do anything with her stubborn grandbaby when she acted like this. Blair brought along her inhaler, just in case. She looked like a Dickensian waif, watery-eyed and thin in her loosely fitting black jacket.

Ellen Schreiber replied to Blair's question with a discussion of Alexander's *character*, a novelistic concept that the girls were beginning to understand, though on their own terms. Alexander knew, Schreiber explained, that Raven was obsessed with a vampire lifestyle. If he *was* a vampire (which was left ambiguous in the story), Raven would have felt compelled to leave her world for his.

"Because he cared for her so much," Schreiber said, "he didn't want her to have to live the lifestyle that he lived."

It was a romantic theme. Our author explained that even though her book was a vampire story, she wanted to emphasize romance over gore.

"Are you gonna write a sequel to *Vampire Kisses?*" asked Mariah. Mariah tugged the hemline of her shiny black skirt, which had hiked up when she sat down. Mariah didn't seem to feel a bit of shame, but Alicia had a look of disgust as her stepcousin spoke. Schreiber only smiled and nodded.

"Yes, I'm writing it now."

"*Oh!* Can we get it?" asked Adriana.

"Is Alexander gonna come back in the book?" asked Blair excitedly.

Schreiber assured us that yes—he would return.

"Yeeaah!" said Mariah, clapping. "The *gothic* guy!"

"Was the bat really Alexander?" inquired Alicia. She was curious about the novel's uncertain ending, which had Raven going up to the lonely, deserted mansion one last time after Alexander's departure. As Raven leans against the mansion gate, down swoops a bat that lands upon the gate and stares at her in a soulful way.[6]

"What do you think?" said Schreiber. "I like to leave that up to the reader."

Alicia felt that the bat with the deep gaze must have been Alexander himself.

Elizabeth had been unusually quiet during our gathering, but suddenly she seemed inspired to ask a question. It bubbled up from thoughts that had been churning inside her, and suddenly everything gelled into the question she most wanted to ask.

"What inspired you to write?"

"To write this story or just to write?"

"Just write."

Schreiber explained, one writer to another, what had prompted her to move into the world of popular fiction. Writing was like an escape for her, something that changed her life when she showed her work to a publisher and they agreed to take it.

Elizabeth puzzled over another question as she thought about her own efforts to write.

"Don't you ever have a feeling that you want to give up or something, really stop writin'?"

"Mostly *not*," our author replied. She really liked to write, and when it flowed she almost had to pry herself away.

"Even like, when your hands start to hurtin', but you want to still type?" Elizabeth continued, "but sometimes do you feel like I don't want to write no more or somethin'?"

Our author admitted that this was not something she usually experienced.

Elizabeth had been struggling to connect the world she knew with that of Ellen Schreiber. Suddenly a question popped into her head, and with her usual eagerness for the camaraderie of a kindred female spirit, she blurted it out before she had a chance to think.

"I know this is off track and all, but when you wake up in the morning is your hair all frizzy?"

On the way back to the girls' neighborhood, after enjoying some chocolate cakes at the bookstore café, everyone was buzzing with a giggly, sugary high. But something else had settled into Adriana's consciousness during the drive back. A word bubbled up from her mix of feelings about this trip to the world of coffee bars, packed bookshelves, arty writing journals and bookmarks, and upscale homes. As we neared the run-down brick townhouse where she and her mother lived in a bottom floor-unit, Adriana spoke the word quickly. *Trash.* It lingered like an echo, in a brief silence that interrupted the rhythms of chatter and laughter on the journey home.

CHAPTER EIGHT

Jessica Finds Jesus, and Elizabeth Finds Love

One morning in late January, I awoke before dawn because of a nightmare about my class. The sky outside was dim with a hint of light, though the moon was no longer visible. It was a chilly morning and damp, and I turned over in my bed and drew the covers closer, shivering.

In my dream, a mad, dangerous woman was trying to snatch the girls away from me. My thoughts in this dreamworld were that some of the girls would never make it to high school. The girls were doing some kind of writing. One of the girls began to speak, saying how hard it was for her to change and do academic work. As I looked upon the girls working, I had the bird's-eye perspective that exists only in dreams. "Three of the girls are going to be taken away by the evil woman," I thought. I feared that I had already lost those three, and that they would not be able to make it in school.

The months of late winter 2004, just like those to come in spring, had a bittersweet feeling to them, for this was to be our

Jessica.

last year of gathering for my weekly reading class. I had plans to spend time at another university the following fall, and I would not be living in the same state. Meanwhile the girls would be going through their own changes. They were on the cusp of adolescence now. Most had turned twelve during the year; Mariah, our oldest, had already turned thirteen. It was a year when we all stood at the crossroads of old and new.

The changes that were coming into our group may have spilled over into my dreams, or maybe it had been my viewing of Catherine Hardwicke's film *Thirteen*—a raw, searing portrayal of one girl's journey into adolescence.[1] The script was cowritten by Hardwicke and a teen girl, Nikki Reed, and based upon Reed's real-life experiences as a thirteen-year-old. The film focuses on the experiences of Tracey, a vulnerable thirteen-year-old sucked into the destructive teenage orbit of another girl, Evie. The two girls smoke, do drugs, steal clothes, and perform blow jobs, at least until Tracey begins to self-destruct by cutting herself and severing the already fragile ties of her family life.

The film is set in a lower-middle-class world, different from the even more stressful setting where the girls in my class were coming of age. But it hit close to home. In the characters of Evie and Tracey, I could see shadowy resemblances to our girls: Jessica and Mariah, our older girls who liked life on the edge; Alicia, who looked small and vulnerable next to them; Blair, who seemed consumed with angry, confused feelings that she herself could not fully comprehend; and sometimes Adriana, who could be distant and depressed on her bad days.

Which of the girls were the three of my dream? At different moments in our work together, as the girls and I sat talking, an unsettled feeling about one of them would creep into my thoughts, its effects lingering well beyond our meeting. Soon the girls would be crossing the threshold of adolescence. I watched the girls closely in the final months of my class, and I worried.

Later that same morning, I walked the short distance from the side street where I usually parked my car to the girls' elementary school. On my way I passed the ground-floor unit where Jessica's grandma lived. On this morning she stood outside on the small cement stoop, a cigarette in one hand. Grandma Kay always reminded me of older ladies from my girlhood in western North Carolina. Her skin was crinkly and pale, which made her blue eyes more striking. Her wisps of gray hair were pulled back in a bun, country-style, and she wore polyester pants and a loose-fitting T-shirt. Grandma Kay nearly always had a half-smoked cigarette in her right hand, and her voice seemed smoky too. She still spoke with the Kentucky twang of her childhood years. Her eyes seemed to twinkle as I approached her, and we exchanged a warm hug. Her eyes did most of the smiling, for she couldn't afford to buy a new set of teeth.

"Hey, how *are* you?" I said as we exchanged pleasantries. Almost right away, Grandma Kay began sharing her worries about Jessica.

Jessica felt unhappy living at home, and she was starting to hang out with an older crowd. She smoked now, and Grandma Kay had finally broken down and given her some cigs. But she had *never* once given her grandbaby any weed.

Grandma Kay's pearly-blue eyes grew misty. She was silent for a moment, as if she were searching for words. I took her hand and assured her I would talk with Jessica. Then I walked away and into the aging school building to get ready for my after-school class. I felt even more weight than usual on my shoulders as a teacher.

It was two in the afternoon, and the girls and I sat together in our borrowed classroom. Outside our windows, the neighborhood children were racing around the school's blacktop playground, some riding bicycles. A child yelled, then came the sound of a kickball slamming against the school walls. Inside, the mood in our small class was more somber for some of the girls. Jessica knew she was in a rough patch that winter, and she looked tired. Small gray circles were visible under her eyes. Over the past summer, shortly before she entered sixth grade, things had clicked for Jessica in my class. She was beginning to find herself on the pages of novels, and she loved writing for our magazine. But in a larger classroom setting, she became dreamy-eyed and distant. She stayed out late at night and smoked and laughed with her friends. In the mornings she felt tired, and besides that school bored her. Then one Friday she didn't come to school at all.

It happened, Jessica told us, when Anna, Jessica's fourteen-year-old best friend, talked her into skipping. Jessica and she were just sitting there talking about skipping, in the way they always shared their secret dreams, when all of a sudden Anna said, "*Yeah,* let's skip!" Jessica sat there for minute, then she said, "*Yeah,* that'd be cool." With all the buildup to adventure, the two never even left the neighborhood. They sat for hours under the viaduct, talking and smoking and giggling like teenage girls.

"We took our cellphones, and we put the alarm on 1:45," said Jessica to the group of listening girls in our Monday after-school gathering. It was less than a week after the eventful day, but already a lot had changed for her. Jessica's voice had a bittersweet edge to it, like a bluegrass song of love and loss, as she told the story.

"We took our book bags and everything else, and we acted like we went to school. An' my mom was out looking for me, an' she had the cops out looking for me."

Jessica knew that the school would be calling home, so she unplugged the house phone. But she was discovered—her mother had to use the phone. Also, Anna's teacher had left a message on the home phone at Anna's house, and there was no way for Anna to erase it. By the time the two girls got to Anna's grandma's, after school hours, the word was out. Anna's grandma told Jessica her mother was looking for her.

From her telling, it was clear that when Jessica was out for the day with Anna, their time together had the delicious feel of breaking the rules. It was the kind of edgy adventure Jessica relished. The girls in our circle leaned forward in their seats as Jessica spoke. Her story felt like a reel of film that, frame by frame, was transporting us into a teen girl world with its mix of pleasure, angry defiance, and anxiety.

"It felt like I was, you know, *older* and everything else," Jessica shared. "But I was just scared. When we was underneath the viaduct we heard some kind of noise."

A few of the girls in the circle giggled.

"And Anna—she had a lighter with her," Jessica went on, half laughing herself. "And her dumb ass gonna light up a cigarette, just sit there and say, 'I didn't hear nuthin'.' I was like, '*Dude,* someone's down here.' She said, 'No, there ain't,' and I was like, 'Yeah, there is.' And then she finally saw this person walkin' past on the railroad track. An' I got my book bag an' I started running. And I was like, '*Anna,* come on *now!*' 'Cause like we're best friends and I worried about her and everything else."

Jessica's voice shifted from comic to melancholic as she shared the aftermath of the girls' adventure. Before the incident, she and Anna had been like sisters, telling their secrets. Now Jessica was forbidden to be with Anna.

"I ain't allowed 'round her until I'm eighteen," said Jessica. "She ain't allowed around me until she's eighteen."

"But you know you're gonna be around her!" said Alicia.

Jessica was crushed by the weight of her loss. "It's like I have tears in my eyes every day, and every night when I wake up, like water drips out of my eyes. We used to be like partners, we used to tell each other *dreams,* our dreams that we had an' everything else. I wish we never did do that because now it's like, I walk over there—"

Jessica's sad thought was left unfinished. Elizabeth and Blair were getting antsy and rudely inattentive. Jessica's lovely blue eyes shifted downward in a mournful way.

"What about the last thing that Jessica shared?" I said, in an effort to keep the girls focused on our group member in need. "Is there anything we can do to help?"

"We can help her make *good* friends," suggested Mariah, who liked to think of herself as steadfast and loyal. "I mean, Anna *is* a good friend, but she can also have other friends."

There was another complication to an already painful story, and Mariah knew the details. After the incident, Anna's father had beaten her.

"That was wrong what her dad does to her," said Jessica, flushing pink with rage. "If William or Tyler gets found somewhere," she went on, speaking of Anna's two brothers, "like if they skip school or something, they won't get *beat* like she did."

"She gets beat," echoed Mariah, who always came alive when stories with a rough edge were shared.

"She got *beat,*" Jessica went on. "Her eye was *black.*"

Anna's father had threatened her, Jessica related. "If I ever catch you *around* Jessica or talkin' to Jessica on your cell or writin' to her," he told his fourteen-year-old daughter, "I'll *punch* you in your face just like I did the other night."

Jessica responded in the neighborhood way. "I told her," Jessica said, "if you wrote tellin' me if he punches you or whatever—cause my uncle already said that he wanted to whoop her dad's ass for already blacking her one eye."

It felt like a scene from *Bastard Out of Carolina,* a novel by Dorothy Allison that I was rereading in anticipation of using parts of it in my class. The story portrays the raw and sometimes painful coming-of-age experiences of Bone, a girl born to a fifteen-year-old waitress with fierce, hard-drinking brothers. For the Boatwright brothers, injustices are settled with their fists. Violence is met with more violence. Other girls in our circle were familiar with the outline of that script, and they were also in on the details of this particular drama. They listened appreciatively as Jessica expressed her dismay that Anna, a girl, would be doled out such cruel punishment when Anna's father wouldn't lay a hand on the boys. This was not a neighborhood ethic, Jessica assured me when I inquired. The girl's father had crossed way over the line, and from now on he would be under close watch.

It was approaching three, and our discussion with Jessica had lasted a long time. The afternoon light was gray. The day was chilly, though you could feel the promise of early spring in a warming sun that kept peeking through the cloud cover. But there was only one hour remaining in my class, and I had planned an activity for the girls. As a way to bring some closure to our class in its final year, I asked the girls to reflect on a question I had first raised three years before, when they were only eight and nine years old: What are your dreams for the future? I passed around the girls' journals and they moved to their favorite places for writing. Jessica retreated to a round table, set near the row of windows. She liked to do serious work by herself; she was easily distracted. Jessica rested her head in one hand, her elbows on the table, and she let out a long sigh. She thought about the life she wanted for herself.

Sometimes when she was by herself, Jessica liked to sit around and imagine the things she would do if she were granted three wishes. Lighting up one of the cigs she bummed off of Anna, she would dream. Her first wish was to be a grown-up. Her second was to be rich and buy five cars. One of these she would drive around the world. Her third and final wish was to become a nurse and help old people at a nursing home or little kids who needed care.

It wasn't long before Jessica had written down these thoughts in her journal. At three thirty I called the girls back to our meeting circle to share their journal writing.

"I'd love to hear what you wrote," I said. "Jessica, could we start with you?"

She blushed with pride. Jessica wore a cute white crocheted top, under which was a pink sleeveless tank top. A black bra strap peeked through the crocheted openings, giving her an older look, like a girl of fourteen or fifteen. Her lips were painted with sparkly pink gloss. Her yellow hair was pulled off her face and secured with a pink clasp. Jessica began reading aloud.

> *I would love to be one of those people who dose the laundry and maintenance person. So there bed room and there bath room will be clean and the whole nurseing home will be spotless clean.*
>
> *The reason why I want to be on the path of my dreams to be a nurse is because I used to help my Aunt down in Indiana. I want to be a maintenance and a laundry person because I know all of the steps how to do it all.*
>
> *The End*

"Why do you want to work with their laundry when some of 'em, like, pee on their self?" asked Blair skeptically.

"I don't know," admitted Jessica. "I'm used to it an' everything else. Not this summer but last summer, I used to help my aunt and everything else." Jessica's baby-blue eyes took on a mischievous glimmer. Suddenly she had a story to tell.

"This old lady chased me down the hall. So I had to run into the laundry room where my aunt was cause I went there to get a pop for us. And the lady chased us down there—she had one of those dirty pamper things," Jessica said, laughing. "And she ran into the door, and my aunt had to scrub the door down and everything else. And I was laughing at her. And she made me pick up all those clothes an' everything else with all them dirty nasty clothes and throw them in the wash an' everything else.

"But the good thing is that you gotta have gloves on to do everything down in that nursing home," Jessica concluded, as if her story required a moral ending to render it complete. Blair looked pensive and puzzled.

"Did you *like* working there?" Blair asked.

Jessica nodded in a mature way, as if Blair were too young to understand.

I'll have to admit that I was puzzled and even somewhat dismayed that the shape of Jessica's *dreams* was so molded by the constraints of a world divided by class: women on her side of the class divide were domestic laborers. And maybe some part of me—the hopelessly idealistic teacher, the dreamer—was also disappointed. I had worked hard for three and a half years to instill a sense of possibility in my students. We had read novels and talked and produced our own magazine. And still Jessica wanted to be a *laundry worker*? Was that dream a little like my six-month stint working in a warehouse, I wondered? Though the work was boring—I put boxes together mostly and filled them with small mail-order items—it felt oddly familiar and comfortable. It was the kind of work that women in my world would have done, close to the domestic labor of the home—women's work. No woman in my extended family had ever gone to college; now *that* was what felt daunting. I decided to probe a little further, to see if Jessica connected education at all with the world of work she envisioned entering.

"What kind of school would be best for you?" I asked.

"Like a maintenance school or something like that," Jessica replied, "dealing with the nursing home. If I do go to practice in a nursing home in Indiana, I know where everything is. I know how to fold the sheets an' everything else, cause I used to help my aunt. An' I just know where everything is, and it's real fun."

"Why is it fun?" said Blair, still looking pensive and a little smug. She saw her own future in nursing—working with tiny, cute babies—but the idea of a nursing home seemed dirty and ugly to her.

"If you was in my opinion of why I wanna be a nurse," said Jessica, "it's because I like helping other people out instead of just helping myself out."

Jessica loved slipping into the domestic role of "helper"; she was often the first and last girl to lend a hand with the table setup and cleanup when we shared snacks and meals. She was a caring, thoughtful girl. Jessica connected easily with other people; her manner was warm and accepting. The anger and risk-taking that were getting her into trouble in school were just a sliver of the Jessica we had all gotten to know in our afterschool group. Maybe a career in nursing could be a good fit to her. But between that endpoint—if a career as a nurse were to become a reality for her—and the knowledge she had accumulated about the world at age twelve lay a long, hard road.

Jessica could feel that she was slipping in school, and it troubled her. She wanted to do well. But the world of friends and flirting and life on the edge called to her in a way that school did not. She found herself drawn to piercings and drugs and boys. She got her nose pierced, and she wore a sweet diamond stud. Then she took the nose jewel out because she felt it made her ugly.

Boys were a source of entertainment but also distraction in her larger classrooms. Jessica really liked boys, but she thought about them while she was in school. It was difficult to get her thoughts wrapped around books and learning with boys there to tempt and aggravate her. She tried to keep her mind focused on her schoolwork, but boys bugged her to the point where she felt like hitting them. Jessica was moody—angry about life at home, where she was miserable, and frazzled from staying up late with her older friends. From the outside, she seemed passive and withdrawn in her classrooms. But on the inside she felt a confusing mix of feelings; she needed to shout it out before she could get a handle on them. She wanted to scream, laugh, and maybe have a smoke—like she used to do with her girl Anna.

Jessica had begun to see changes for herself as she read novels and watched films such as *Whale Rider*. She had become a leader in my class. But the pressure of being a disadvantaged student in need of basic, remedial instruction overwhelmed her in her regular classrooms. Sixth grade was a benchmark year, and her teachers were under intense pressure to get students such as Jessica ready for the big March tests. In her crowded classrooms, where teachers were already pushed to the limit trying to get even half of their kids test-ready, Jessica fell between the cracks.

Her rage became passivity. She started to give up. Without the middle-class privilege of tutoring, or the upper-class opportunity of a private-school education with small classes or even all-girls schooling, Jessica slipped into a dreamy state of removal. Sometimes she fell flat asleep at her desk.

The Monday after our conversation about dreams, I found Jessica's homeroom class in the auditorium. The kids were rehearsing for a Wednesday performance led by the music teacher; everyone—or almost everyone—was up on stage. But not Jessica. There was some kind of conflict brewing; the other kids were begging her to come up and read one of her poems, but Jessica refused. She looked red-faced and unhinged. Later I learned Jessica's version of the story. The songs the class was singing were babyish and "gay." Plus her throat hurt. When she refused to go up on stage, cussing neighborhood style, Mrs. Stevenson kicked her out of school for the rest of the day. I knew the details of Jessica's story were partial. Mrs. Stevenson was a strict, traditional teacher, but she was also fair. She would be intolerant of cussing but unlikely to send a kid packing for it. But for Jessica it was just one more day of feeling as though school didn't work for her. She couldn't even imagine herself on stage filling the hall with her poetry, like a singer.

Jessica ran out of school that day, and onto the streets. She did not even return for the girls' literature class that she held so near to her heart.

Elizabeth had once loved reading. In a household with ten kids and not enough money to feed all of them, she was the one with two bookshelves full of her books. But in the long four months since her twelfth birthday, Elizabeth had felt *bored* with reading. As a matter of fact, most things about school bored her lately.

She kept getting lost in thoughts that sent her mind in weird directions.

One day, right after her baby brother Luke died—he would have been the eleventh child—Elizabeth had tried something strange and new. The ashes from his tiny body were in an urn, for he had been cremated. In a rare moment when no one was around, Elizabeth moistened the tip of her index finger in her mouth, stuck her finger in the ashes, and ate a small bit of him. Afterwards she kept wondering if some part of this small person was now living inside of her. It felt disorienting, like she couldn't be sure any longer if she was truly alone in her own body. Even her body felt strange to her, like it had its own alien ways. She had grown tall, as tall as most of her teachers now, and she couldn't sit still. Whenever she tried to sit down with a book, she would lose her mind because the whole thing was so boring.

One night that winter, Elizabeth's dad, in a rare moment of concern, asked why she didn't read anymore like she used to. When Elizabeth offered her explanation—she just didn't *like* reading anymore—he countered with his.

"You've got your mind on that dumbass Zack," he said in his growly voice.

"Yeah, Dad," she replied soberly.

The problem was this: her dad didn't like redheads, and Zack was a redhead.

She asked her dad, "What if Zack dyed his hair?"

"That'd probably be better, but I still don't trust him," he said.

There had been trouble from the moment Elizabeth met Zack. Zack didn't really know her that well, and he had called her a slut because she was hanging out with Mariah and starting to act like her too. Her older brother had called Zack's mother a slut, and the two boys had gotten into it. Zack ended up the winner: he beat the crap out of Elizabeth's brother. Their dad thought it was typical, because redheads were assholes. Elizabeth was beginning to view men in uncertain terms. She hated men, as a general rule, but Zack was one in a million—he wasn't no asshole. Zack was more gangsta, letting his pants droop in the urban style. He told Elizabeth he'd run away and get married with her if he had to. "*Fuck* him," Zack told her. She thought about the idea of running away, because she wanted to have a redheaded baby. They looked so cute until they grew up and got ugly.

One afternoon Zack tried to walk Elizabeth home after the two had met up after school. Her dad happened to drive by in his green van, and he stopped.

"You come over here and *fuck with* my daughter ever again and I'm gonna kill you! I'm gonna get my gun," he said.

"Oh brother!" said Elizabeth.

"I'm going to kick your ASS!" said her dad to Zack. Zack turned red.

"Dad, STOP!" Elizabeth said.

"I don't care," he said. "I don't like fucking redheads!"

All of these events seemed to be on Elizabeth's mind when we sat together on the first Monday of February, discussing romance and love. Valentine's Day was just around the corner, and Elizabeth framed her opening greeting with a showstopper: Tell us about your boyfriend or your secret admirer. With Zack tucked away in her own thoughts, Elizabeth leaned back in her armchair and listened with a new kind of smug interest.

"I don't have a boyfriend," said Blair, "and I don't got no secret admirer either. I'll buy *myself* a rose."

A hooting sound arose from the circle of girls.

"I ain't got no boyfriend *no* more—I'm single," Adriana said.

Jessica whispered a boy's name.

"I dumped his ass!" said Adriana, with a laugh. "I ain't got no secret admirer," she added, smirking with her new freedom.

"I think I'm gettin' roses for Valentine's Day, I ain't for sure," said Jessica, next in our circle to share. "But I'll tell you guys, when we come back to group. I'll tell you if my *guess* was right."

Jessica was blushing. Could she have been thinking about the last time she and her boyfriend had been together, I wondered. She had shown us a photograph of the boy, his chest bare, with its tiny area of red pimples. She was his blonde, blue-eyed beauty.

A softly muttered comment was spoken in our circle.

"Oh, my God, *shut up!*" Jessica said. She was still blushing. Her large baby-blue eyes had come alive in a way that was rare in a school setting.

The next girl in our circle to share her greeting was Mariah. "I'm single," said Mariah, who was the last girl to share. "But I have a secret admirer," she went on. "I can't tell nobody, cause ya'll would get—"

The other girls looked stricken with their lust for details.

"Okay, my secret admirer is Russell Stallard [a few girls drew in sharp breaths], but right now I am like in SO much trouble over him."

Alicia had the doubtful look on her face she got when she called Mariah on one of her stories.

"You said, you told me that in front of Sean and Tyler and all them cousins."

"I did, but—"

"He's your secret admirer and you like 'im but you go around talkin' about 'im all the time."

"Alicia," said Jessica, like a patient big sister, "you say to yourself when you're in love with that person that you don't really mean it."

"Yeah, exactly," confirmed Mariah. "Anyway, he got in trouble because I called him 'cause I was really bored. And my family don't like 'im because of somethin' that happened between my dad and his dad."

"Can I say something?" said Elizabeth. It was her turn—we had come full circle—but she felt compelled to ask for the floor anyway.

"Zack wants me to be his girlfriend, but I said I can't cause my dad don't like 'im so we're gonna be secret boyfriend and girl-friend without nobody knowing."

Mariah nodded her head in an understanding way and shifted her weight on the loveseat. Her romance with Russell was every bit as complicated as Elizabeth's with Zack. Some things had happened before she even came into her adoptive family. Her adoptive father had a fight with Russell's father.

"My dad said that if he wouldn't stop harrassin' my brother my dad would shoot 'im," Mariah said. "And his dad said that if he wouldn't stop harrassin' his *son* that he would shoot him. And it's just goin' back and forth, back and forth."

It seemed so Shakespearean to me—these stories of adolescents and their feuding families. I thought about the Romeo and Juliet story and the closest thing to it that I was sure the girls knew: *A Little Romance,* the film we had watched one year earlier around this time. It was a contemporary spin-off of the classic story.

"This sounds familiar to me," I said, always in search of ways I could forge connections between the girls' everyday experiences and the books we had read or, in this case, the films we had seen. "Do you remember *A Little Romance,* the movie where Lauren was sneaking out to be with her boyfriend, Daniel, and how her parents didn't want her to be with a French boy like him?"

Elizabeth remembered the story in vivid detail. "That mom, she thought there was something wrong with that boy."

Her blood seemed to boil with the thought.

"*Man,* that's what gets on my nerves! Man, I get so freakin' mad!"

"Russell is the man of my *dreams,*" said Mariah, growing more confident and animated by the minute. "When I go to my junior prom, I'll probably be with Russell Stallard."

At this, Blair began to think aloud about her prom. She could picture her dream night, and she began to share the details. It would start with a very *sweet* prom date who knew how to treat a lady. Then it went on with the details of the memorable event. The pretty, light-blue dress with a scarf she held around her arms. The very pretty, light-blue shoes. The excitement and happiness she would feel.

"You're a copycatter!" said Alicia, with a tone of mock indignation.

"How?" asked Blair.

"'Cause if I go to the prom I was gonna wear the same thing. Copycatter!"

"I would feel happy too," said Mariah, "because—." Suddenly she felt shy, a rare thing for her in my class.

"Say it!" said Alicia.

"It's because I *love him,*" said Mariah, blurting out the words. Elizabeth let out a quick gasp. Jessica smiled knowingly.

"It's just the way I got feelings for him."

My thoughts drifted back to the previous summer, when I first learned of Mariah's budding romance with Russell. Mariah, Alicia, and I had gone out one steamy August afternoon to see a film in air-conditioned comfort. Afterwards we went to a pizza parlor for a late lunch, and Mariah spoke of her new boyfriend.

Beaming, she shared how this summer was her dream come true: Russell had asked *her* out. She had been asking him out before, and he had always said no. She had seen him often when they hung out around the neighborhood pool with other friends. One time Mariah and Jessica had been hanging out with Russell when he turned to the girls and said, "Which one of you wants to suck my dick?" Russell's nickname among Mariah's peer group was Mr. Blow Job. He was thirteen years old.

"He acts like a *big baby*!" said Alicia in her high-pitched voice.

"And you wanna know what?" Mariah went on, happy to have pulled Alicia into the orbit of neighborhood business. "You never know who got Margie—"

"I know!" said Alicia.

"Well, Andrew is not neither one of them kids' dad."

"We know who Brianna's real dad is," said Jessica, who had been listening excitedly. "Some dude that lives down in California or whatever."

"Okay, we're gonna move on," I said, donning the mantle of literature teacher. It was time to turn to the afternoon's reading selection.

"No, wait, wait, wait!" said Alicia impatiently. "Because what's her name, uh, she told Logan that he was the dad of them. He said, 'Nuh uh.' And Audrey went to get a blood test. And it came out that—"

"—Let's talk about, *let's talk about* that later," I said impatiently. Our time together each Monday was always too brief, and a short story awaited us.

That February evening, on the way home to my apartment across the Ohio River, I replayed in my head the afternoon's discussion about young love. I kept returning to how Shakespearean in plot and feeling the girls' stories were. For Elizabeth and

Mariah, all the elements of the Romeo and Juliet story were there: the secret romance, the raw feeling of young passion, the feuding families, even the street fighting. The girls had loved *A Little Romance*, but what did they know about the Shakespearean tale that was the basis for the cinematic spin-off? As I crossed the bridge that separates southern Ohio from northern Kentucky, the question began to gel in my mind: What if the girls in my literature class could read Shakespeare?

It was one of those moments in the long history of my class when some issue or topic touched a personal spot in my heart. I thought back to my experiences in middle school and even high school. Not once did I ever so much as crack open Shakespeare's plays in any of my English or language arts classes. This was only one of the gaping holes in my K-12 education and something about which I feel ashamed even to this day. I had no idea if I could even cope with Shakespeare's language myself, much less use his original work with a group of sixth-grade girls. Some of the girls, Jessica and Alicia among them, still struggled with basic literacy skills. But the stubborn and rebellious part of me wanted to give these girls, the daughters and granddaughters of hard-working laborers, the kind of education *I* didn't have. By the time I had pulled up to the apartment building where I lived, I had decided. It wasn't a question of if but *how*. We would work with William Shakespeare's *Romeo and Juliet*. I got on the Internet that night and found a copy of the play online. I began to read the verses. It was the first time in my life I had read the play for myself.

Deciding you are going to teach a more difficult piece of literature is one thing. Figuring out how you are doing to do it is another. For days afterwards, I struggled with the question of how to present a whole new kind of literature to girls who would be sure to get in my face if something turned them off. On the other hand, my girls could be impassioned learners when something really grabbed them. Where was the hook that could excite these loud, strong-willed girls about Shakespeare?

Then I remembered: There was a luscious cinematic version of the story, directed by Franco Zeffirelli, featuring teen actors.[2] It was a little dated, from the late 1960s, but timeless in its faithful adherence to the play itself. I bought a video copy of the film, sat down with a Barron's Simply Shakespeare paperback copy of the play, and mapped out a plan.[3] We could watch the film in sections and work with printed excerpts from the scenes we had first watched on screen.

The following week, I shared my teaching idea with Mrs. Stevenson, who in sixth grade was still the girls' language arts teacher. In a generous gesture—the big March tests were just weeks away—she offered to let me try out my ideas with her entire class of sixth graders, which included my girls. I mapped out a week's worth of lessons, rearranged my university schedule, and took over the girls' English class for the whole next week. I was able to schedule some real actors from a local theater to join us on Friday and stage some scenes from the play.

I was worried and anxious at first, particularly about students such as Jessica. She missed the first day of the unit, when I introduced the characters and story and showed the opening scenes of the film. She walked in the next morning looking disgruntled and out of it. There was some vague story about a doctor's appointment—another slice of neighborhood business not intended for a teacher's ears. But I was undaunted. On the second day of the special week, I pulled Jessica and two other students out of a computer class where they were practicing testing skills and had them watch the scenes from act 1 they had missed. By the time we got to act 2, Jessica and everyone else was with us. By act 3, she was completely hooked. Even Blair, who had started to miss one or even two days of school nearly every week, was in school and on time every single day. She had discovered some new things about herself—that she could like sensitive films (like the arty version of *Romeo and Juliet* we watched) and that she could read and speak a new kind of language.

By week's end, the girls had chosen their parts for a stage performance of scenes from the play. Our Juliet for the famous balcony scene was Alicia, the group's doll-faced comic actress. Blair performed the role of Juliet in the tomb scene, when Juliet awakes from her drug-induced sleep and discovers Romeo, dead from poison. Blair read her lines quickly and in monotone. She held a piece of paper folded into a pointed shape—her dagger.

> Thy lips are warm.
> Yea, noise? Then I'll be brief. O happy dagger!
> This is thy sheath;
> There rust and let me die.

Blair crumpled to the ground, a tragic heroine. It was the most special moment for her in the week. She liked being Juliet, she said, because it was fun and a little weird.

Our Elizabeth, one of the most irreverent voices in my class, chose the part of a servant in the house of Montague. In an early scene, she got to bite her thumb as an entourage of Capulets walked by. Biting your thumb, Elizabeth learned with delight, was the equivalent in Shakespeare's day of giving the middle finger. She walked around the hallways of her aging brick school building for days and days after the staging, biting her thumb whenever it struck her fancy. It gave her, I suspected, the giddy, powerful feeling she got when she cussed or got smart with someone—a new way of getting in your face.

Adriana was cast as Benvolio, Romeo's friend. And then there was our Jessica, who by the end of the week was laughing and having fun with her lines. She got the role of Nurse to Juliet, which meant she had to speak in a bawdy, brassy voice like the one she used out on the streets. She had to imagine herself as the Nurse and believe firmly in herself as she sang out her lines in a loud voice:

He's dead, he's dead, he's dead!
Tybalt is gone, and Romeo banished;
Romeo that killed him, he is banished.

At the end of the day's work on stage, our visiting actors would select Jessica as one of the students they thought would do well in a summer Shakespeare theater camp for middle-school youth. She loved everything about the week, as did Adriana and Alicia, who would take two of the summer scholarships offered to three lucky students. Jessica did not end up pursuing acting; other things called to her in the neighborhood—her friends, her summer romance, working to earn a little of her own money. But for one week in her troubled life in school, Jessica was in love with a Shakespearean play. The crazy, beautiful world of Juliet and Romeo was as rich and dramatic as her own world just outside the walls of a money-starved public school.

The rest of the month of February was slow and unremarkable. In the third week, the neighborhood had its last dusting of snow. Cincinnati is not known as a city of harsh winters. *Up South* was the term used by some to refer to a city on the divide between the Appalachian south and the Midwest. The muddy waters of the Ohio River are its most fertile asset, and barges move slowly up and down the river even in winter. In late February and early

March the sky turns an unchanging pale gray, punctuated only by an occasional cold drizzle. On the Mondays of my class, our steam radiator worked overtime with its concerto of clangs and hisses. During those long weeks, I tried to introduce short pieces of fiction that might lift the girls' spirits. We read selections from Julie Orringer's collection *How to Breathe Underwater;* I had been struck by the way she captured the wonder and fragility of adolescent girlhood.

Then spring came to the neighborhood. The forsythia bushes bloomed their technicolor yellow, the trees produced tiny lime-green leaves, the rains were gentle and soft, and the afternoon breezes were warming. It was then that something happened that was, for Jessica, amazing and wonderful. She was *saved*.

Jessica was at church one day when her aunt turned to her. "Do you want to get saved?" asked her aunt. Jessica wasn't sure what being saved was, so her aunt explained. Then Jessica was like, "Yeah, I want to get saved!" Jessica went up to the front of the church and got saved. Then she came back to her seat, crying. She was like, "Thank God, I just got saved."

March had been a troubled month for our Jessica. Early in the month, she had been taken to court for the first time in her twelve years. The official story was that she had been called into court for truancy, due to days such as the one earlier in the school year when she had skipped with Anna. But dangling from the official tale were murky details, hanging like threads of a frayed garment. There was the rumor that Jessica had cussed out the local community police officer. There was the story that she had lied about her birth date. By the time Jessica got to court, her mom was told that Jessica needed a lawyer, or she might end up with a sentence that prevented her from driving until she was twenty-one. Jessica chose to get a lawyer. It was a serious moment, but Jessica managed to infuse adolescent whimsy into the court appearance.

"I was bored," she later confessed to her sisters in my class. "Then I ran into all my best friends—it was funny!"

Her friend, she told us, once he spotted Jessica, was like, "I remember that girl Jessica." Jessica glanced over at him and sang out in her street voice: *"I know you!"* She was tripping out. Then her mother said anxiously, "Sit down, sit down, *sit down*—'fore they come out here."

Once Jessica got her moment with the judge, she confronted a mean dude. When he talked, spit came out of his mouth. Jessica referred to him as Slobber Mouth. But the judge was fair with the punishment he doled out, Jessica felt. Every day now, someone from the probation office called to make sure she was in school. After school, she had to go home, and someone always called to check in on her there. In the summer weeks she would have work detail.

"It feels like I'm a little *kid* again, like I'm real little," Jessica later admitted.

But after she was saved, Jessica shared with our group, it felt like she started her life all over again. When she walked down the street, everybody was staring at her as if she were glowing. It was like there was sunshine from the heavens or from Jesus, shining down upon her. Jessica felt a sense of peace. Her friends felt happy for her. Jessica wrote a poem in the journal she kept for my class.

Sometimes I feel sad because it feels like
I am missing something in my life.
I feel lonely sometimes.

Now I am happy because I gave my life to God
And people can see me glow.
I feel loved, cared for, and safe.

They just make me forget about what I am sad for.
My family has grown and come together,
Like flowers bloom together and grow in the sun.

Peace will come someday on earth.

I was no stranger myself to the notion of being saved. I grew up in the Bible Belt, where, driving along a mountain road, you could come upon a sign with a simple message: Jesus Saves. In the summers when I was small, I often spent two weeks in vacation Bible school, coloring pictures of Jesus and singing songs: "Jesus loves me, yes I know / For the Bible tells me so."

People were always getting saved in the small mountain town where I grew up. I knew the script well. There was the moment of emptying yourself out and admitting your sins. Then there followed the tears and a flood of happy feelings. If I had been a little less stubborn and a lot less questioning, I might have tried it myself, to just open my heart and let Jesus in. I prayed once in a while, but I was more curious than repentant, hungry for knowledge and adventure but not sure what was out there for me. But when Jessica shared the news on a spring afternoon in my class, I wasn't surprised. Jessica was a girl in search of peace and love, but some part of her was also drawn to extremes. The joy of being saved was the right counterpart for a girl who, in her darker moments, could be drawn to things like weed and piercings and hanging out on the streets until past midnight. Neither was I shocked when Jessica shared yet another epiphany on a beautiful April afternoon. Soon she would leave us. Jessica was moving to Florida.

It had long been her dream to move to a more peaceful place, somewhere like Indiana with its green vistas and quiet towns. Now just months shy of her thirteenth birthday, Jessica's dream was finally going to come true. Still, the other girls had confused feelings about the whole affair.

"I feel mixed—I don't know," said Blair. "It's all different kinds of feelings." Blair looked sad, even though the move could lead Jessica in a better direction.

Jessica had mixed feelings too.

"I'm gonna be happy in a way," she said. "But theeennn [she drew out the word], most of my feelings are gonna be sad 'cause I'm leavin' some good an' special people here. An' it's really gonna hurt me. It's gonna hurt me because I've been in this school for a long time."

Suddenly a silly mood seized her. "It's gonna hurt, it's gonna hurt me *so* bad." Jessica was beginning to sound like a Motown singer. She laughed at her own comic performance.

"It's gonna hurt me so bad to leave these people back in this *nasty* neighborhood," she said in her giggly version of a soulful song.

NAH-sty. There was the drawled-out word again. I didn't really believe Jessica's tale about leaving. Over the years I had heard similar stories from girls, and they rarely turned out to be true. These stories were more like a psychic safety valve. You could always dream of leaving, moving to a place with palm trees or verdant hills, rather than worry yourself sick about an urban homeland that had gone ghetto. Most of the girls dreamed of a future that would put them on a road leading out of the neighborhood.

"Why is the neighborhood *nasty?*" I asked, in my usual probing style.

"'Cause it's, it's like—you see all kinds of prostitutes and everythang around here," Jessica replied, speaking with her gentle rural twang. "You see drugs and everythang."

"But you think it's going to be better in Florida?" I asked.

"Yeah, I think my life is gonna change—really big."

Jessica insisted that she was going to visit us—probably on weekends, about once a month or so. Still, Elizabeth was starting to feel the familiar sense of crushing loss. Another friend would be leaving her. She looked bleary-eyed and angry.

"I feel really sad that she's leavin', and I feel like I'm about to cry," Elizabeth said. Blair and a few other girls were still acting giggly, having given in to the flip side of their sadness.

"I don't want her to leave!" Now Elizabeth was flat out sobbing. "I *don't*. She's my best friend; I don't want her to leave!"

The box of tissues was hauled out. Jessica soaked in the stormy emotion that her story of leaving had left in its path. Her eyes looked pensive in an older, wise way, as if she knew where her destiny lay.

In her collection of personal essays, *Skin,* Dorothy Allison writes about her experience of moving to Florida. She tells the story in an essay about growing up in Greenville, South Carolina. When she is thirteen years old, her stepfather goes down to Florida and finds work. He comes back with a U-Haul, and the family packs up and leaves that same night. "The night we left South Carolina for Florida, my mama leaned over the backseat of her old Pontiac and promised us girls, 'It'll be better there.'"[4]

"I was only thirteen," says Allison about the experience. "I wanted us to start over completely, to begin again as new people with nothing of the past left over. I wanted to run away from who we had been seen to be, who we had been."

When I was still a girl myself, I too left, trying to get away from a family life so troubled with anxiety and craziness that it threatened to choke off my future. I had little to guide me but my improbable and ill-defined dreams, but off I went—to get a college education, to travel to France. What a struggle this all was, but what a journey too. Now here I was, trying to be a teacher for a girl hoping to create her own way of leaving. The neighborhood troubles Jessica dreamed of escaping were different than the ghosts of my family life. But the impulse was the same. You try to get away before it gets *you*. Jessica could almost look at the sad, sorry women on the streets and think to herself: If not for Jesus and my own resolve, there I would be, hooking for weed and money. She knew *she* deserved better, a better life than that, and at the age of twelve, Florida was her hope. But it's always tougher to leave than you think, and I knew Jessica would struggle, even if her imagined journey came true. She would have to find herself all over again in this new place, and there would always be the bits she had left behind.

None of us really knew at the time where all of these changes would lead, in these months when Elizabeth found love, Jessica found her Lord, and all of us—even I—read Shakespeare's *Romeo and Juliet*. But for now, there was a new feeling of hope and giddy anticipation in my classroom. The girls were turning twelve, the neighborhood had become a ghetto, and my students were starting to imagine a way out in whatever form this might take. On April nights, Elizabeth stole cigarettes and smoked, studying the small patch of world she could see from a house perched next to a weedy lot near an old-industry ghost town. She dreamed of the day she could leave with her red-haired boy, Zack. Jessica walked the neighborhood with a new resolve and peace, her head held high against the nasty things she saw. And at home in my apartment, I did the small things I could do as a teacher. I poured over my books, and I searched for stories that might speak to the dreams of an adolescent girl in the other America.

CHAPTER NINE

Blair Discovers a Voice

Dorothy Allison's coming-of-age novel *Bastard Out of Carolina* is set in Greenville County, South Carolina, which was in the year 1955, we learn from its young narrator, Bone, "the most beautiful place on earth."[1] It is a land of weeping willows and black walnut trees—a southern landscape that in the drippy heat of summer pulls its inhabitants out onto porches and crusty, baked earth. Bone's people are poor whites. She is born to a fifteen-year-old waitress, Anney, who was seduced by a sweet-talking black-haired boy. Anney is unconscious at Bone's birth, and the job of creating an official story to fit the murky details of Bone's lineage is left to an aging granny and an aunt named Ruth. When they are asked for the father's last name, "Granny gave one and Ruth gave another, the clerk got mad, and there I was—certified a bastard by the state of South Carolina."[2]

"The real meaning to bastard is—your parents were not legally married when you were born." It was Mariah speaking, with her usual sense of drama and urgency. We had been working with excerpts from Allison's novel.

"I'm a bastard!" said Alicia.

"I'm a bastard," echoed Mariah. "I'm a bastard. I'm *proud* to fuckin' say it. I'm a bastard."

"You know, my only cousin that is *not* a bastard," said Alicia, "is the baby that Margie is carrying right now, 'cause her and Xavier are married. That's my only cousin that's not a bastard."

"My whole family's a bastard," remarked Adriana.

"What does this word mean to Bone?" I asked.

I was hoping to help a group of young readers probe into the meaning of a word that holds such power for Anney, Bone's teenage mother, and eventually for Bone herself as she comes into awareness of the frozen class position into which she has been born.

"In the beginning of the story when Bone was born," replied Blair, always happy to be the smart learner she was, "she said, 'I'm officially a bastard out of Carolina.'"

"And they had to burn that little suckin' thingy," Alicia said with an air of disdain, referring to the birth certificate stamped with the word ILLEGITIMATE.

"No, what does the word mean for *Bone?*" asked Blair, feeling puzzled about her own question. The art of delving into the layers of possible meaning beneath language and story in a novel lay just beyond the reach of these girls on the cusp of adolescence. Still, they found themselves drawn to strong words such as *bastard*, and they experienced a giddy sense of power as they debated its meanings.

It was a soft spring afternoon in late April. The streets were filled with local children who had bolted outside as soon as school was out for the day. Elders with their cigarettes and young mothers with babies had already set their folding chairs on the stoops and sidewalks in front of their brick rental units. The scent of flowering forsythia was in the air. On such a lovely afternoon you could not even detect the smells of waste from the barrel-stripping company nearby or from Mill Creek beyond that. Our classroom windows were cracked open about six inches so that the spring air could make its way into a room that had been tightly sealed against the long winter.

This was the spring when Blair turned twelve, and the long weeks of winter and early spring had felt crazy to her. Most weeks in sixth grade, she stayed home from school one day, sometimes two. Blair felt confused about all of this. On the days when she didn't go to school, when she was at her house sometimes she wished she had gone to school, because it was no fun being at home when everyone else was at school. But most of the time she just didn't like school.

When she discovered the voice of young Bone telling the stories of her life, Blair had a different feeling. She wanted to speak out about the world she knew so well. The girls and I sat with our copies of chapter 1, in which Bone's grandmother urges her daughter, Anney, to forget about the "damn silly paper with the red stamp on the bottom."[3] "If Granny didn't care, Mama did. Mama hated to be called trash, hated the memory of every day she'd ever spent bent over other people's peanuts and strawberry plants while they stood tall and looked at her like she was a rock on the ground. The stamp on that birth certificate burned her like the stamp she knew they'd tried to put on her. *No-good, lazy, shiftless.*"[4]

"What do you think about this passage?" I said, after calling the girls' attention to it in their copies. "Dorothy Allison takes words like *trash*—words that could be used in name-calling and insults on the streets—and she uses them to create the story about Bone and Anney in her book."

I looked around at the faces of the girls, noting their expressions ranging from puzzled to pensive.

"What does the word *trash* mean to you?" I said, hoping to make connections to the girls' own experience.

"You're TRASH," said Blair.

"It *means people call you trash*," said Alicia, her face hot with the thought. "They, they, they think you're just *junk*. Like you AIN'T NUTHIN'. You're *white*—"

"—like you ain't got no money or nuthin'," interrupted Adriana.

"Yeah!" said Alicia. "You're poor. You ain't got no food or whatever. It's like, you're, you're GARBAGE. You ain't got *nuthin'*!"

Blair thought about the way some people in the neighborhood threw their candy wrappers and empty pop bottles right into the streets. She found this disgusting. Then she thought about the rapper Eminem. Blair thought he was sizzling hot, and she had a photo of him shirtless and dressed in jeans. She had watched a bootleg copy of the film *8 Mile*, in which Eminem plays Rabbit, a character modeled on his own life growing up on the forlorn outskirts of Detroit. Emimen's character lived in a single-wide trailer with his beer-drinking, unemployed mother. They couldn't afford much, because, as Blair knew, everybody who lives in a trailer park is poor.

"Some people down here are white trash too!" said Blair. "I am too, but I don't live in a garbage can or trailer."

She smiled and laughed lightly.

"I'm not!" said Adriana, feeling smart and ready to get in someone's face.

"I'm not!" echoed Alicia.

"I'm white, I'm not trash," said Blair, who even as she spoke seemed to feel puzzled about the layers of meaning that could cling to a word she heard all the time on the streets.

To make this adult novel accessible for a group of sixth-grade girls, we worked with excerpts rather than trying to read it from beginning to end. That would have been far too difficult and exhausting for girls such as Alicia or Jessica, who sometimes even struggled with young adult novels. For their benefit, but for all the other girls' too, we also worked with clips from a made-for-television movie version of the novel. I didn't find the film adaptation anywhere near as strong as the rich and raw storytelling language of Allison's novel. But at least it helped create a visual context for some of the scenes that we also read in Allison's words.

"Let's talk about some of the connections you are making with the story," I said. Mariah was the first to respond.

"A little bit of Bone's family reminds me of my biological family," she said.

"Can you say more?" I said.

"'Cause on my birth certificate my mom didn't put my dad's name down because she didn't want him to be my dad."

Alicia sat next to Mariah on our loveseat. She closed her eyes for a moment and thought back to a scene in which Anney, Bone's mother, was getting strangely dolled up one night, with her bitter, glassy-eyed husband looking on helplessly. The family had run out of money for rent and food. Anney's two little girls, Bone and her younger sister, were eating crackers with ketchup in a vain effort to keep their bellies full. That night, Anney donned a tight-fitting red sweater, panty hose, and black high-heeled shoes. She applied red lipstick to her lips.[5]

"She was going to be a prostitute," Alicia remarked about the scene.

At Alicia's school, the entire class of sixth-grade readers had been deemed—by virtue of the end-of year proficiency test results—weak at making *inferences*. With her knowledge about the facts of female poverty and prostitution, Alicia shot out this inference effortlessly. She sounded smart and sure, in a way that wasn't always revealed on tests that hardly drew upon the world that Alicia knew so intimately.

"I didn't know her mom was a prostitute," remarked Adriana, who was comfortably perched in an armchair. Adriana was clearly impressed by Alicia's insight.

"She wasn't a prostitute until she needed to make money," said Alicia. "That's when she took her daughters to their aunt's house because—" Alicia paused briefly, "—she went to go sell her body so she could make money. When she was in her little red thingy."

Alicia took a moment, then returned to my original question.

"So no, I don't have no connection," Alicia insisted. "The only part I have with a connection is that her mom's a prostitute and *my* mom is too."

"How did you infer that her mom was a prostitute?" I inquired. I couldn't help but be struck by the paradox: Here was a young reader deemed in need of remedial work on making inferences, a higher-level reading skill, slipping so easily into inferential reasoning. I was curious to know if Alicia was aware of her skill at reading beyond literal meaning.

"Easy!" she shot back, as if I were the stupid one.

"Look at the clothes she was wearing!" said Mariah.

"Look at how she was dressed," said Alicia. "And that guy—you can just tell, because when would she get all dressed up? She *never* dressed up. And she did her hair, all kinds of makeup and clothes and stuff on."

"Can't you tell by that?" Alicia asked incredulously. It was one of the many sad ironies of reading and social class difference that Alicia's knowledge and ability would never be so visible in the unfamiliar narrative terrain of standardized tests.

Less than a month had passed since Blair turned twelve, but already things felt different for her at home. Blair had always been her Grandma Lilly's little baby. There was a tradition in Blair's family. When you were a baby, you slept by your grandma. And if another baby came along, you had to scoot over. Blair's half sister had slept with Grandma Lilly until the age of nineteen. And when Blair's little niece came along, Blair had to move over. Now she slept on the end of the bed, and little Angie slept by Grandma Lilly. In her family, you just had to scoot over and when you got too big, you had to get out of the bed completely. All this felt weird to Blair. She was growing up.

Sleeping arrangements were not the only things that were different. When she was a little girl, Blair had been the one in her house who was a tattletale. Her half brother, gangly and looking for fun and trouble, would break things. Then Blair would tell, and he would hit her. But lately she didn't do that anymore because she didn't want to get hit.

We talked about some of these changes on a balmy day in the last week of April. Blair was our group's leader, and as the leader for the afternoon she had a choice seat: one of the armchairs with its inviting cushions. Our reading selection was from *Bastard Out of Carolina*.

"I don't tell on him anymore," said Blair. "Only if my grandma asks who did it. 'Cause he'll break something hitting me. But if he's not in the room I'll tell. And I'll tell my grandma not to tell him that I said it. 'Cause if she tells him that I said it, later on he'll remember and he'll hit me. So I'm not telling on people now."

Blair sat tall in the armchair, looking sure of herself. Her hair had gotten long enough over the spring that she could put it up into a tight bun. Some people said she looked like a dancer, with her sharp cheekbones and long narrow neck. Her ears were pierced, and she wore fake diamond earrings.

Mariah sat in the other armchair, next to the loveseat where Alicia, Jessica, and Elizabeth were scrunched together in cozy comfort. Blair's words and those of Dorothy Allison resonated with Mariah. She shifted in her chair and folded one leg under the other. She wore a blue tube top, and over that a loose-fitting white T-shirt. Her nails were also painted blue, and the nail polish had begun to crack at the edges.

"My biological father used to *beat* on me," she said in her low, throaty voice. "Like I have *scars* from where my dad used to burn me with cigarettes. I have a bunch of scars. I probably have more scars than anybody in this class."

Daddy Glenn, Bone's stepfather in *Bastard Out of Carolina,* is a working man. The son of middle-class respectable folks, he marries Anney, a pretty blonde waitress with a sweet smile and rough-talking, hard-drinking brothers. Glenn finds work at an RC Cola plant, swinging flats of bottles onto his delivery truck. He is a smaller-sized man with huge hands—hands that work, that hungrily reach out for Anney, that unleash their fury against men who cross him, and that ultimately lash out at Bone. "I looked at his hands," we hear Bone's inner voice say, after Daddy Glenn has squeezed her arm too tightly. "No, he never meant to hurt me, not really, I told myself, but more and more those hands seemed to move before he could think."[6]

Daddy Glenn's hands symbolize the physical but also deeply emotional power of a working man—certainly for Bone, a young girl, but even for Anney, who stands by helplessly on the other side of the bathroom as her daughter is beaten. It is a sad aspect of life among the working poor that women do not always feel able to walk out on their men, even when they are abusive. In part this is an economic reality, born of knowledge about the difficulty of making ends meet without a man in the household. There are also the tortured attachments that women form to men such as Daddy Glenn, who is sweet-talking one minute and brutal the next. There is a long tradition of looking past the excesses of men who unleash their anger on those who are more vulnerable: hoping it won't happen again, justifying ("that's how men are"), even pretending things are not as they are. My mother stuck with her man after she had to get between him and the baby crib, trying to make sure he wouldn't beat his own child. It is a problem that has run through the lives of poor women and girls—my mother's generation, my generation, now that of the girls in my class.

"I have a scar that goes from here to here where my dad tried to cut me with a knife," said Mariah, holding up one arm. With her olive skin already darkening from the April sun, I could only see the faintest of lines.

"He molested you?" asked Alicia.

"He tried to," said Mariah. "I had staples in the back of my head, 'cause I was in the tub and he wanted to take a shower so he pushed me out and I busted my head. And I had to have *staples.*"

Elizabeth nodded with understanding. One afternoon she had slipped on the stairs at school and hit the back of her head. At the children's hospital, they had put in three large staples. The whole experience freaked her out.

"And I was abandoned when I was little," said Mariah. She spoke in a solemn voice that conveyed many things at once: anger, sadness, resignation.

These were the most painful of facts and feelings, but Allison's storytelling had opened up a new door for Mariah.

"I could turn my story to fiction," Mariah said to us, as she contemplated the work of another writer of stories. We had decided to create another issue of our magazine, *A Girl's Word*, and Mariah was beginning to ponder what she might contribute.

"So one idea for the magazine," I said, "is for you to turn your life story—your family story—into fiction, like Dorothy Allison. Your story may not be something you would want to tell everybody, but you can tell parts of your life story by making it into a fictional piece."

Mariah nodded.

Blair thought of Mariah's story and young Bone's in *Bastard Out of Carolina*.

"My idea," she shared with us, "is to make a story about how my mom was, how she was a drug addict and my daddy was a drunk. And they both left me, and my grandma took me.

"That's my idea," she went on, "of how I can make a fiction story where, how this girl's parents left her and her grandma took her in.

"That's my idea," Blair repeated.

If Blair and Mariah were beginning to find parts of themselves on the pages of a novel such as *Bastard*, they were also beginning to comprehend the power of fiction for sharing their lives, so that others could read and learn and understand. "The need to make my world believable to people who have never experienced it," writes Dorothy Allison, "is part of why I write fiction. I know that some things must be felt to be understood, that despair, for example, can never be adequately analyzed; it must be lived. But if I can write a story that so draws the reader in that she imagines herself like my characters, feels their sense of fear and uncertainty, their hopes and terrors, then I have come closer to knowing myself as real, important as the very people I have always watched with awe."[7]

Of all the characters we had studied in fiction and film that year, Blair had found herself most drawn to a young girl in Jim Sheridan's film *In America*. I had taken Blair and her friend Adriana out to see the film to celebrate Blair's twelfth birthday. The film's narrator, Christie, a girl of about eleven, is an Irish immigrant who has moved to America with her family. With a hand-held camcorder, Christie records their first year living in New York's Hell's Kitchen. An astute young artist with an eye for social complexity and emotional nuance, Christie was an interesting point of identification for Blair. Always an avid reader, Blair was beginning to ponder the possibility of recording *her* life—if not in film (for she had no camcorder), at least in words. Sometimes at night, amid the social theater of her grandma's bedroom, Blair wrote down her thoughts in a journal. She had discovered that she was a good writer for a young person. She could hold onto her memories by recording the stories of her life and her family.

"My brother and some of 'em are like, sometimes they act like bums," said Blair. "And my grandma'll tell 'em, 'Oh well, you should've went to school.' My brother Ronny should still be in school, but he's always asking my grandma for money. And Kyle—he hasn't been going to school."

"What do you want for your life?" I said. "What are your dreams?"

"I want to be the first one to go to college," said Blair without hesitating for even a moment.

"So you're going to go to college?"

"Yeah. My grandma went to college and nobody else went to college. And my grandma don't want me to end up like everybody else."

Blair began speaking slowly and deliberately. "She really has her hopes up for me. So if I don't go to college that'll be a waste of her hope.

"I really want to go," she said, looking straight ahead, as though she could see some part of this imagined road ahead.

The next morning, Blair stayed home from school.

Her half brother Kyle had been up nearly all night watching movies in the living room. He came in and out of Grandma Lilly's bedroom to get things, keeping everyone awake. When morning came, Blair couldn't drag herself out of bed in time to catch the bus.

All day long, Blair mostly stayed in her grandma's bedroom and watched television. From outside, the sounds of cars, shouts, and occasional wild remarks from the local crazies drifted in through the front-facing windows that opened onto a sagging porch. Inside, the world moved more slowly. Grandma Lilly lay in bed, answering the phone when it rang and directing things. The babies in her care cooed and cried. A small mixed-breed terrier jumped in circles for attention. The television blared daytime drama and talk shows. Blair read and slept and watched TV. It was weird the way things were but also nice to be with family. The day was marked with the rhythms of aunts, nieces and nephews, and half siblings moving in and out of the front bedroom. Blair soaked in the neverending human drama, and she thought of the world less than a half-mile away where somebody was trying to teach her classmates how to succeed in school.

PART III

Leavings

CHAPTER TEN

At Sixteen

At sixteen, I already had one foot out the door of the small town where I had grown up in the Blue Ridge Mountains. Behind me were two years of service industry jobs. I started working at fourteen, and by fifteen I was spending my summers in the hot, steamy dishwashing room of a nearby summer camp. The cooks, black women in their forties and early fifties, and I were there to do our paid labor and serve others. But I was more spirited than I was demoralized. I felt like a hungry young bird, wanting the security of a good meal but wanting even more to fly. When the scholarship to a local two-year college materialized, I was not even seventeen, and I had only the vaguest notion of where my journey to college would take me. I just knew I wanted to go somewhere, for I felt the pull of destiny.

Sixteen is such an important year in a girl's life. So when the girls who had spent four years in my class turned sixteen, I decided to find out where they were, and whether they had realized any part of the dreams they had had as young girls.

The biggest question of all for me was this: What impact did our small class have on the girls I had taught? Had our class helped them navigate the troubles and turmoil of a poor, white community that had once been a beacon of hope for Appalachian migrants, but was now a ghetto? Since so many of my students saw—as I had at their age—leaving as their best hope, I wanted to know if any had taken those first shaky steps toward a different kind of life. Had Jessica departed for Florida, or Mariah for Tennessee? Had Elizabeth found love, and had Alicia found a substitute for the family that drugs and the street had stolen from her? Was Adriana any closer to her dream of traveling to other countries? Had Shannon become a high-school basketball player, or maybe a high-school journalist? Was Blair still writing?

My hope for every girl was that she would finish high school, hardly a given in their slice of America, and go on to either a two- or four-year college. So I also wanted to find out if any of the girls were closer to taking some of the uncertain steps toward college I had taken around their age.

I had been through a lot of changes myself in the years since I left, when most of the girls were only twelve. During those intervening four years, I made a major decision, as much a leap of faith as a logical move from one opportunity to a better one. Leaving behind the security of a tenured university post, I quit my job, packed my belongings, and moved to North Carolina— my native soil. I believed that whatever gifts, experiences, and knowledge I had could be put to best use in the culture and region I knew so well. I landed in the Durham-Chapel Hill area, a place crammed with creative writers, university researchers, and scholars. From there, I plotted the next phase of my work— this time as an independent writer and educational advocate for girls and young women in Appalachia. But even in the midst of all the upheaval, I never lost contact with the girls from my class. We kept up twenty-first century style: emails, text messages, and for me, discount airfares that took me back to Cincinnati as often as I could manage. Still, our time together was too short during my visits, and my financial resources weakened as I learned new ways of earning a living without the security of a tenured university position. Our visits grew more infrequent and improvisational.

Fragments of news led me to wonder and worry about the girls from my class. A series of emails from Adriana made me aware that she was extremely unhappy in her local public high school and that she wanted to explore an all-girls Catholic high school with a college prep curriculum. Phone calls were made; I became an intermediary, helping her navigate a voucher application, since she was otherwise alone when it came to advocating for her education. Text messages from Elizabeth revealed other news: she had moved, she was in foster care, then she was living with relatives. From Mariah, I heard only second-hand news, but it was also troubling. There was talk of her embarking on a journey back to her family in East Tennessee, a family setting that had been too unstable for her to live in as a child. I tried to piece things together from these fragments of stories, until one day I decided I had to know more. I made plans to leave my new home in North Carolina for a long visit, to learn all I could about the lives of the girls who had once been my students. They were sixteen now, with the exception of Mariah. She had turned seventeen that year.

So in 2008, eight years after Blair had begun reading Stephen King and I had begun teaching my class, we came together again. The girls and I met in coffee shops, restaurants, parks, and the girls' homes—wherever we could find a quiet place for me to listen. They had once been like sisters. Now they led separate lives that sometimes tangled in the ways of the neighborhood. From these snapshots of my students on the cusp of young womanhood, I was able to learn some of the answers to my questions.

Probably every teacher like me, those of us who hope to help America's poorest children have a real chance at opportunity, has confronted the question: What can one teacher really do in the face of so many crushing obstacles? What I learned from my students' stories at sixteen should serve as the grounds for unerring hope, but it also reveals disturbing truths about how we educate our most vulnerable girls and young women. I learned that our small class had planted an important seed for change within each and every girl. Every single student had learned to *want* a rich and meaningful education. Most of my girls wanted to go to college, something virtually no one in their families had ever done. But I also learned that the seeds that I had planted, that *we* had planted together, were taking root in the most impoverished of soils. My students had to endure things in their early teens that would have traumatized the most emotionally sturdy and mature adult. Without the regular support and intellectual challenge of our class, my students had lost one more connection to the world of formal education—the only real ticket out that most poor or working-class girls have. And sadly for them, public education fell far short of helping my students realize their potential. At a critical turning point in their lives, the poets and fiction writers, readers of Shakespeare, and literary critics from my class were floundering in the shadow system of schooling for the poor.

In these next chapters, I move in and out of these stories, no longer a teacher, now just a caring adult, listening and trying to understand. I have no ready blueprint, no quick-fix solution to the uphill struggle faced by my students in adolescence. Many of them would have struggled to find themselves in any formal educational setting, as they struggled even in the nurturing class I created. But from these girls' stories, and my own, I can offer smaller openings and pathways, both reasons for hope and ways we can make things better. The resounding message from this group of girls in their sixteenth year was that they looked back upon our class as the *kind* of education they wanted. What was it about our experience that gave these vulnerable girls a reason to believe in their possibilities, and to work hard to achieve their dreams? And what happened to these girls—and why—when our class ended when they were twelve?

My story of the girls' lives at sixteen begins with Blair Rainey. I had worked hard in the years following our class to make sure that this gifted reader and writer got on a track toward college, her Grandma Lilly's dream for her. A snapshot of Blair on her sweet sixteen birthday shows something different: a girl who was lost in her public high school and confused about how to get to the place that both she and her grandmother wanted her to find. But her story reveals how even a student who might appear, from the outside, to be giving up can have big dreams for her future. Such a student can also have what I possessed at the same age: intelligence, grit, and a great deal of curiosity about the world. And still she can falter and become lost, a dropout. As troubling as Blair's story may be, it is not inevitable. If we listen closely, we can discern her belief in the promise of education, even as she moved further and further away from the public high school that was her best chance at getting out.

When Blair awoke on the morning of her sweet sixteen birthday, she realized that suddenly the world had changed. She was sixteen now, and she could get a job. The day had begun late for Blair, as did most days. She awoke around eleven, still groggy from the night before. Everyone had stayed up late watching *Jeepers Creepers*: her half brother had managed to get a bootleg copy. It wasn't Stephen King, but it was scary enough to keep everyone riveted to the television in Grandma Lilly's bedroom. The movie told the story of the Creeper, an ancient demon that arose every once in a while to feed off human bodies and renew itself. In one scene, the Creeper ripped out the back of a young guy's head so it could take his eyes. It was kind of weird, but it was a good movie. Everyone had stayed inside to watch it except for Blair's mother, back at home after a round of winter rehab. She had been good for three months, but on the eve of Blair's birthday, her mother was on the sidewalk running her mouth and yelling at everyone. Blair's half brother dumped his mother's beer in the house and put grass in the opened beer can. Blair's mother stormed back into the house acting the fool.

"If you wouldn't call me *crackhead*, I wouldn't want to smoke!" she screamed at Blair and her other biological children living in the house.

"You can't blame us!" yelled back Blair, furious but determined to ignore her retarded mother. The movie was more interesting.

But that morning, things seemed different to Blair. The household needed her help: the only person working was her older half sister, who at age twenty-five had three children, an unemployed live-in boyfriend, and part-time work at Taco Bell. That morning, Blair told Grandma Lilly that she wanted to fill out job applications and get a work permit.

"You don't need to work—let the older people work," her grandma said from her perch in bed, leaning to one side so she could keep an eye on the six younger children she was babysitting—her great-grandbabies.

"You know, I'm trying to get independent and stuff," said Blair. "I want to buy myself stuff instead of asking you."

Grandma Lilly was always talking about how she needed money to pay the bills, but now she slipped Blair a fifty dollar bill for her birthday.

"You keep it," Blair said.

Her grandma said, "No, you better take it and get out of here."

As soon as she could get her shower, Blair went to the mall with her half sister. She budgeted like any savvy shopper: forty dollars for a full nail set, leaving ten dollars for gas and two slushies.

At one thirty that afternoon, Blair sat in an Asian nail salon getting a full set of acrylic nails applied to her fingertips. The day was warm for late March, and Blair wore a black T-shirt with the word CRAZY on the front, followed by three dictionary definitions of the word. She studied the nail attendant with a distant expression as he worked. The female nail attendants had all been busy with other customers walking in from the shopping mall corridor outside. Blair got the only boy, a young man of about twenty with a Vietnamese name and fingers nearly as slender as hers. As the attendant began applying shiny black polish to the acrylic nails, now firmly attached and filed to a half-inch, Blair thought about the day ahead: window-shopping in the mall with Grandma Lilly's fifty dollars, hanging at home, a cake that night for dinner. The birthday gift had given Blair's mother something new to yell about. *Her mother didn't get anything on* her *birthday*. Blair replayed the dialogue from the morning.

You're forty-six years old and you want your MOM to buy you a present?
Blair could picture the day when Grandma Lilly passed, and her
mother would find herself on the street again. Blair's half sister
would kick out everyone who couldn't pay rent and clean up the
house.

She watched intently as the nail attendant painted orange,
yellow, and bright pink designs with quick strokes of his brush,
replicating the design she had chosen. Her hair was drawn into a
tight bun, like a dancer. Blair was taller now, nearly her full height,
but still rail thin. She could pass for a dancer with her long neck
and a complexion that was pale and translucent. She didn't have
a boyfriend at the moment, and she didn't know why. There
was no point rushing—that much she knew. Also, there weren't
many guys around who were boyfriend material. When she was
younger, Blair had dreamed about her prom night and a boy
who knew how to treat her right. As the attendant continued
painting intricate designs on her black nails, Blair thought about
the birthday wish that over the fall and winter had replaced her
little girl visions of prom night romance: She *wanted out* of her
neighborhood.

Sometimes when she was alone in her bedroom—Blair had
moved into an upstairs room of her own now—she thought
about the kind of neighborhood where she wanted to live: clean
and nice, but not so stuck-up that people didn't talk to you.
Maybe it would be like some of the neighborhoods she saw on
television. Those were *really* nice, though she didn't know where
they were. She had been only as far away as Kentucky and Indiana, which you could reach by car. One time she had been to a
neighborhood in Lexington with big houses. But she was not the
kind of person to want to live there with *those* kind of people. If
she had the money and opportunity, Blair would take her two

half sisters and their six children with her. She didn't know if she would get out of Cincinnati, but if she did, she didn't want to leave anyone behind.

Grandma Lilly had always wanted to get everyone out of the neighborhood, but she had never been able to do it. She herself was once successful. She had gone to business college but ran out of money to pay for it and quit. Then came Blair's mother and after that the grandchildren. Grandma Lilly had taken care of grandkids for twenty-five years. Now she was barely able to get up and whoop the little ones—a fourth generation. Still, she had high hopes for her special baby, Blair. She wanted Blair to finish school and go to college. But in the ninth grade, when Blair was only fourteen years old, something had happened that made everything more complicated. She had stopped going to school.

Blair herself was confused about how it happened. Eighth grade had been a good year for her. She had an English teacher who loved teaching literature and creative writing. Blair read more novels and wrote short fiction. And around the same time, two other changes occurred: she fell in love for the first time, and she began writing poetry.

It started in the spring when Blair was thirteen years old. At first Vinnie was just a friend to her. The two of them played football in the empty lot next to her house, and after that they would chill and talk. Then her half brothers and their friends started leaving Blair alone with Vinnie. The two smoked and shared secrets. When Vinnie reached for her hand one after-noon, Blair felt happy in a strange new way. Soon after that she began writing poems in a spiral notebook she had bought at Walmart. She filled up one page after another, and then started another notebook. One of her half brothers, a boy of seventeen, discovered the poems and showed them to his friends. Her half brothers had always been mouthy and disrespectful; when she was younger they always beat her up. Now they looked for new ways to put Blair down and humiliate her. But she had learned not to take the bait—she knew them too well. "I don't care if you want to read them," she said to her half brothers, "but don't do it behind my back." One day her younger half brother, Kyle, said to her: "It was funny at first, but actually you write a lot of good poems."

The year Blair entered ninth grade was when things began to unravel. The world of high school was new and foreign to her, even though she went to school in the same building. The neighborhood elementary school, which had provided a K-6 education for generations, had first added middle grades and now had become a high school as well. The decision was prompted by a crisis in dropout rates—at least 60 percent, and often more, of neighborhood youth in any given year—and a belief that educating youth in their own familiar neighborhood would help them stay in school. Blair was to be part of the first graduating class in what had effectively become a K-12 school. But in her high school classes, Blair felt unsure of herself and lost. She had found herself in poetry, especially her notebooks filled with poems that told of her life and her strong feelings about Vinnie. But she was lost in math and science, and things got rough for her. When she was still in middle school, her math teacher would sit down and explain things until they made sense. In ninth grade, she fell behind in math, her weakest subject. In the early weeks of September, when high school began, she said to herself, "I'm going to do this." But she slipped further back, and once she was down it was hard to get up. Even her English class wasn't working for her. Her teacher, a fresh transfer from another school, acted cool and cussed and taught historical facts about Shakespeare. For Blair, this wasn't writing really. She wanted to read novels and write poems, and maybe write a book of her own someday.

At first Blair stayed home on Fridays, and sometimes on Mondays too. One cool fall night in the end of October, she stayed up late, eating her TV dinner at eleven and watching a horror movie on television with her brothers. At two in the morning she needed to go to the kitchen for a soda pop, and she had to cut through the living room where her mother slept on the couch. Without thinking, Blair flipped the light switch, and the single ceiling bulb lit up the room. Blair's mother rose up in groggy anger. Her hair, which hung to her shoulders, was streaked now with gray. It was matted and wildly loose; her eyes were half open and bloodshot. Her mother was court-ordered crazy.

"TURN OFF THE FUCKING LIGHT!" she yelled.

Blair felt mad too, but she turned off the light and stepped gingerly around the small pile of poop her brother's dog had deposited on the floor. One more thing for her mother to yell about the next day. On her way out from the kitchen, Blair slammed the refrigerator door shut.

The next morning she overslept again, and the morning after that too. Finally Blair decided it was better to stay home the whole week. When she got herself up to go to high school the next Monday, her English teacher would not let her work on the end-of-unit assignment about Shakespeare. "You weren't here," he told her, "so you can't do it." She failed the assignment. Her self-esteem was low, and now she was feeling depressed most of the time. Nothing felt like it mattered as it used to. She smoked weed and liked it. In November, Grandma Lilly decided Blair needed some counseling. Blair saw a counselor in a local public clinic, who referred her to a psychiatrist for testing. She was diagnosed as bipolar and given two antidepressants. The pills calmed her down, and after that she didn't think about things as much anymore.

In the following months of what would have been Blair's ninth-grade year, she stayed home. Each morning she awoke around eleven and smoked her first cigarette. Blair was no breakfast eater; she rarely ate until around one, when she heated up a frozen dinner and enjoyed a can of Pepsi. Some afternoons she hung out with Vinnie, who had left school himself and started work at the local Krogers. But love changes fast at fourteen: one day Vinnie was nice, then suddenly he wasn't. He cussed at her; she cussed back. One afternoon in April, when the air had turned soft with spring, Blair told him that she hated him. She was just mad, but after that things were different. Vinnie acted all toughy-tough, but inside he was a softy. They broke up, and almost right away he had a new girlfriend. By summer his girlfriend was pregnant with Vinnie's child and threatening to beat up Blair. Blair ignored the girl when they passed on the streets. She refused to hit a pregnant sixteen-year-old, even if the girl was a bitch.

At two o'clock on the day of her birthday, Blair sat in one of the nail salon's oversized chairs, waiting to have her toenails filed and painted black to match her new set of acrylic nails. The chairs provided a light back massage for a quarter, which Blair didn't have at the moment. Also she preferred to hold on to spare change; she might need it when she and her half sister enjoyed their fruit slushies later that afternoon. Blair held out her hands, admiring the nail artist's handiwork—a full set, black with bright orange, pink, and purple designs painted on with whimsical strokes. She wiggled her feet in a tub of warm soapy water, enjoying the moment of luxury. Next to her, a woman in her twenties adjusted her MP3 player and sat back in the massage chair, now set into motion. Blair's nail attendant appeared with his small bottle of black polish. Blair was savvy with money, and she had talked him into adding a pedicure for free. She leaned back in her chair as he began working, drying her feet for the pedicure and polish. She let her eyes close halfway and her thoughts drift. She could picture the reaction of everyone back at the house when she walked in freshly manicured with her birthday full set. She glanced over at her half sister, seated near the windows and enjoying *Cosmo*. Blair felt grown-up—a young woman having her nails done.

Back at home, Grandma Lilly lay sideways in bed, half-raised, and barked out orders to the young children in her care, three from one granddaughter and three who belonged to another. Between changing television channels, answering the phone, and whooping the kids who were acting out, she had another mission for Blair's birthday afternoon. There was now an online charter high school program called ECOT, the Electronic Classroom of Tomorrow, and to Grandma Lilly it looked like Blair's only remaining chance for a high school diploma. And everyone, including Blair herself, knew she needed a diploma to get into college. Grandma Lilly picked up the phone to call the person listed on the information brochure that Blair's high school had mailed her.

At the beginning of what should have been tenth grade, Blair had decided to give high school another try. She had been in counseling and on medication for months. She was a year older and felt stronger. When school started again in the fall, she said again to herself, "I'm going to do this." But after only a few short weeks, she fell behind with her schoolwork, especially her math.

Then her ex-boyfriend and his girlfriend, now the mother of his child, began hassling and bullying Blair. She felt afraid in school, even though she was prepared to beat the girl's ass. Even with counseling and Grandma Lilly's tough love, Blair gave up. The high school truancy officer gave her work detail: she had to ride in a van to pick up trash in another neighborhood. But one morning, her grandma was sick with a stomach virus, and Blair needed to stay home and help look after all the kids. At 10:30 that morning, a police car appeared in front of the house. An officer came to the door; he slapped handcuffs on Blair's wrists then led her away to the police car out front. Grandma Lilly watched from her bed, crying tears of anger and despair. Blair had always been her baby, since the days when she was tiny enough to fit in a shoebox. Grandma Lilly was a *strong* woman. But she could hardly bear to watch as the officer put her baby in the back of his car and drove away.

The juvenile facility where they took Blair was a boring place. She sat for hours and watched television. After a while she got up to go to the bathroom. The officer in charge of the place screamed at her.

"WHAT are you DOING?"

When she explained, the officer told Blair that she had to ask permission to go to the bathroom.

It was 2:15 p.m., and the nail salon was bustling. All of the pedicure chairs lined up against one side of the wall were now occupied by clients. The two-year-old child of the woman listening to her MP3 player whined miserably. Blair glanced briefly at the toddler and then turned her attention back to the nail attendant, who was painting her toenails with black polish. She extended her arms in front of her for a moment; it felt good to stretch after sitting still for forty-five minutes. She had slept on a new mattress the night before, another of the special birthday presents. Her brother had taken her old king-sized mattress, thrown on the floor after its set of box springs broke. It had taken up nearly the whole floor of her room. At first nobody would help her carry out the mattress, then one of her half brothers claimed it. He had a girlfriend now and could have slept at her place, but for some reason he still preferred sleeping on Blair's old mattress. His old bed had been the couch.

Blair closed her eyes and thought about the new computer she would be getting soon. Maybe it would come later in the spring, or over the summer. She wasn't sure. The same brother had gotten his own computer too for the online high school program. He wasn't sure how the program worked though, because he never really started it. Now the ECOT high school people were asking him to send back the computer, because he was going to drop out or go back to the neighborhood high school or do something else. Blair didn't really know what. She could picture the booklet that the ECOT people sent. She had been in Grandma Lilly's bedroom doing what she always did in the afternoon, watching television and helping with the little ones, when the packet arrived. It explained what you had to do: take this online class, sign up for these credits. Blair was supposed to be in the tenth grade but they had put her in ninth. If the computer came before summer, or maybe by the fall, she might be able to finish ninth grade by the middle of the year and move on to tenth. She couldn't remember how many months were in the school year. Was it six? High school seemed far away now, but she knew it was something Grandma Lilly wanted for her. High school was the first step, and Blair knew her grandma wanted more. She wanted her baby to be the first one in the family to go to college.

Sometimes when she was alone in her room writing in her spiral notebook, Blair thought about college. College was something she would like, Blair thought. Everybody did their own thing, and that was better. Nobody worried about what other people were taking. She would sign up for English classes and study writing. College would be an opportunity, but first she would have to get a scholarship or one of those financial aid deals. Her family didn't have the money to pay for that kind of thing.

College was a long way off, and Blair knew she would first need a diploma to get there. And there was one other thing she knew for sure: she was not dropping out.

She was *not* dropping out.

The other thing that Blair knew about herself was that she was going to be a writer. As a matter of fact, she had a book of poems half-finished already.

The writing thing started when she was in the afterschool and summer class for girls, in sixth grade, when she was really confident. At twelve, she was a motor mouth, a strong reader, and a young writer. It was weird, how things can change; Blair admitted to herself. Even so, her writing stuck, and she filled one notebook, and then another and another. She and her grandma had come to the conclusion that a publisher might want to make these into a book.

Writing wasn't a definite career in Blair's mind. Still, she wanted to write at least one book of poetry. The way she saw things was like this: first you wrote one book and you got *that* money, then it took a while to write another book. She wasn't sure she could support herself that way. She would have to get a side job. Working in a factory or warehouse or behind a food counter was okay when she was young, but she didn't want to be there forever. She had a feeling that she was meant for bigger things. When she thought about her book of poems finding its way to a publisher, the world outside her neighborhood seemed closer somehow.

The nail salon attendant finished his work and blew a hair dryer across the fresh coat of black polish on her toenails. Blair stood up stiffly when he was finished, then admired the handiwork. Following him back to the front desk, she counted out the bills: forty dollars—a good deal for a full set and a toenail job. Admiring the fashionable effect of black nail polish with her leather thong sandals, Blair walked to where her half sister sat.

That night there would be a family gathering with a cake made by her half sister. Grandma Lilly would give Blair a charm bracelet with a heart-shaped charm. They would all stay up until the late hours, eating birthday cake and watching Stephen King's *The Shining* and laughing. It was fun and crazy, and nice to be with family.

At the age of ten, Blair Rainey was an impassioned and precocious reader of Stephen King books. At the age of twelve, she was beginning to see herself as someone who could put the crazy and weird story of her life into written form, by turning it into a work of fiction. By fourteen she had fallen in love and become a poet, with dreams of publishing her first book of poetry. At sixteen, she was a high school dropout, rising late to smoke her first cigarette, then take her tiny dog, a terrier, out for a walk on the stretch of street where her world convened. I have often asked myself in the years since I first met Blair, so small then, even frail-looking, what effect my four-year class had on her. It seemed to me like a special moment in her childhood, a time when many things were possible even for the granddaughter of a bedridden woman struggling to get by on social security, and the daughter of a mother who was in and out of rehab, crazy with anger and the fog of drugs and alcohol. As Blair grew up, the roots that tied her to immediate family seemed to wind ever more tightly around her, even as these same roots and some new tendrils tied her down to the neighborhood she dreamed of leaving. She grew more aware of her circumstances, and yet ironically less able to leave them behind in the way her grandmother wanted.

"You were born to go college," I once said to Blair, then in early adolescence.

"I was born in the wrong neighborhood to go to college," she replied in her quick, no-nonsense way.

When I was just one year older than Blair, I fled a family that was crazy in its own way, though in a different way than Blair's. I went off to college, where I struggled to find a sense of meaning and purpose for my young life. It took years before I found what I was searching for: the college classroom is not set up as a safe, nurturing environment for a dreamy-eyed but naïve working-class girl. Blair was at sixteen stumbling about in her own search for a meaningful life. She had her passions—she wanted to write poetry and study English—even if she had only vague notions about how to get to the place, college, that could help her achieve those dreams. Blair would have struggled in any high school setting—that much I know from having been her teacher for four years. The weight she carried on her young shoulders—the anger, the depression—was too great for things to be otherwise. But my firm belief is that she was open to the possibility of an education and even to the personal change that graduating would have entailed, if only public school could have met her needs. It takes a great deal of effort and educational expertise for a girl born into severe poverty to have a real chance at the dreams of her grandmother, herself unable to help her granddaughter carve a pathway leading to college.

In many ways, our small class was a glimpse of what could have been possible for a precocious and spirited, if troubled, young girl. For those years, Blair attended a literature and writing class more like one for the gifted, and yet one that had its unique features. Twelve-year-old girls in suburban America—the girls who have access to programs for the gifted—do not have the experiences that would allow them to read Dorothy Allison, or even Stephen King, with such insight and potential for learning. And the ripple effects of this kind of educational experience are still uncertain. Many things had changed for Blair at sixteen, but not her grit and determination, even her stubbornness. Her resolve was clear: she was *not* dropping out, even though by any external standard she had already left school. Blair was soon to enter a shadow system of schooling that exists for the poor and working classes, where online high schools, alternative schools, and GED programs exist to offer the most basic ticket, a diploma, even if they do not come near the quality of a first-rate high school learning experience. In the midst of it all, she clung to the idea that someday she might become a published poet. She wrote poems, she smoked her cigs, and she dreamed of a day when she could leave the neighborhood, taking her family with her in search of a better life.

CHAPTER ELEVEN

Girlhood Interrupted

High school stopped working for Shannon around the middle of her pregnancy, two months before she celebrated her sixteenth birthday. It was winter then, and the trees had lost their leaves. It was cold outside, often gray, and Shannon felt nauseous. She was stressed out, and always in a bad mood from her schoolwork. Her baby's father, a boy of sixteen, had left town as soon as they learned she was pregnant. During her pregnancy, he called just once to ask how the baby was, then she didn't hear from him again. Only Shannon's good friends from school, Kristin and Tammy, were supportive of her. They were there through the best and the worst of times, right by her side no matter how much of a bitch she was. Her teachers didn't seem to care. After her son was born at twenty-three weeks and died hours later, Shannon blamed the baby's dad. When Shannon got pregnant, he had told her that he wished she *and* the baby would die. Four days after her baby's death, Shannon had to take the big OGT, the Ohio Graduation Test. She did badly on the test, and soon after that she dropped out of school.

Shannon shared all of this with me in a quiet corner booth, off to ourselves, in a Cincinnati restaurant with a Scottish décor and menu. We had placed our orders: a pasta dish with salmon for me, an oversized burger and side of homecut fries for Shannon.

"Did you get to see your baby?" I asked gently.

Our waitress had taken our orders and brought a tall glass of Diet Coke for Shannon. Her long blue eyes, outlined with just a touch of eyeliner, widened and she smiled. Shannon's features had softened and matured since I last saw her, and she looked pretty in a serene way. Her expression was that of a Madonna.

"Yeah, and he was the cutest thing. He was just so adorable. Like looking at him, I was crying. They were tears of joy, 'cause of seeing this beautiful little thing, seeing this beautiful little baby boy.

"And then, he was born with a smile on his face, and you could tell that he was *so happy*. And you could just look at him and tell that he knew that I loved him with *all* my heart. And he was just so beautiful. He was so *small*."

Shannon shifted her weight in the booth. A male waiter walked by dressed in a Scottish kilt, and she looked sideways at him, curiously. She wore her usual attire: jeans and a loose-fitting T-shirt. Shannon was never a girly-girl. But she had adopted a touch of teen fashion. Her jeans were flared and had a whimsical design around the ankles—sprays of color, like a Jasper Johns painting on denim. Shannon's father had told her, she said, as she left the house that she looked like trash on Perry Avenue.

"You got a chance to hold him?" I said.

"Yeah," she replied. "And he was holding my finger, and right before he died—I had just got done dressing him, and I was holding him, and then he *grabbed* my finger. And he was squeezing my finger real tight. Then he just took one last breath, and about five seconds later—after he grabbed my finger and took his last breath—the nurse checked for the heartbeat and there was no heartbeat."

The waitress brought our food. Shannon's plate was piled high with a bulging hamburger and a mound of fat, fresh-cut fries. The waitress left, and we continued talking as each of us got to work on a filling late lunch.

"Why didn't they decide to put him in an incubator?" I asked. The baby weighed only twelve ounces at birth and was not considered viable. I knew practically nothing about premature infants, and I was trying to imagine something so tiny breathing on his own.

"Their excuse was that I'm young. They didn't want to tie me down with a kid, and if he would've lived, I would've spent the rest of my life taking care of him for the rest of his life."

Shannon held a reluctant bottle of Heinz ketchup upside down over her fries and shook. She looked for a moment like a girl, determined to douse her fries with ketchup, then her face softened once again with a womanly expression. Her blond hair was pulled off her face by a clasp, so that her eyes and cheekbones stood out.

"But I told them, 'That's a mother's *job.*' Why be a mother if you're not going to spend the rest of your life taking care of what you *created?* That's a mother's duty, a mother's *job.* But they was like, 'Well you're still young, you still got your whole life ahead of you.' I was like, 'Okay, this *is* my life.'"

Each of us ate our food, mulling over Shannon's words. I twirled the pasta on my plate with a fork, while she lifted the plump burger and ate hungrily. The pause gave us time to reflect.

"Were you in love with the baby's dad?" I asked.

She thought for a brief moment. Then she replied, "He was my second love."

Shannon had had one young romance that stretched on for five years. Then she met Tyler, and the trouble started. He took her virginity, and she wound up pregnant. Unbeknownst to Shannon, he had another son with a girl in Kentucky, and he had walked out on her too. Tyler was sixteen.

"What drew you to him?" I said, wondering about the romantic pull of this improbable prince.

"His personality, and his *smile*. He was constantly making me laugh and smile. I could be in the worst mood and he would come over and start making me smile. It was so sweet."

"But he just left," she added wistfully, following the comment with a french fry dipped in ketchup.

Less than one month after she turned sixteen, Shannon dropped out of high school and enrolled in the local GED program. It hurt her mother deeply. Shannon's mother worked in the school cafeteria, and she was also studying at night to get a two-year degree so that she could become an instructional assistant. Shannon's mother understood the implications of dropping out in the new, unforgiving economy. For her, there was only one option for Shannon: high school, high school, or high school. Shannon just wanted out of the building where she had attended school since she was in kindergarten. Her father would not let her leave the neighborhood to attend a different high school. At first, the local GED program felt strange, and Shannon was lost without her support network, her friends. Then she got used to working on her own. Now, if she had other things to do during the day, she could study for the GED test at night.

I thought back to the Shannon we had gotten to know in my literature class. She was not the most voracious of readers, and sometimes she could be downright lazy. There had been times I had to push her to stick with a novel and finish it. She could take on an air of passivity and drift into a dreamy state, or even nod off into a light snooze.

"Do you feel like you have enough self-discipline to do your schoolwork on your own, and not do something else?" I said, remembering her dreamy expression as she stared out the window instead of reading her novel.

I laughed softly. "I mean, sometimes in my class I had to really push you."

Shannon smiled serenely. "I've grown up a lot since I've had my son," she said. "And I don't goof off as much as I used to. Like, I put the most important things before anything. It's a big change compared to what I was used to. It's a lot harder, like you have less time for *you*. It's the fast track of growing up."

It was two in the afternoon, and the restaurant was fairly empty. A bartender dried glasses at the bar, readying himself for the early evening crowd. Our waitress walked over to check on our progress. We were among her few remaining lunch tables. She took our plates—Shannon had cleaned hers and I had eaten as much as I could—and promised to bring us dessert menus. Shannon and I both had a serious sweet tooth.

"Do you see yourself finishing school and getting your diploma?" I said as soon as our waitress walked away.

"If it's not getting my high school diploma it's getting my GED," Shannon said firmly. "I see how hard it is for my dad to get a job without his high school diploma or GED. I see how hard it is for my brother and his wife—they have kids. I don't want to end up like that. I was raised a *lot* better than that."

Shannon straightened for a moment, then resumed her familiar way of sitting, her shoulders forward, her head tilted slightly to one side.

"I was raised with my parents telling me, 'You can do better than that. You *deserve* better than that.'"

I thought back to our weekly reading class, where I had worked so hard for four straight years to instill a love of literature, reading, and creative writing. That love hadn't always come easily for Shannon, and she saw herself as more of a writer than a reader. But I was curious about the place of reading in the life of a girl who had dropped out of school.

"Do you read books still?" I asked.

Shannon smiled and turned her head briefly in my direction. "Yeah," she said. "I'm actually reading this book called *Girl Interrupted*. It's about this girl who ends up in the psych ward."

"I saw the movie," I said.

Shannon nodded. "Yeah, it's a really, really good book. And it actually made me realize a lot of things that I was doing before I got pregnant, and how stupid they was. It actually helped me mature a lot."

Our waitress brought back the menus, and Shannon began to study hers as she spoke.

"But I'm still constantly reading books and like, even when I was pregnant I was reading books to my son while he was still in me. I'd read chapter books to him."

When she had finished studying the last page of the menu, Shannon said: "I think I'll order cheesecake."

The waitress came back and took our dessert order: cheesecake for Shannon but nothing for me. I was still full from lunch and too engrossed in Shannon's story to be interested in dessert. Shannon looked pleased with herself. It had been a long while since she had eaten cheesecake, she said, and it was one of her favorite things.

"You used to talk about being a journalist," I said, thinking back to our magazine. "Have you thought about writing lately?"

Shannon twirled the straw in her Diet Coke playfully. "I don't really get into writing as much as I used to. It's just not my thing anymore."

Our waitress brought to the table a huge slice of cheesecake, floating in a raspberry concoction and dribbled with a swirl of chocolate. Shannon began eating almost immediately, as if she had not eaten in months. Her shoulders were still slightly hunched forward.

"When we produced our magazine," I said, studying Shannon as she ate, "you created a beautiful piece about girls having power. It was the opening piece."

I could picture Shannon's creative essay vividly. It had been an ordeal to get her to complete it. I had had to sit close by, asking questions and offering words of support to keep her going. Once she got a draft completed, she was as proud of her accomplishment as any writer could be. She knew that her words expressed her strongest feelings and her beliefs. *Girls have power over what they wear and do and how they act. Girls can gain power by having a future and a career and by keeping their minds focused on school. Girls should be respected, and men should not disrespect girls' power.*

"Do you feel like you have power over your life?" I said.

"Yeah," said Shannon, using her fork to cut a large bite of cheesecake.

"Do you feel like the guys you have known have taken power away from you?"

Shannon thought for only a moment as she savored the morsel on her fork. Her look was serene and determined.

"There's been times when guys have taken power away from me, but guys can only take power away from a woman if the woman allows them to. If you don't allow a guy to take power away from you, then they cannot take that away from you. I don't think I've let a guy take power away from me, like when I got pregnant and lost my virginity, I let him take my innocence and my power away from me. But after I got pregnant and had my son, I don't let nobody take power away from me. Like every time a guy tries to, I tell 'im, 'This is *me*. I'm a strong woman.'"

Shannon finished the last bite of her cheesecake, then pushed the dish away. She wiped her mouth with the back of her hand and leaned back in the booth. Our waitress, who had little to do at this hour, came by to take Shannon's empty dessert plate. Shannon leaned forward on her elbows.

"I'm my own person," she said. "I'm pretty much the same old Shannon, but I'm a lot more mature than most of them girls."

I nodded. Shannon had always been an outsider among the girls who had joined my class. She often sat by herself and worked by herself. She liked to hang around with boys and play basketball with them. Sometimes she seemed to feel more comfortable being with boys. Now that she was growing up, she said, she thought it would be nice to find a boy who would stick by her side through everything. While some girls thought that doing every guy around was cool, she preferred to spend quality time with one individual guy. After having her baby, she had met such a boy. He was a sweetheart, always giving her compliments and telling her she was pretty. He was a little older, about twenty-one. But sometimes he acted more like a kid than Shannon did at sixteen. Her boyfriend had a little girl of his own, a daughter of eighteen months. When his baby's mama kept him from seeing his child, he goofed off as a way of keeping his mind off things.

Outside our restaurant window, it was beginning to rain. It was a warm afternoon in May, but heavy and gray with clouds.

The rain fell lightly at first then began to come down harder. The two of us watched the pouring rain for a moment then returned to our conversation about Shannon's life since our class ended.

"Now that you've had one baby, do you feel like you want to wait to have more?" I said with a hopeful tone. Part of me was still looking for an opening to nudge her toward education, something I saw as the real source of power for her.

"I want to have kids while I'm still young," she replied. "But then again I want to wait until I get my life together. Right now I'm just trying to go with the flow and see how things work out."

Shannon felt fine about staying in the neighborhood so she could be close to family, and in this way too she was alone among the girls who had joined my literature class. Other girls dreamed of going away—to Florida, Kentucky, Tennessee. Mariah had already left for the Cumberlands, a place she saw as beautiful and peaceful. But Shannon knew the neighborhood like few others did. She lived only one block from the school; she was in the neighborhood 24/7. It would be easier to imagine staying if it weren't for the cops, who harassed her for being a minor out on the street. Once a friend of hers had sold some weed and made nine hundred dollars. The girl had spent her money on clothes. It was a tough way to live, Shannon thought aloud, but sometimes a girl had to do it to get by. Still, when people made out the neighborhood to be bad, she thought about how no place was perfect. A lot of the stories told about Perry Avenue were not true. There was the story, for instance, that you heard gunshots every night—a story that was perpetuated on the evening news.

"You probably hear a gunshot about *once a week,* maybe two, three times a week. But I mean, there's not a gunshot every night," said Shannon.

Shannon stretched her arms briefly in front of her. She wanted to smoke a cigarette. Our waitress came once more to take my payment. I thought about the months ahead, summer. Four years earlier, when Shannon was not yet in her teens, we had spent the summer together reading books and talking about the girls' dreams for their lives. Now that summer was nearly here I tried to imagine how Shannon would spend her days and long nights. Would she hang out on the stoop of her house, smoking and watching the human drama unfold in the neighborhood? Her father didn't like her straying far from home. One night, a sexual predator had tried to follow her when she was out walking. She was scared shitless that time, crying, and she called her mother.

"What are you going to be doing over the summer?" I said.

Shannon replied, "Probably spending time with my brother's kids, because I don't have a kid of my own to spend time with."

Her brother's girlfriend had been young when she had her first baby, only fifteen. Since then she had matured a lot, and now she was one of the best young moms in the neighborhood. It took a lot of maturity, Shannon knew, to go from being a fifteen-year-old girl with one kid to being a twenty-four-year-old woman with four children.

Shannon smiled faintly, looking relaxed and sure of herself. "I'm planning on having more kids, especially a boy." She laughed lightly. "I was dedicated to having a girl, but then once I had a boy, now I just want a boy so bad."

The rain outside was heavier now, so we readied ourselves for the walk from the restaurant to the downtown parking garage where I had parked my car. For Shannon this was easy: she slipped on her zip-up sweatshirt and pulled up the hood. I struggled with a plastic bag I had, trying to forge a makeshift rainslicker, but it was no use. Only minutes after leaving the restaurant, we were getting drenched, especially me. I yelled to Shannon, "Let's go to the museum!"

On the way to my car sat Cincinnati's new contemporary art center, a building noted for its architectural beauty, with a gorgeous children's museum on the top floor. The place had vivid memories for us. When the girls were in my class, we once went there on a summer day, and the girls had laughed and squealed as they went from one hands-on exhibit to another. Now Shannon and I piled into the museum lobby, soggy and giggling. We headed straight for the elevator—admission was free due to some construction work—and arrived at the sixth-floor UnMuseum.

In one corner of the children's floor was a space for making art. There was construction paper of all sizes and colors, and there were markers and crayons. I followed Shannon's lead as she found her way to one of the surfaces for drawing and painting. We both set to work quietly, using crayons and cheerful markers. I created a girly picture of my garden back in North Carolina, with its old stone wall and pink climbing rose that I had planted. Shannon drew hearts on the front of a piece of construction paper that she folded, like a card. On the back, she drew more hearts and wrote her childhood name: Shannie Sue. She thought she might give the drawing to her new boyfriend, but she wasn't sure.

CHAPTER TWELVE

I Deserve a Better Life

It was not the case, I learned, that all or even most of the girls who attended my four-year class were school-leavers by the age of sixteen. In spite of their family histories—most of the girls' mothers had dropped out of school—the majority were more like me. Against all odds, they clung to the idea of getting an education, even going on to college. At sixteen, four of the seven girls saw some kind of college in their future, even if they had only a vague notion of where they might go or how they might get there. When you grow up without the economic security enjoyed by middle-class or affluent students and without the cultural capital of seeing others around you finish high school and go on to college, a lot of what happens in young adulthood just happens *to* you. I don't remember ever thinking of my life at sixteen in terms of real, concrete choices. Instead, I took the SAT test one Saturday afternoon and, months later, got a letter offering me a free ride at a nearby, two-year college. It never occurred to anyone, least of all to me, that I could explore other options: apply to a four-year college, do college campus visits, make choices. So, all during the four years I taught a group of girls facing similar obstacles, I tried to instill a sense of possibility. They had the right to dream, but they had to stay in school and work hard and fight for their dreams. For many of my girls, this sense of possibility stuck. They clung to the hope of a future that included education, in spite of bone-crushing losses. Among these girls were Alicia and Adriana. At sixteen, the two were all but orphans—the streets had claimed their mothers—and they were also college-bound girls. For these girls, the road ahead was clear: they deserved a better life than the one they had inherited.

When she was ten years old, Alicia, the sweetheart girl with elfin eyes and a huge, open smile, had lost her mother to drugs and the street. She was placed with her grandparents, then that fell apart too. They beat her brothers and treated her more like domestic help than a daughter. One day in middle school, after our program ended, Alicia couldn't take it anymore and called child protective services from a phone at school. A social worker was assigned to the case, and her grandparents lost their rights to custody. Alicia spent one week with a foster family before she was placed in the care of an uncle and his wife. They became her new family.

When all this was happening, Alicia thought things were going to be really hard. But she discovered that things weren't as hard as she had imagined, and she became determined to have a better life. She wanted to go away to college someday. Like many of the girls who had been her sisters in my afterschool class, her journey so far had taken her only up the hill from the old neighborhood. A narrow road that began at Perry Avenue and wound its way up one of the steep hills that defines Cincinnati's geography led to a neighborhood only marginally better than the old one. There was still trouble on the streets, but some of the side streets, such as the one where Alicia now lived, were better. Every morning she traveled down the hill to attend high school in the same building where she had attended kindergarten. She hated the old neighborhood around the school now. Things had gotten so much worse down there. It had gone from cigarettes and weed to all the other things: percs and vics and crack and cocaine. She didn't want any part of it anymore. She didn't even want to talk to her mother, who was back from a fresh round of rehab. Then one afternoon after high school, Alicia was walking to a corner store with a friend to get a soda pop, and there, at the bus stop, stood her mother.

It was around three on a quiet November afternoon. The warm days of early fall were lingering well past their time. Alicia's mother wore no sweater or jacket, just an oversized, ripped-up flannel shirt, baggy pants, and torn shoes. She looked like any homeless person waiting for the bus that would take her to the nearest shelter. Alicia's mother had once been a woman with lovely, shoulder-length auburn hair and striking gray eyes, oval-shaped and beautiful. She was not very tall, but she was sturdy and strong. And she was fearsome. When she got into fights, she *always* won, even with dudes. She and Alicia's father fought many times. Alicia could recall the time that one of her mother's guys, Dan, came over for a visit. Dan's picture was among those laid out in a glass table that held photos of friends and family, and seeing Dan, Alicia's dad went off. He and Dan started fighting in the middle of the room and broke the glass table. Then her mom started beating the crap out of her dad, and her dad started beating the crap out of Dan, then Dan started beating the crap of her dad, so her mom started beating the crap out of Dan for beating up her dad. It was *crazy*. In those days, her dad would never hit Alicia's mom back. One day her mom smashed his leg in the door, and after that, things changed. Her dad started drinking, and soon he started hitting back. When he went to jail, Alicia wondered why the cops hadn't taken her mom instead.

When Alicia's mom first got out of her latest rehab stay, she had been huge, over two hundred pounds. Since then she had lost the weight. She was still only thirty-five years old, but her teeth were black, like they were about to fall out. Her face was sunken and gray from the effects of crack. She walked up to Alicia, who was still near her friend.

"Don't be mad at me, don't hate me today," said Alicia's mother.

"Why not?" said Alicia. "I hate you every day."

Her mother laughed lightly. "Just don't hate me right now."

Alicia knew how to tell when someone was high. Her mother was twitching; her eyes were glassy. Alicia looked her mother up and down.

"You're high, ain't you?"

Her mother laughed again. "No, I'm not high," she said sarcastically.

"Why are you laughing?" said Alicia.

Everything had become a game for her mother, and she lived in a fog. She no longer knew her children's ages for sure. She hadn't been part of their lives for seven years. Alicia didn't think her mother would ever wake up from her drug-induced haze.

"You look *bad*," said Alicia, in a way that was both sad and angry.

Her mother said, "I feel it."

"Well you look it!" said Alicia. "I mean, look at you. Did you look in the mirror lately? You still haven't even straightened up after all these years. You've done lost us. You have nowhere to stay. You're down here *selling* your body for money just so you can buy your drugs."

Alicia spoke very quickly. The muscles in her neck and throat tightened, and she was trembling, but she continued:

"When are you going to realize? One day you're going to freakin' overdose and die."

"Don't say that!" said her mother. She was no longer laughing.

"For sure you're going to die one day. Just like Kelly. Do you want to end up like Adriana's mother?"

Kelly Turner, Adriana's mother, had been found dead in an alley the year before. She and some drug-using friends had gotten a bad batch of heroin. By this time Alicia strongly suspected that her mother was on heroin too. Heroin and crack had become the biggest street drugs; before it was always weed and painkillers. This much Alicia knew: a girl would do *any*thing for heroin, *any*thing she had to do.

Alicia went home that afternoon, a Friday, to her new family up the road that led out of the old neighborhood. She liked it where she lived. Her uncle and aunt did things as a family on the weekends. They cooked out, went to movies, or ordered pizzas to watch a movie at home. Her family had gotten small: she had lost her mother, her father who was in and out of jail, and then her grandparents. Everything from her childhood had been lost—her toys, photographs, her old books, most of her clothes. She had been through a lot for a girl who had yet to turn sixteen. But that evening, as she sat on the stoop of her home, enjoying one of the last of nights she could sit outside that fall, she was filled with a determination that replaced her tears. She was *not* going to let things stop her. She was *not* going to let her mom and what her mom had done pull her down. She was going to *push* herself and go for what she wanted. She would finish high school and go to college to become a nurse or pediatrician, someone who cared for children.

Alicia went to the movies that evening with her brother, his friend, and her aunt and uncle. They laughed and had fun, and she loved the feeling of being with family.

When she was in my afterschool and summer class, Adriana had been a girl with big plans for her life. A road trip by bus to Las Vegas had left a strong impression on her. She had wanted to travel and see the world outside her small neighborhood. She had wanted to float in a swimming pool and read her Stephen King novel. There were so many things she had wanted for her life, and—at the age of fifteen—this had not changed. Now that she was soon to be a young woman, she wanted to be successful and travel the world. The idea of being a photographer or a journalist appealed to her; those were things she had been exploring in my class. And of course, after high school she wanted to go to college. She could picture herself going to college in New York, maybe even living in a loft. Everywhere she went around the neighborhood, Adriana was a commanding presence. She was a pretty girl with a voluptuous figure and luminous violet-blue eyes, which she outlined with black eyeliner. Her hair was dyed black too and carefully straightened each morning. She knew who she was and what she wanted for herself. But in the world of a girl growing up in a poor neighborhood, stuff happens and dreams can be fragile. The past four years had been horrible, and Adriana still struggled to comprehend how things had changed, and why her life was so hard.

It all started in the form of a small white pill, the same pill that had stolen Alicia's mother from her. When Adriana was in middle school, her mother, Kelly, had begun crushing prescription painkillers such as OxyContin. She was a weak woman, and that was how she ended up on the heavy drugs: she lost control of things. One afternoon, Adriana returned from school to find that she had been abandoned. Her mother had left her. Adriana was fourteen years old.

Her father had been out of the picture for so long that Adriana really didn't know him; he was a stranger. So for three months she moved in with a friend of hers, and her friend's grandmother allowed her to stay. Then she moved in with her boyfriend's family. For months she had been talking with Bryan at school, and their relationship flourished. When she was with him, it helped her get her mind off her mother. When they were apart, she thought about how he was the person she should be with, and she felt happy with the thought. But one April morning, her ninth-grade year, an officer came to the door of her English classroom to pull Adriana out of class. She soon learned why: her mother had accidentally overdosed on heroin, and her body had been discovered in an alley.

The moment didn't seem real to Adriana.

Now she was completely alone, orphaned, and without a parent or even guardian. Her boyfriend's mother wanted to adopt her, but her father decided to claim his custody—and the social security check she started getting when her mother died. A police officer was sent to pick up Adriana at her boyfriend's house. Once again Adriana moved, this time to a household of strangers: her father, his girlfriend, and an assortment of kids, one of whom was trouble. Adriana had to share a bedroom and a bed with one of the girlfriend's kids; she had no room of her own. She was seriously depressed; she cried every night. She so much wanted to be happy, but she knew she was going to have to wait for happiness. She could not stand living in a house where she was not treated like family, even though her father was living there. The other kids who were looking for trouble tore up her things and stole from her, even her clothes. She cried and told her father how she felt.

"You expect me to leave somebody I've been with all these years?" he said.

He chose his girlfriend over his daughter. Adriana's life was so stressful that she frequently cried until she was exhausted. "I can only take so much!" she confided to one of her good friends. Only her dreams kept her motivated.

"You'll be eighteen soon—you just wait," she said to herself. "Everything's going to get better eventually."

The future. That was what gave her hope.

Life at home was hard, and school didn't work either. Her grades slipped after her mother died, and Adriana no longer pushed herself in the same way. She had once been seriously interested in writing and photography. She read novels and excelled in reading. Now she got Cs even in English. But Adriana knew she was cut out for bigger things. Her close friend, Christy, saw her life only in terms of the present. Christy wanted most of all to get a big-ass truck, customized with pink and black paint, put some beer in the back along with some of her friends, and drive off. But Adriana was different, for she had aspirations and wanted to be famous. One day she got into it with Christy at school when Christy called her a fake-ass bitch. Adriana popped Christy in the mouth. "She's just a person I could care less about," Adriana said to her other friends. By the time the two of them moved up to high school in the building where both had attended public school since kindergarten, the two girls were headed down different educational roads. By tenth grade, Christy had dropped out and loved her new freedom. But in the same year and at the young age of fifteen, Adriana made a different decision. She decided that she wanted to apply to a college prep high school for girls, run by the local Catholic diocese. She could study foreign languages there. They would push her, she knew, and help her be a success.

Adriana contacted me. I did some research and made phone calls. Adriana qualified for a school voucher, because her neighborhood K-12 school was listed as being in a state of "Academic Emergency," the lowest category on the ladder of public school accountability rankings. All students at the school were theoretically eligible to use their public funds to pay for a private school education. But this still wasn't easy, especially for a girl such as Adriana who had no real parent: no one to fill out the many forms, no one to go with her to the school for an interview or help her work through all her insecurities. Even a student with legal status to a voucher still had to be accepted by a private school. And this wasn't easy, because the voucher did not fully cover the costs of tuition, even for a Catholic high school. Getting accepted was more like getting a coveted scholarship slot, and there were only a small number of these available each year. Still, even with the limited help I could provide, Adriana was accepted by the college prep high school for girls. She couldn't believe the news at first. For once, it seemed like her dreams would come true.

She would prove everyone wrong and become famous. Some day she hoped to find her own way, maybe even write a book of her own, telling others about the incredible story of one girl's life.

In her essay "Life Is Hard," written for my class when she was only ten years old, Adriana had peered into her future with a maturity and insight that was hard to associate with such a young girl. *When I turn 18 it will be hard,* she wrote. *I'll be in college with a job. I would have to work all the time. [At] 16 I would first get a job and when I got my paychecks I would put half of it up to save for college.* Now that she was nearly sixteen, what she most wanted was to be eighteen so she could legally have her own life. "I can't wait until I'm a woman," she wrote in the place she where she still confided her closest secrets: her journal.

But for now she was still a girl.

At the age of sixteen, when Elizabeth and Jessica looked back at the years that had gone by since our class ended, all they could see was trouble. For Elizabeth, things started at home, at the end of the cul-de-sac where she was taken after school each day in her father's green van. For Jessica, the trouble came from the streets, in a form that had haunted her since the latter years of my class. She smoked weed, hung out, cut school, and got wild. For these two girls, Jessica and Elizabeth, hope came not in the guise of school, as it once had for me, but in forms of solace and salvation that they had found earlier as girls. With everything in her world spinning so fast she couldn't understand it, Elizabeth once more found true love. And Jessica—she found redemption, this time not with Jesus but in rehab. In the midst of it all there remained the memory of what they had once felt in a class where they could read and write like smart girls, girls with dreams. With this and their own resolve to have a better life, the two looked into their futures with a mix of hope and anxiety.

The spring of Elizabeth's sixteenth year was a time when she was restless and uncertain, but still she had dreams for her life. Among other things she wanted to climb to the top of that big tower in Paris, the one you could see in movies and posters. She wanted to get her first job and make some money. There was even a chance that she could make hundreds of dollars as a model. Elizabeth had grown tall and was reed thin, with high cheekbones. When she sauntered up and down the streets after school, boys' heads turned. "You lookin' *good*," said a black dude one afternoon in early May, when she paraded down the street in a pair of jeans that hugged her long, thin legs. Elizabeth was looking for fun and looking for love. But what she wanted most in the world was the thing she had lost: a family.

The year that she turned thirteen, her father had been jailed for a terrible crime. The gruff, stern patriarch had messed up his own life and fractured his family by doing a horrible thing: he had had sex with an underage girl. This might have gone on, unspoken and secret, but the girl had gotten pregnant. Off he went—to jail—with the children, now ten of them, sent to different foster homes. It was as if Elizabeth's worst nightmare, that she would be alone, had come true. Elizabeth was fostered by some relatives, and everything in her life changed. She felt lost and alone and angry. She cut herself.

One day when she was fourteen, she had carved into her arm the words: *I hate my fucking life.* The scars were still there two years later.

Elizabeth missed the way things had been with her family, even though things weren't perfect there either. Losing her family was like being inside one of those nightmares in the horror films and books she enjoyed. She knew she was smart and capable of big things, even college if she wanted. But all around her people put her down. Her dad had tried to put her down when she was younger. He thought she was going to be a piece of shit. But in her new household things were even worse. People compared her to her mom, who was pregnant at fourteen. "You're going to be just like your mom, a fucking slut," they would say.

Elizabeth knew that wasn't so; she didn't want to have kids until she was thirty. But still the words ate away at her, until she felt like she wanted to choke someone or hurt herself. When she cut herself, the blood coming out felt like screams that others could not hear. She didn't cry every single night in bed, but she cried. She tried to imagine who she could be, and how she could prevent the past from ruining her future.

High school was not easy for a restless, willful girl who had trouble understanding the dizzying and dramatic turn her life had taken. For one thing, school felt *boring*. It was so boring that during a practice run of the OGT, the Ohio Graduation Test, a crucial rite of passage for getting a diploma, she put her head on her desk and fell flat asleep. None of her teachers bothered to wake her. She felt afraid. Mostly she was afraid she wouldn't pass the big OGT in the spring and that other people's words about her would come true. She wandered the hallways of high school feeling lost and getting into trouble. One day she got into a fight with another high school girl. Elizabeth was so angry at the girl that even hearing her voice made her feel sick. She wanted to choke the girl. One day she couldn't hold it in any longer. Then— *wham!* She popped the bitch in the face. The girl got a fat lip, and Elizabeth got a month's suspension. Later she laughed about the whole affair. "Hos got mouth!" she said to a good friend, when her friend asked Elizabeth why she did it.

Elizabeth remembered a time when she felt a sense of accomplishment in school. She had helped produce a magazine, read long novels, and dreamed that she could be the one in her family to make it out. That seemed far away now, and she struggled to see a place for herself in school. She needed some money, so she got a job as a grocery bagger in a Krogers supermarket. After that she was tired at night and let her homework and her grades slip. Around the same time, just a few months after her sixteenth birthday, Elizabeth found Lillian.

Elizabeth was this kind of girl: when she fell for someone, she fell *hard*. And Lillian was not her first love. Her very first love was a boy named Derrick. Then there was a girl named Miranda, and finally Lillian. Elizabeth didn't understand all the things she felt for Lillian. She felt hypnotized by Lillian's smile and her eyes. She was crazy in love. Lillian was also good at doing certain things. They made out and kissed everywhere they could. And the two had sex: they had sex on the couch, they had sex on her stepsister Jill's bed, they had sex on her stepsister Deidre's bed and her stepsister Shelly's, and then they did it in the pool, the kiddie pool, the twin girls' bunk beds, then they did it in her aunt's room, and then they went downstairs to do it in the laundry room. They did it in Lillian's dad's van, and then they went to Elizabeth's back porch, and they did it in her bed and on the couch and on the porch rocking chair.

Love had its dark side too, and it was painful sometimes. The two of them had terrible arguments about things that Elizabeth didn't really understand. When Lillian would make eyes at another girl, Elizabeth felt a stab of jealousy in a heart that had already been broken by her family. She tried to look past the bad days, and she dreamed of moving in with Lillian.

There was a special place that she liked to go with Lillian and other friends. Less than half a mile from the big house where Elizabeth now lived with her foster family was an overlook where you could sit in the evenings and watch the darkness fall over Cincinnati. On warmer evenings in April, the two of them would bum a ride to the overlook and sit, smoking and sharing secrets and laughing. At those times, when twilight had come and the lights down below were flickering like fairy lights,

Elizabeth's heart felt full again. She was no longer alone, and she felt happy. For the moment, she didn't have to wonder where she belonged. She would take a drag on her cig and pass it to Lillian. The two lovers were together, and they would follow their hearts and be strong.

The big change in Jessica's life happened in the year after she turned sixteen. All that year, and even the years before that, she had wandered the neighborhood hustling money for weed or for a drink. The whole neighborhood had gotten crazy. You could walk down Perry Avenue and hear the sad drunks and drug users. Jessica smoked weed herself and felt lost and afraid, like she didn't have anything in her life. Then one day in early June, she woke up and realized she wanted a better life. She went downstairs, where her mom was sitting on the couch enjoying a cig, and said, "Mom, I need rehab."

"What?" her mother said. "What do you mean?"

"I really want to quit smoking weed," Jessica said.

Her mother took Jessica to rehab, signed her in there, and Jessica's new life began.

When Jessica thought back to that day, she couldn't believe she had done it. The beginning had been horrible: they strapped her down and gave her medication, like in a psycho ward. She *felt* crazy in there at first, but then things changed. Every Monday she would get together in a room with the other teens in rehab and talk about her feelings. She had a counselor. After one month of this she was clean; she couldn't even stand being around weed anymore. In July, when she was out walking around the neighborhood she felt like a different person. If she spotted someone rolling up a joint, she just walked away. The people who smoked weed were throwing their lives away. And she *deserved* better. She had dreams: she wanted a better life for herself.

One afternoon during the last week in July, she sat in front of a friend's computer, doing the same things she always did: looking at MySpace, sending out emails to friends. When she came to her friend Nicole's MySpace page, Jessica gasped. Nicki had posted pictures of her college; it was in Florida, not far from the beach.

"Oh my God! It's beautiful!" said Jessica as she scanned through the photos. One time she had been down to Florida herself. The drive had taken her family one long day—through Tennessee and Georgia, and finally into Florida itself. When she got there, exhausted and yet excited at the same time, she saw palm trees and a beach that stretched for miles. "This is *my* place," she had said to herself. It was peaceful down there, and green. It was the most beautiful place she had ever seen.

Now that she was sixteen and thinking of all kinds of possibilities, Jessica sometimes dreamed about the kind of place she wanted to live. She would picture a farmhouse, maybe with three acres or so. Her cousin Darrell lived down in Kentucky and built houses. Her grandpa, who had moved up from Kentucky when he was only a boy, talked sometimes, when he was out on the stoop making popsickle stick wishing wells, about going back down there himself. Jessica pondered all of this: if her Grandpa went down to Kentucky, she might go with him. Maybe after college, maybe five or six years down the road, she would start a family. She wanted to go away, to refresh her mind and meet new friends. Jessica wanted to study at a college, and she was going to force herself to go—at least for one year. She might become a nurse and work in a children's ward. Or she might become a hairdresser.

When Jessica was a younger girl, she had started to find herself in novels and in the pages of her own poetry. Everyone in our afterschool and summer class told her: *stay in school*. Graduate and go to college. She didn't understand things at the time, but now she could see her future. She had said to herself on the day she walked out of rehab: "I deserve it, I deserve a better life than what I got raised up in." Since that time, her whole life felt better. Jessica read books. She read more books than she had ever read in high school, which she had left shortly after the beginning of ninth grade. When she entered her neighborhood high school and saw that it wasn't for her—too many rough kids and teachers who didn't care about her—she had signed up for ECOT, the same online high school that Blair's grandmother had begun to explore. ECOT had mailed her a computer, and now she could work at her own pace. Jessica read books and worked online every morning, and soon after she turned sixteen she also began working at a pizza place in the afternoon. She saved money: she wanted a car and her own apartment. She wanted to emancipate herself legally and live on her own.

At twelve, Jessica had dreamed of the places she wanted to go and all the things she wanted for her life. She still thought about those things all the time: a beach with palm trees, their leaves gently moving in the ocean breeze; a pasture in Kentucky with trees and pretty rolling hills. A place where you could find peace, away from a neighborhood that had gone bad and almost dragged her down with it. She had been dreaming of these things for so long, and lately she had begun to think about college too. She would stick it out with her ECOT classes, then she would go away. She didn't want to go to college close to home. Maybe she could go to that place in Miami, where her friend went to school. They had hurricanes, that much Jessica knew. But it looked nice, and now that her life had changed she looked upon her dream-scapes with a new feeling of possibility and hope. She would move away and be happy; maybe she would meet the man of her dreams. Each morning she would wake up and say to herself: "*Now* I got something to show for all that I'm doing and all that I have accomplished in my life."

CHAPTER THIRTEEN

The Road Out

The journey home to the land of her birth started for Mariah with a phone call to her mother. One afternoon, shortly after a blood relative visiting the city had given her her mother's house phone number, Mariah decided to place the call. She was fifteen at the time, a freshman in high school. She had gone through a lot in the two years since we said our goodbyes in my literature class for girls. Her stormy emotions, and especially her anger, had followed her into middle school, where the drama of adolescence only fueled her outbursts. Through it all, she dreamed of returning to the place where she truly belonged: the Cumberland region along the Kentucky–East Tennessee border. She longed to be reunited with her birth mother, who had gotten off drugs and set up a household with her boyfriend, a man in his thirties with teenage children of his own.

Soon mother and daughter began talking over the phone. Mariah shared her dreams of returning to her birth mother and the place where she belonged. Six months later, she decided to make the journey to a new life in the country. She told all her friends and her adoptive family in Cincinnati: "I'm just going home." She was sixteen years old.

On a raw January afternoon, with a fresh blanket of snow on the ground in Cincinnati, I made the trip south to the Cumberland to talk with Mariah. The road from Cincinnati began as a four-lane highway and ended as a narrow mountain highway, curving around hollers and hills dotted with single-wide trailers. Further south the snow disappeared, and I breathed a sigh of relief: I wouldn't have to drive on icy mountain roads. The nearest town to Mariah's new home was Whitley City, Kentucky, fanning out along a single stretch of highway dotted with fast food restaurants and a Walmart. Past it, the narrow lane cut through the lush green hills, one of them naked and jagged at the top from strip mining. The road followed a mountain stream and passed by clusters of trailers and brick homes. Most were plopped on an acre or more of land; country folks like their independence even if they also lay claim to being from a community. The houses were graced with assorted vehicles: cars, a pickup truck or two, a four-wheeler. In one of the mountain coves sat the small brick house where Mariah, now seventeen, lived a strange if quiet life. She was under house arrest.

I arrived at Mariah's home, a one-story ranch house with two cars and a four-wheeler out front. Three dogs—a pit, a tiny mixed terrier, and a boxer mix—greeted me as I stepped out of my car and walked stiffly to the door after the long winding drive.

Inside the house, which everyone entered through a side door leading to the kitchen, I was met by Mariah's birth mother and two of the counselors assigned to Mariah. I waited for Mariah to arrive on the school bus while the three exchanged pleasant goodbyes and the youth counselors made their way out. The kitchen was small, with a linoleum table against one wall. The house smelled of cigarette smoke. On the living room wall, plainly visible from the kitchen, were new photos of Mariah with her mother. The family resemblance was there: the sharp cheekbones, the lovely hazel eyes. Then in walked Mariah, and we exchanged a joyous hug. After clarifying logistics—we would share an early dinner and then I would bring Mariah home—we drove off to Huddle House. Mariah was under strict court orders to return home by six, and not one minute later.

At the Huddle House, Mariah and I each enjoyed the kind of meal we liked. For Mariah there was a burger with a side of fries and a large pickle. For me dinner was a fish fry with slaw and french fries as well. As we ate, we talked of all that had passed since our literature class ended over three years before. Mariah ate quickly, and she spoke fast too. Her voice had changed. She spoke with a rural Kentucky accent now, stretching out her vowels in a way we had never heard in Cincinnati. She sounded more like a mountain girl than the urban street-savvy teen we had come to know in my class. But her voice was still resonant and a little throaty as she told the story of coming home.

"Every girl wants to be with her mom." Mariah reached for the large pickle on her plate and bit off a chunk of it.

"When I was in Cincinnati, I'd hear everybody going, 'Well, my mom does this and my mom does that.' And it *hurt* to hear about that because I was never with my mom. I never had those times with my mom when I was little. And I missed my mom so much."

I thought about the other girls in my literature class and their mothers. Only two of the other girls, Jessica and Shannon, were living with their birth mothers. All the other girls had lost their mothers to drugs, neglect, and the debilitating impact of poverty on intimate families; their fathers were generally never in the picture to begin with. They were orphans in one sense, though their extended families had stepped in and tried to fill the gaps left by parents who had lost control of their lives. Mariah was not that different from the other girls, but she had lost her mother at a younger and more vulnerable age. Her child's heart had never fully healed, and it had kept pulling her back to where she felt she belonged.

Even so, she had left a lot behind in Cincinnati, along with the streets and their torments. There were her two girls, the darling little daughters of Mariah's adoptive siblings. The oldest was in kindergarten and could write her name now. Then there were our girls, her sisters who had once been part of the Monday afterschool class. Mariah had loved her distant stepcousin Alicia like a sister. Mariah missed Alicia's comic side, her laugh and goofy, wide smile, and even the way Alicia would moan and groan about every little thing she did.

"Alicia can be a smart one, buddy!" Mariah remembered about her friend. But so could Adriana, Blair, and Elizabeth, our other motormouth girls.

"*Them four* together, look out buddy!" said Mariah about her sisters in the literature class, softening and drawing out her vowels.

The rural landscape that greeted Mariah on the day of her arrival in the late spring of her ninth-grade year was beautiful and welcoming. And on the steps of the side porch leading into the kitchen of her mother's house sat William.

"He's my big teddy bear, that's what he is," said Mariah. She slurped her Diet Pepsi through a straw. "He's about six foot seven, he's really tall. He's about 250 pounds but most of it's muscle."

He had once worked with Mariah's new stepfather in construction. But business was slow, and both men were temporarily out of work. William was looking for work, as he had quit school. After getting a GED, he thought he might go to a school for electricians, because a friend had told him that there was good money in working on the poles that fed electricity into the veins of the cove. The trailer where William lived was on a hill, up a dirt road that connected to his parents' homestead.

Mariah had not fallen hard and fast the way she often did for boys. This was a slow and sweet romance. When they first began going out, Will was, she said, stuck up her butt 24/7. It took two more rounds of dating for him to win her over. Then things began to change for her: Mariah began to see her own life in terms of their future. She dreamed of a wedding.

"What makes him so special to you, that you want to get married to him?" I asked, in between munching on my fries. I always felt a mixture of happiness and worry when the girls shared their romantic dreams with me. Mariah was still only seventeen years old. Could she possibly be ready for marriage? I remembered that marriage had been her dream since the earliest days of our literature class.

"Me and Will have this kind of bond, you know? He likes me for who I am. He doesn't want me to be somebody that I'm not. I can tell him things, personal things. He gives me advice about— He's straight and personal, to the point about what I have to say about something. And ever since I was in juvenile, and everybody talked bad about me and put me down, he was there to bring me back up."

Mariah paused long enough to take another long drink through her straw. Her food was nearly gone now; she ate quickly and heartily.

"He was there to bring me back up. He's been there from day one. He's brought me off the floor to where I am now. I hit rock bottom, and he was the only one there."

The trouble started for Mariah soon after she arrived in rural Kentucky. She felt like an outsider even among her own blood kin. The family resemblances were there, and so were other things that she came by honestly: a temper, a mouth on her, a rebellious spirit. Mariah's wild spirit was something her birth mother wanted to tame before things got out of control. All of this was so different from what Mariah had hoped for, and everything felt wrong. She felt unwanted in the very family where she should have belonged. Things got even worse one afternoon when she and a boy tried some drugs and ended up having sex in the basement. For Mariah it was rape, but she refused to press charges against the boy, who had yet to turn eighteen. She told people about the incident only after she thought she might be pregnant. For Mariah's mother, it was part of a larger pattern of disruptive behavior, one that her mother wanted to put an end to before things spun out of control. By late September of her tenth-grade year, Mariah was in a maximum-security juvenile detention center for what was characterized as disorderly conduct, with ninety days tacked on for perjury. She would spend her seventeenth birthday in juvenile detention.

"I mean, I *come here* to get away from going down that road," said Mariah. "And it seems like I'm going straight *down* it."

Her journey to the juvenile detention center took her past Whitley City and into the Kentucky countryside. Down a small road with two locked gates was a facility with a "Welcome" sign in front. The facility was grouped into ten-bed units that separated male and female youths. She would not leave until December.

"We didn't have *bars* for our doors," said Mariah, looking satisfied with her dinner. There was a new roundness to Mariah's face and body. She had put on weight with the good country food.

"No, we had metal doors. And when them doors shut there ain't no way of getting out. 'Cause you can't escape. The first night I was in there, when them doors shut——." Mariah paused long enough to drain her glass of Diet Pepsi. "It tears you apart. You're inside that cell and you look out that little window you got, and you look into the sky, and you say: 'I wonder if anybody else is looking up, or if anybody else is caring and crying the way I am?'"

Mariah had always had a way with words, and a special gift for driving them right into the soft spots in my heart. I felt overwhelmed. I mean, this was the girl who in sixth grade was absorbing teen vampire novels and reading Shakespeare. It all seemed so unfair, as though she had entered a shadow world not unlike that of the old television show *The Twilight Zone*. But even as I struggled to wrap my thoughts around the craziness of it all, I found myself consumed with curiosity about the ordinary, everyday things. I asked the question that was always at the center of my thoughts and worries about the girls once they left my class:

"Did you have school in there?"

Education in juvenile was reduced to its most minimal of forms. On Monday through Friday, Mariah would get up at five thirty. First there was gym and morning rec. Then came breakfast at seven thirty. After that, she got her books and sat in her cell until two thirty. Mariah showed me one of her school texts, a social studies book, to explain.

"You take a book, you flip through it, and——see them questions?" She had opened the textbook she carried to a page with end-of-chapter questions.

"Yeah."

"You answer them on your own."

"And that's school?" I said. "There's no teacher?"

"There's a teacher that comes around and helps you if you need help. You come out and face your door and you put your hand on the lock and wait to be called. And there's this thing you have to learn how to say every time you walk through the hallway. And it goes: *Ladies and gentlemen, while in line there should be no laughing, talking, smiling, or giggling. No looking inside the windows, wings, pods, especially Control. Males or females. Stay one block from the wall, one block between two feet, two blocks from you and the other resident. If you have a question or redirection raise your hand. The staff will get to you at the next designated area.*

"You have to say that every time you move out in the hallway. *Every* stinkin' time!"

Even after Mariah got out of juvenile, she belonged to a different educational system. One thing I began to realize as I followed the complicated lives of my girls after they left my class is that there exists a shadow system of high school education for young people living in the margins of access and opportunity. There are online high schools, GED programs, and "alternative" schools that coexist alongside the public and private high schools that offer a real chance at democratic access. After her stint in the jail system, Mariah entered this shadow world of schooling.

"It's easier," said Mariah of her new alternative school. "It's not like a regular high school. It's basically for dumb kids, like kids with mental problems, or bad kids."

My thoughts drifted back to some of the moments from our literature class: reading a novel by Alice Hoffman, producing a literary magazine, performing scenes from Shakespeare's *Romeo and Juliet,* watching an art film and having a heated discussion about it. Hardly a class for dumb kids or kids whose motor-mouths could not be focused on books and literature. So much had been lost for a girl with dreams and intelligence.

"Do you ever see yourself going back to regular high school?" I asked.

"I'm afraid that if I go back to the high school now I'm not going to graduate," said Mariah. Our waitress walked over to check on our progress, and Mariah handed her an empty plate. I worked on my serving of fries and picked at the fried flounder. My appetite had disappeared.

"I miss our girls' class," said Mariah wistfully. She still had her signed copy of *Vampire Kisses,* a beloved artifact from our time together.

"Me too," I said, as I pushed my half-eaten plate to one side and checked my watch. We had to leave by five thirty to make certain Mariah didn't miss her curfew. The last thing I wanted was for her to have more trouble at home.

"Our class had a big impact on my life. It helped me figure out what I was going to do in my life."

"What are your dreams for yourself now?" I asked.

"Beyond high school, I'm going to go to college," she said without a moment's hesitation. "And I'm going to get my nursing degree. And I can work in the county hospital."

Mariah shifted her weight in the booth where she sat across from me, and smiled. "And I don't want to be stickin' the babies, because I'd cry myself!"

Our waitress came over with menus and placed them so we could ponder dessert choices. Mariah and I looked at one another and shook our heads in unison. We were stuffed.

"I miss Alicia so much," said Mariah. "I had this dream the other night, where I was having my wedding. I had her as my maid of honor because she's like my sister. And I was thinking, wow, I have a best friend down here but she doesn't compare to Alicia. No way and no how."

Mariah had begun plans for her wedding, which would take place days after her eighteenth birthday. She had picked out her wedding dress online, and her ring too. After the wedding, the couple might travel to Cincinnati for a honeymoon.

"Now mind you, I'm fixin' to be married, and Will's best friend is probably going to be his best man. I told my mom, I said, 'He can't do that to me!'"

Mariah was speaking in her old breathless style, spurting out the story like there was no tomorrow.

"And my mom goes, 'Why?' And I said, 'Because I'm going to be saying *I Do* to somebody else and not William.'"

Her hazel eyes flashed. She paused, and I knew I had to prompt her.

"Why?"

"Because of Rob Ayres. I've had the hots for him ever since I've come down here. He's the pretty boy. He's got blond hair, baby-blue eyes, he's got a good six-pack, and he's got a tan."

Mariah took a deep breath, satisfied with herself. I laughed, then got out my wallet to pay for our meal. It was time to get her back home.

On the way back, I got a little unnerved by the sharp curves on the mountain road leading to Mariah's house. I kept glancing nervously at the dashboard clock as it neared six. It was dark outside; evening came early on a January day. Finally we arrived, three minutes late. I walked inside with Mariah, prepared to explain that it was my slow driving that had made us late. Only her mother's boyfriend and his son were there, playing video games in the living room. They seemed unfazed and indifferent. Mariah and I said our goodbyes, hugging, and I walked back into the cold winter night.

The night sky was vivid with starry patterns, so clear in a sky untainted by city lights and pollution. It had been years since I last looked up at an Appalachian night sky, and I had forgotten how the stars sparkled in the formations I had learned about as a girl: the Big Dipper, the Little Dipper. I soaked in the nakedness of the drive back, feeling anxious on the unforgiving roads with hardly any other cars in sight. I was spent and unhinged by Mariah's story, so that it wasn't until I was back on a four-lane highway that I could feel myself relaxing to the soothing hum of the road.

In the year I was seventeen, I had taken the only road I knew away from a family life that entrapped me and a small town that seemed dreary and unchanging. For Mariah, the road I was driving had taken her in the opposite direction. She had gone back home to find herself, back into a family that was as strange and crazy as they were hers—her blood kin. The roads leading from our childhoods always seem to find their way back to where we began. I had no more left my small mountain mill town than Mariah had found her dream family and her unlikely prince, William. Each of us was, in our own way, a girl with big dreams. I wanted for Mariah the kind of college education that could give her books and literature and tools for critical thinking. These could in turn, I hoped, open new doors for her in a world that was closing, like the metal door of her cell, ever more tightly around her. But Mariah saw things differently. She would marry

William and help him get his GED. They would get the trailer and his mom's car.

In so many ways, our literature class was only a small moment in the lives of Mariah and all the girls I taught. And there was surely a lot working against us. By the time they crossed the threshold of adolescence, Alicia, Adriana, and Blair had lost their birth mothers to the streets. Elizabeth had lost her family. And Mariah had begun the tenuous course of return to the mother she had lost years earlier. They were like sisters in my class, and maybe this was part of its power for them. Sometimes it is the very smallness, the intimacy, of an educational encounter that gives it the chance to change your life. I was certainly naïve going into my class, and I had my own lessons to learn. But for a few magical years, I think we were doing it—creating together an educational experience that could prove life-changing for girls who had so much else working against them. For those years, Mariah and the other girls were readers, critics, creative writers, and thinkers. This is surely their birthright in a nation that prides itself on education as the pathway to opportunity.

The generation of Appalachian migrants who moved north to cities such as Cincinnati in the postwar decades had dreams like those of any poor or working-class Americans. They dreamed of creating better lives for their children than the lives of poverty they had inherited.

Maybe the ghosts of some of these rural migrant workers inhabit the physical remains of this story from America's labor history. The girls in my class certainly believed in ghosts, and brought them to life in their rich storytelling. If so, these ghosts must be deeply saddened to see what has come of their backbreaking labor in factories and warehouses. The truth is that the landscape inherited by my students *is* haunted, by social and economic forces that are all too real. The life choices of my students remain shackled by the hard living that their grandmothers and great-grandmothers fled when they left poor counties in Appalachia. In certain ways the options of girls today are even starker, and their family lives more fractured by the demise of working-class jobs, the growth of a street-drug problem, and the historic inequalities in our public school system. In such a landscape, too many obstacles can come between a girl and her dreams. Unless she stumbles her way into a two- or four-year college, as I once did, she can lose her one chance to become a poet, a pediatric nurse, or a journalist.

I have sometimes thought about why I was able to leave behind the world I knew and find my way to college by the age of seventeen. My mother and father were too bogged down in residual pain from their own childhoods to attend to the needs of a precocious young girl. And my brother was too disturbed as a kid to do what I did: create my own future in spite of everything. Every face I turned to for love and support only reflected back the anxiety, anger, and trauma of lives that were themselves damaged long before I was born. I must have early on summed things up pretty well: I was for all practical purposes on my own by the time I was old enough to leave the house on childhood adventures. The road to college felt like any other journey, like the one I would later take across the Atlantic Ocean to France, with only enough money to get there. It's easier to leave when there is so little holding you back. Then there are the idiosyncratic factors of personality traits and character. I was by any measure an unusually resilient child. I had a lot of grit and determination, and maybe even more importantly, a big imagination. I was an example of what some psychologists would refer to as an invulnerable child—able to read the fine-grained nuances of psychic or material neglect, adapt myself, and land solidly on two feet, even thrive.[1]

Conservatives love to cite life stories such as mine, the atypical story of a working-class kid who climbs her way out of a hardscrabble life and up the ladder of social mobility, as an example of universal attributes that all disadvantaged people should possess. But it would be a huge mistake to generalize from my idiosyncratic experience. And it would be further folly to ignore the fine gradations of social class. When you are looking at the narrow range of opportunities for a poor or working-class girl, small differences can have big consequences. Unlike me, the girls I taught didn't have the relative luxury of a family with stable working-class jobs. By the time they came into the world, those jobs were gone from their community. As one of their neighborhood elders poignantly said, "There ain't nothin' here no more." My students were growing up in a community of extreme poverty, a ghetto. They too had grit and intelligence, but the road between their lives and college was even longer and more tortuous than mine had been. There is only so much that even the most resilient girl can do to untangle the web of stress, material neglect, and hurt that can entrap her in America's poorest neighborhoods. My students needed a great deal of help to reach their full potential. Dreams alone are not enough to lift the most vulnerable out of poverty and carry them to the better lives they deserve.

What was it about our class that allowed girls such as Elizabeth and Jessica, Mariah and Blair—girls who would probably have struggled to find themselves in most educational settings—to attach themselves to literature and learning? First there was its small size, and the intimacy that ensued from meeting week after week, year after year. In a cultural setting where family is at the center of life and of personal identity, we straddled a border between a family-like setting and a classroom. It has always struck me as one of the ironies of our public school system that the students most in need of small, intimate classes, with expert teachers who have the full resources they need to teach effectively, are those least likely to ever receive that kind of education. Someone manages to find a body of research with the thesis that class size makes no real difference to student outcomes; and suddenly we have an argument in support of inequalities that have been there to begin with. Yet class size certainly makes a difference to the parents who can afford to send their children to elite schools, with their lower ratios of students to teaching adults. The size of our class and our long history together made a big difference to me as a teacher. I was able to get to know each of my students in a way that would rarely be possible in a larger middle school. I knew their families, to the point where I could move easily between their worlds and the world I was trying to create in my class. I knew the underlying stories beneath Blair's frequent absences or Mariah's resistance. And over time we developed *trust*, something that doesn't come easily to a girl who has had so much taken from her, even her childhood.

There was one more thing that made our small class bigger in terms of its meaning, and that was its focus on stories and literature. You can certainly find some works of fiction in most fifth- and sixth-grade classrooms. Every English teacher has to teach reading and language arts, and many of us drawn to this profession manage to sneak in our beloved novels, even if the mandated curriculum does not specify their inclusion. But I had the flexibility and the authority, given our class's existence on the margins of the regular school day, to focus my teaching around fiction and story in a way that has become ever more difficult in today's classrooms. Having no funds other than those I could raise, I wrote grants that allowed me to buy exactly what my students needed: a particular novel, a camera for telling the story of their lives, the tools for creating a magazine. I was then able to fine-tune my teaching exactly to my students' needs and interests. My discovery of the raw power of stories of hauntings and horror led me to shift course, and use those books as a productive teaching tool. My awareness of the girls' lives led me to a novel by Dorothy Allison, hardly what you would find in a mandated curriculum for sixth-grade girls. My students' vibrant storytelling—their tales of fights, family feuds, and love—led us to Shakespeare. Who could have planned things this way in a curriculum geared toward preparing the daughters of hard-working laborers for their end-of-grade tests and working-class jobs that no longer exist? In certain ways, things have gotten worse for students whose lives and experiences do not fit a standard course of study, with its precise measures of proficiency and achievement. Worse in certain respects, but not profoundly different from what history has accorded us. The girls I taught had experiences in school that were eerily similar to mine growing up.

I was in some ways naïve to think that something as simple as books and stories could help my students forge a better future in the unforgiving world that awaited them. But as a teacher you have to start somewhere, and why not with something that is truly basic and yet full of intellectual possibility: the stories that shape our lives, and the works of literature that allow us to imagine a world different from our own?

If I could change one thing about the class I created, it would not be its content or even its curriculum. I might make small adjustments to these, like any devoted teacher of literature. But on a larger scale, I would have—if only I could have—continued our class through the tumultuous years of early adolescence. We would have held our class through the terrible times when Alicia and Elizabeth went into temporary foster care, when Mariah was contemplating a return to her birth mother, when Jessica was starting to turn to the street, and when Blair was losing her fragile connection to school. The changes I was making in my own life, as I too returned home in one sense, made such a continuation impossible. Like any devoted teacher, I have had to accept the limits of what one woman can do. But part of me remains the curious girl I once was, barefoot on the dirt roads leading from our house to places I could hardly have imagined as a girl. I have stored this teaching journey in a travelogue of experience and learning. Of late, I have begun working with girls in those critical middle school years, and not too far from the small mountain town where I grew up. My journey is not yet over.

Can a girl growing up in one of our nation's old-industry ghost towns, the daughter or granddaughter of poor Appalachian migrants, really have the chance to achieve her life dreams? My resounding feeling after striving for years to make this possible is one of hope. I know from my own teaching odyssey how difficult this can be. But I also know how possible it is to create educational experiences that can have a lasting impact on young lives. The girls in my class were clear, their resolve unfaltering: They *wanted* better lives. It was painful for me to watch these girls form strong attachments to books and writing—things that could help them forge life-long connections to reading and to school—but then give up on public school itself. Looking at things through their eyes, I would say that each of the girls was striving for a meaningful and rich education, wherever she could get it. My hope is that all of the girls will someday find those educations, perhaps by paths as twisted as my own improbable journey through public school, into college, and finally back into the America that shaped my childhood—this time as a teacher.

Epilogue

It has been twelve years since I first laid eyes on a thin, eight-year-old girl, Blair, and four years since I last spent significant time with her and my six other students. When we last met to talk and share stories about their lives and mine, the girls were sixteen, about to enter young adulthood. Now most are twenty: they are young women. We stay in touch through text messaging and email, though less frequently than in the past. My former students Adriana, Alicia, Elizabeth, Jessica, Mariah, Shannon, and Blair are busy building their own adult lives, and for three of these young women, creating better lives for their children.

Sadly, the economic and social inequalities that darkened their childhoods have only become worse in recent years. The city today is third in the nation in terms of the percent of children living in poverty. Only Detroit and Cleveland are worse: over half of the children in those old-industry cityscapes are growing up in poverty. With 48 percent of its children today growing up poor, many of them in areas of severe concentrated poverty, Cincinnati is much like its kindred cities to the north. The dead-end nature of life in an extremely poor neighborhood has not been lost on my former students; as young adults, they know that a ghetto is no place for a young woman to build her future. With the exception of Elizabeth, all have left the old neighborhood, though most have not gone far. They have moved to safer ground: more stable working-class communities that are close enough for visits with family and friends.

From my vantage point as a teacher, I am immensely proud of the distance my former students have come, given the hardships they endured as young girls. Against all odds, three of the girls were able, with grit and determination, to get the most fundamental of tickets out: a high school diploma. Adriana became the first member of her family to get a diploma, and she did it all on her own: a degree from a competitive Catholic high school with no help from her family and a baby by her senior year. She graduated at seventeen and by eighteen had moved out of the old neighborhood. Today she works hard to finish at a postsecondary school for hairstylists and to make sure her child, a lovely little girl, never knows the streets that claimed Adriana's mother. Mariah, too, has a baby and a high school degree. Both were products of her new life in Kentucky. Things didn't go as Mariah planned: her marriage to her high school sweetheart ended painfully in divorce. But now she lives with the father of her baby girl, a toddler who is as feisty as Mariah herself. She is making plans for a two-year college program, the arrival of another baby, and a house big enough for her growing family.

Alicia, once our group's tiny comedienne, is also the proud recipient of a high school degree. Now a happy and devoted Army wife, she has moved away from the city with her husband. College may lie ahead, and someday, she hopes, a family of her own.

She stays in touch with family and friends, including some of her sisters from our class.

For my other four students, getting a high school diploma has proved to be more daunting. Shannon struggled for years in her GED program but finally gave up. Then she discovered an online source that would issue a diploma for a minimum of work and a payment of $299. In two weeks she held a diploma in her hand. As I once did, she packs boxes in a warehouse, but she has bigger plans for her life. In love with a young man who has family in a blue-collar neighborhood, she hopes to enter a college program and build a life away from her old neighborhood. Shannon's hopes for a better life are ones shared by Elizabeth, but the door of opportunity has been harder for her to open. In part Elizabeth has suffered from the rigidity of the school accountability movement. Always a bright and impassioned girl in my class, she is a few points on a state-mandated test away from getting her high school diploma. She aced the reading and writing parts of the Ohio Graduation Test but has failed, twice now, to get a passing score in science. She lingers in a murky borderland between minimum-wage jobs and the college classroom. She needs her diploma to enroll in college, something that is still her dream. And now the stakes are even higher: single and pregnant, Elizabeth needs the security of an education and a decent job so she can care for herself and her baby.

Jessica too has struggled with high school completion. Her efforts to get her diploma through ECOT, the online charter school, failed when she didn't get the close, personal help that students can receive from teachers who are more than disembodied replies on a computer screen. She has joined the large numbers of students nationally who enroll in online high schools, only to drop out before graduation. For now, family is her solace and her focus. Jessica is engaged to a mechanic, tending to her elderly father, and looking forward to the day when she can live far away from the old neighborhood. I often think of Jessica when I work in the mountains, directing a summer program for girls in the beautiful southern Appalachians. I long for the day when I can introduce Jessica and her sisters from our class to a part of the world that shaped my childhood, and that is connected to their family histories as well. Jessica and I plot ways for her to visit me in a place where I know she could find peace.

Blair had a similar experience with online high school after her Grandma Lilly enrolled her in ECOT. Blair's stint was even shorter than Jessica's, closing down yet another shot at a high school degree. As a last resort, Blair turned to a local GED program but has not yet completed her high school equivalency. Now twenty years old and living with her fiancé up the road from the old neighborhood, Blair works the night shift at a large downtown warehouse. She cleans several floors—exhausting but steady work that pays the bills. She still hopes to go to college someday and has thoughts about a community college that offers GED and college classes. For now, she sleeps until midday, smokes her first cig, and readies herself for a night job cleaning one of the buildings where, when morning comes, prosperous Cincinnati and the new global economy meet.

In recent years, the lives of poor and working-class whites have come under increased scrutiny in the media and on the op-ed page. As I write, a new book by the conservative pundit Charles Murray has sparked considerable conversation about the Americans who live on the other side of the class divide. Murray's book *Coming Apart* deals in generalizations based on attributes culled from statistics and on his somewhat iconoclastic studies of two white communities, one working class and one upper middle class. The problems of the white underclass, he argues, are due more to the demise of traditional American values—hard work, family and marriage, education—than to the economic forces that have turned old manufacturing communities into ghostly cityscapes.

I'll leave the social scientists and critics to rebut the spurious thinking at the root of Murray's portrait of the disenfranchised working classes. As an educator working in the trenches in a poor white community, I perceived a more complex reality than that offered by Murray. From up close, things look different, and more difficult to paint broadly in terms of clichés about morals, culture, and even—for some—intelligence. I am reminded of the words of Todd Gitlin, who in the 1960s spent years interviewing people in Chicago's Uptown neighborhood—once (like Cincinnati's Lower Price Hill) a beacon for poor whites from Appalachia. As he writes in his book *Uptown:* "A deep and passionate engagement with one life matters more, teaches more than a nodding acquaintance with ten or a door-to-door survey of a thousand, if the passion does not obscure one's faithfulness to what one sees. Better to let some people stick in your throat."[1]

Some days, from my vantage point in the middle-class world where I now live, I cannot help but marvel at the voluminous help that the more affluent young receive as a standard part of their apprenticeship in the new global economy. For four years, I tried to give a sliver of this opportunity to the girls in my class, and I watched as they struggled, sometimes resisted, but then flourished in a class just for them—gifted girls. I hope that I have been faithful to what I have seen and experienced myself, a daughter too of the working classes. From inside these lives, I have seen some of our most cherished common values: strength, courage, and the hope for a better life. My students still dream of becoming nursing assistants, college students, poets, stylists. What they most need is not more virtue, but more opportunity. Once their teacher, now a writer, I hope that the dreams of poor and working-class girls can shed light on the truths of these still mysterious lives in America.

NOTES

INTRODUCTION

1. "Blair Rainey" is a pseudonym, as are the names of the six other girls (and their immediate relatives) whose lives are portrayed in this book. The pseudonyms were in most cases chosen by the girls themselves. Nearly all of the photographs which appear here were taken by the girls themselves, some as staged self-portraits.

2. John Dawson, quoted in Todd Gitlin and Nanci Hollander, *Uptown: Poor Whites in Chicago* (New York: Harper and Row, 1970), 203.

CHAPTER ONE

1. *America's War on Poverty*, vol. 1, *In This Affluent Society* (PBS Video, 1995).

2. Barbara Zigli, "Prejudice, Stereotypes Are Painful Obstacles," in *The Urban Appalachians*, 10, a reprinted set of articles originally published in *The Cincinnati Enquirer* (May 3–11, 1981).

3. The three paperbacks *(The Haunting, The Horror,* and *The Final Nightmare)* in the House on Cherry Street series (New York: Scholastic, 1995) were written by Rodman Philbrick and Lynn Harnett.

4. Stephen King, *Rose Madder* (New York: Viking, 1995), 317–18.

CHAPTER TWO

1. Cynthia Rylant, *A Blue-Eyed Daisy* (New York: Aladdin Paperbacks, 2001).

2. Ibid., 15.

3. Rodman Philbrick and Lynn Harnett, *The Final Nightmare* (New York: Scholastic, 1995), 15.

4. Kate DiCamillo, *Because of Winn-Dixie* (New York: Candlewick Press, 2000).

CHAPTER THREE

1. Paul Tough, "The Alchemy of OxyContin," *New York Times Magazine,* July 29, 2001).

2. Sabrina Tavernise, "Ohio County Losing Its Young to Painkillers' Grip," *New York Times,* April 19, 2011.

3. Tough, "The Alchemy of OxyContin."

4. Kristina Goetz, "The OxyContin Pipeline," *Cincinnati Enquirer,* February 25, 2001.

5. Rodman Philbrick and Lynn Harnett, *The Haunting* (New York: Scholastic, 1995), 47.

6. Ibid., 50.

7. Jane Prendergast, "Queen City Barrel has history of problems," *Cincinnati Enquirer,* August 20, 2004.

8. Michael Maloney and Christopher Auffrey, *Social Areas of Cincinnati: An Analysis of Social Needs,* fourth edition (Cincinnati: University of Cincinnati Institute for Community Partnerships, 2004).

CHAPTER FIVE

1. The importance of the distinction between Us and Them in working-class communities is articulated in Richard Hoggart, *The Uses of Literacy* (Boston: Beacon, 1961).

CHAPTER SIX

1. Alice Hoffman, *Aquamarine* (New York: Scholastic, 2002), 100–101.

2. Francine Prose, *After* (New York: Joanna Cotler Books, 2003), 330.

3. Niki Caro (director), *Whale Rider* (South Pacific Pictures, 2000). See also Witi Ihimaera's originating story, *The Whale Rider* (New York: Harcourt, 1987).

4. Alice Kaplan, *French Lessons: A Memoir* (Chicago: University of Chicago Press, 1993), 139.

CHAPTER SEVEN

1. Ellen Schreiber, *Vampire Kisses* (New York: Katherine Tegen Books, 2003).

2. Ibid., 5.

3. Darren Shan, *Cirque du Freak* (Boston: Little, Brown and Company, 2000), 60.

4. Tanya Gold, "Why Have Teenage Girls Been Bitten by the Edward Cullen Bug to Devour the 'Twilight' Novels?" *The Guardian*, Friday, November 13, 2009.

5. Ibid.

6. *Vampire Kisses*, 196–97.

CHAPTER EIGHT

1. Catherine Hardwicke (director), *Thirteen* (20th Century Fox, 2003).

2. Franco Zeffirelli (director), *Romeo and Juliet* (Paramount Studios, 1968).

3. William Shakespeare, *Romeo and Juliet* (New York: Barron's Educational Series, 2002).

4. Dorothy Allison, "A Question of Class," in *Skin: Talking about Sex, Class, and Literature* (Ithaca: Firebrand Books, 1994), 19.

CHAPTER NINE

1. Dorothy Allison, *Bastard Out of Carolina* (New York: Penguin, 1993), 17.

2. Ibid., 3.

3. Ibid.

4. Ibid.

5. Ibid., 74.

6. Ibid., 70.

7. Dorothy Allison, "A Question of Class," in *Skin: Talking about Sex, Class, and Literature* (Ithaca: Firebrand Books, 1994), 14.

CHAPTER THIRTEEN

1. The phenomenon of psychological adaptation and resiliency on the part of some children is discussed in E. James Anthony and Bertram J. Cohler, eds., *The Invulnerable Child* (New York: Guilford Press, 1987).

EPILOGUE

1. Todd Gitlin and Nanci Hollander, *Uptown: Poor Whites in Chicago* (New York: Harper and Row, 1970), xxv.

Text: 10.75/15 Janson

Display: Janson

Compositor: Westchester Book Group

Printer and binder: Maple Press